Power in Practice

Power in Practice

Adult Education and the Struggle for Knowledge and Power in Society

Ronald M. Cervero, Arthur L. Wilson,

and Associates

Foreword by Michael W. Apple

 JOSSEY-BASS
A Wiley Company
San Francisco

Published by Jossey-Bass
A Wiley Imprint
989 Market Street, San Francisco, CA 94103-1741   www.josseybass.com

Jossey-Bass books and products are available through most bookstores. To contact Jossey-Bass directly
call our Customer Care Department within the U.S. at (800) 956-7739, outside the U.S. at (317) 572-
3986 or fax (317) 572-4002.

Jossey-Bass also publishes its books in a variety of electronic formats. Some content that appears in
print may not be available in electronic books.

Library of Congress Cataloging-in-Publication Data

Power in practice: adult education and the struggle for
knowledge and power in society / Ronald M. Cervero, Arthur L.
Wilson, and associates; foreword by Michael W. Apple.—1st ed.
        p. cm.—(The Jossey-Bass higher and adult education series)
Includes bibliographical references (p.   ) and index.
    ISBN 0-7879-4729-6
    1. Adult education—Social aspects.   2. Adult education and
state.   3. Educational equalization.   4. Cervero, Ronald M.
I. Wilson, Arthur L., date–.   II. Series.
    LC5225.S64 P69   2001
    374—dc21   00-011644

FIRST EDITION
HB Printing 10 9 8 7 6 5 4 3 2

Contents

Foreword

In the old mill town on the east coast where I grew up, it was hard to miss the ways in which relations of inequality structured our daily lives. Because of the impoverished nature of the city, caused in part by capital flight, there were constant struggles to challenge these relations in nearly all its institutions—in schools and colleges, in labor unions, in community organizations, in families, in government, in health care, in the justice system, and elsewhere. It was clear to me and many other people that education inside and outside of the community's formal institutions was central to the multiple projects of interrupting dominance. It is to the credit of the authors of this book that I was immediately reminded of my first involvement in the role of education in the processes of political/economic/cultural transformation when I read it. The book feels "real" in two ways. First, it is grounded in the realities of differential power. Second, it is not content to simply throw slogans at educational problems. That is, its chapters are serious contributions, ones not content to engage merely in the rhetorical artifice that has characterized too much of the recent literature on critical pedagogy (Apple, 1996, 1999). Because of this, I believe that all those who are concerned with democratizing education should welcome this book. Let me say a bit more about this.

While some may deny it, we are not an equal society. Our social system is crisscrossed by axes of class, gender, race, age, nationality, region, politics, religion, and other dynamics of power. All of these produce differences, some of which are more strongly experienced than others, depending on the situation. However, these sets of social differences are *not* isolated. They interact with each other in a complex nexus of power relations. And because social power is clearly not distributed equally throughout society, "any set of social relations necessarily involves power and resistance, domination, subordination, and even struggle" (Fiske, 1987, p. 17). Notice that the quotation begins with the words *any set of social relations.* This needs to be taken quite literally, I believe, especially when one is talking about the central sets of institutionalized social relations in this society—including educational relations. The recognition that educational activities—and the curricula, teaching, and evaluative policies and practices that structure the daily events that go on in them—are among the most central of these institutionalized sets of social relations is not new, of course. But our understanding of what this means has grown massively over the past decades. This growing recognition—and what it means in terms of critical theories, policies, and practices—constitutes much of the core of this book.

There is a "simple" set of questions that underpins a good deal of critical work in education: Who benefits from the ways education is organized? Whose knowledge and ways of knowing are considered legitimate or official? Whose knowledge is not? What is the relationship between the inner world of educational theories, policies, and practices and the larger society? How is power constituted, and how do we think about and change it? Who is the "we" here? Whose voices are heard?

Obviously, this list of questions could and should be expanded. And just as obviously, these questions are anything but simple to ask or to answer. They require a considerable amount of conceptual and empirical sophistication—and a good measure of practical political/educational experience. They require a detailed and complex understanding of the relationship among economy, politics, and culture and an equally detailed and complex understanding of the social movements and groups that constitute this society. They involve difficult issues surrounding theory, ideology, and politics, about whom research is supposed to serve, and ultimately about one's own appraisal of the multiple struggles for social justice in an unequal world. And, not least of all, they should also be grounded in an unromantic—but still hopeful—sense of what actually does and might go on in educational programs (Carlson & Apple, 1998).

Such critical theoretical, political, and educational theories and practices underpin the chapters in this book. Yet the authors are not simply doing theory for theory's sake. Let me say something about both why I say this and how I approach theory. I am not interested in theory as a subject in and of itself. Unfortunately, critical theory has become something of a "substitute." The production of endlessly refined accounts of supposedly new perspectives has created a situation in which theory has become an academic pursuit of its own. Yet in the process of "politicizing the academic," all too often what has happened has been "academicizing the political" (Apple, 1999). Let me hasten to add that there are positive aspects to this. We absolutely need to constantly interrogate our accepted perspectives—including the perspectives that are accepted as given within the multiple critical communities in education. However, I am impatient with some of this activity. It is all too often not connected—except in the most ephemeral ways—to the most important political, economic, and cultural issues of our time. As Said (1996, p. 73) says, "The question of oppression, of racial oppression, the question of war, the question of human rights—all of these issues ought to belong together . . .; as opposed to the massive, intervening, institutionalized presence of theoretical discussion." "Doing theory," especially in its most arcane forms, enables the "knower" to comment from on high, unmuddied by the pollution of and dangers from ongoing and concrete economic/political/cultural mobilizations in education or elsewhere.

Of course, theoretical interventions are important. And they do count as political work themselves at times. But I fear that for too many people within the multiple critical educational communities, this may be the only political/educational work that is done. It is a bit reminiscent of Bakhtin's discussion of the function of balconies during carnival in Europe hundreds of years ago. The affluent were both attracted to and repelled by the cultural, political, and bodily transgressions that accompanied carnival. The smells, the noise, the possibility of loss of control, the undercurrent of danger, all of this was fascinating. But the powerful could not let go of their safe havens. The balcony was the creative solution. The carnival of the streets could be experienced—vicariously. The sights and smells and sounds could be safely lived—and commented on, which also had its own politics of pleasure—from the balcony overhanging the street. One could be in and out, almost-participant but mostly observer, at the same time (Stallybrass & White, 1986).

The universalism of the intellectual who stands above it all, observes, and deconstructs the positions of others has of course a long tradition in education and elsewhere. Adorno's vigorous attack on such "innocuous skepticism" is telling here. As he put it, such a standpoint "calls everything into question and criticizes nothing" (quoted in Osborne, 1996, p. xiii). Even though there *is* much to question, my own position—and that of the many people who have contributed to this book—has little in common with such innocuous skepticism. Unlike, say, Karl Mannheim's view of the unattached intelligentsia where the relative classlessness of free-floating intellectuals enables them to stand aside from the political and ideological struggles of the larger society and to look at the "interest of the whole" (Osborne, 1996, p. xiii), my belief is that we are *already* deeply positioned. We must attach our criticisms to identifiable social movements that aim, expressly, to challenge the relations of differential power in education and the larger society (Apple, 2000).

Indeed, this is one of the major elements that gave the great Brazilian educator Paulo Freire such legitimacy. He not only focused on and wrote about a particular kind of educational/political praxis but also himself engaged in the hard and disciplined (and sometimes dangerous) work of putting theory and practice together. He had actually helped build programs that were not meant to be simply rhetorical. If critical educators too often sit on the sidelines, much of what gave Freire's work its meaning—its concrete connections to lived struggles in "favelas," in rural areas, among (the identifiable, not abstract or anonymous) large groups of oppressed and exploited people, and so on—is vitiated. Theory is not connected to social movements in which the writer herself or himself is involved (in part because the writer herself or himself is unconnected in any meaningful and organic way to large-scale social movements). Critical pedagogy becomes something we only write about and study. Here I must admit that I am suspicious of those individuals who have appropriated Freire's language and name but who themselves have never been engaged in putting such work into concrete practice (Apple, 1999). The same needs to be said, I believe, about those authors in education who are now influenced by Foucault. He was not simply a brilliant commentator on the complicated ways the dynamics of power organize our lives. He was also more than a little active in movements to alter them (Eribon, 1991). Balconies get built when we forget this.

I do not want to be misunderstood here. I am *not* claiming in any way that there is not crucial political/intellectual value in serious academic work; nor am I taking a vulgar pragmatist position here. Indeed, like Freire himself, I believe that we must be critical of a position that is antibook and antitheory. And like him, I "prefer knowledge that is forged and produced in the tension between practice and theory" (Freire, 1996, p. 85). Paulo Freire better than anyone knew both intellectually and bodily what was at stake in the struggles over literacy, culture, economy, and power. And he more than almost anyone else I knew understood that "naming the word and the world" was part of an ongoing and never-ending struggle in which we could never be satisfied with abstract commitments. They had to be acted on, embodied, lived. The editors of *Power in Practice* have brought together authors who understand this. I hope that reading these chapters enables you to go further in your own understanding—and action—as well.

MICHAEL W. APPLE
John Bascom Professor of Curriculum and
        Instruction and Educational Policy Studies
University of Wisconsin, Madison

References

Apple, M. W. (1996). *Cultural politics and education.* New York: Teachers College Press.

Apple, M. W. (1999). *Power, meaning, and identity.* New York: Peter Lang.

Apple, M. W. (2000). *Official knowledge* (2nd ed.). New York: Routledge.

Carlson, D., & Apple, M. W. (Eds.). (1998). *Power/knowledge/pedagogy.* Boulder, CO: Westview Press.

Eribon, D. (1991). *Michel Foucault.* Cambridge, MA: Harvard University Press.

Fiske, J. (1987). *Television culture.* New York: Methuen.

Freire, P. (1996). *Letters to Cristina.* New York: Routledge.

Osborne, P. (Ed.). (1996). *A critical sense.* New York: Routledge.

Said, E. (1996). Orientalism and after. In P. Osborne (Ed.), *A critical sense* (pp. 65–86). New York: Routledge.

Stallybrass, P., & White, A. (1986). *The poetics and politics of transgression.* Ithaca, NY: Cornell University Press.

Preface

We are living in interesting times, for adult education matters more now than ever in our lives. Over the last twenty years, adult education has moved increasingly to the center of the many institutions that make up the social, political, economic, and cultural fabric of our lives. Because of this increasing visibility and importance, we now see more clearly that adult education has a significant role in the distribution not only of knowledge but also of social, economic, and political power. We can no longer believe that adult education is a neutral activity in this continual struggle for knowledge and power. As the visibility and importance of adult education increases, it becomes more important to ask the right questions about our work as adult educators. When we engage in these myriad educational efforts, we are often so "busy" doing the work that we often neglect to ask ourselves what ends we are working toward and why. However, adult educators cannot continue to believe that we are experts in the process but have no stake in the consequences of our efforts. At the heart of our work as educators, we need to keep our focus on the central political and ethical questions: who benefits from and who should benefit from the programs, practices, and policies of adult education? These are not new questions, of course, for they have been asked often throughout the history of adult education. What *is* different now is not the questions but rather the stakes involved in answering them. As adults increasingly participate in educational activities, as adult education increasingly becomes central in our personal and social lives, it matters more than ever how adult educators respond to the struggles for knowledge and power in society. Understanding and acting in the face of this struggle for knowledge and power is what this book is about.

Along with this increasing importance of adult education in society, there has been an explosion in the literature that seeks to address these questions of who benefits and who should benefit from adult education. This literature has focused primarily on showing that adult education is caught up in the conflicts of our economic, cultural, social, and political systems. As exciting as the writings have been at the theoretical and philosophical level, many adult educators have shared Mike Newman's frustration with the abstract level at which issues of power are discussed in adult education. As he says, these frustrations "lead me to go looking for writers on adult education who will provide detailed case study and locate their theory in time and place" (1999, p. 217). In our attempts to link power and program planning practice (Cervero & Wilson, 1994, 1996), we found that the issues of power and practice, although pervasive in adult education, are rarely discussed. We therefore agree with Newman that there is a gap in the literature, and as a result we have produced this book.

We began our search for authors who were equally passionate about the need for understanding how and why power operates in the practice of adult education. We have been heartened by the response of the adult educators who chose to join us in this volume. Indeed, in seeking others who might work with us on this project, we found many adult educators around the world whose practical and intellectual work has been striving to move the conversations in adult education in this direction. Although these adult educators practice in many different social institutions, offer multiple approaches to the analysis of power, and express different social visions, all agree on the importance of seeing adult education as a site of struggle for knowledge and power. We believe it has been fruitful to bring these diverse educators together in one place and thereby create a forum for expanding this new conversation. It is our hope that many other adult educators will join us in seeking better practical and intellectual answers to the question, What now? in the struggle for knowledge and power in society.

Purpose, Audience, and Scope

Our purposes in writing this book are to understand how the power relations in the wider society are manifested in the concrete programs, practices, and policies in adult education, and to offer educators ways of acting in the face of these power relations. In order to accomplish these purposes, we invited the authors to make explicit their own political and ethical agendas when investigating a specific adult education program, practice, or policy. Thus, we see the unique contribution of the book as the explicit connection made between theories of power and educational practice, and what this connection can tell us about educational practice. We hope that by making this explicit connection between power and practice, the book can benefit two primary groups of readers. The first audience comprises practitioners who are responsible for adult education in the classroom, who provide leadership for the many types of organizations and groups that provide adult education, or who work for agencies that develop and implement policy about adult education. We hope that the book illuminates the reciprocal relationships between these practitioners' everyday work and the wider social, economic, cultural, and political systems of society, thereby providing a clear connection between the "what for" and the "how to" of adult education. The second audience comprises educators who are pursuing graduate degrees in adult education and related fields, such as higher education, public administration, and social work. As we explain in Chapter One, the theoretical frameworks used in the book are typically discussed as abstractions in graduate education. We hope that the practice orientation of the chapters helps these educators better understand the theories as well as be able to make use of the theories in their own educational work. We think the book would be most useful in foundation courses, issues courses, and courses that focus on the varieties of theories and issues around power.

The two fundamental choices we had to make for the book regarded which sites of adult education practice to include and how to organize these sites in the book. We selected the sites of practice to demonstrate that power dynamics work at different levels (from the classroom to institutional programming to global policy formation) and in different domains (such as employment settings, higher education settings, and community organizations). We also wanted to select sites of practice that cut across geographical boundaries so that we could reveal the universality of the struggle for knowledge and power in adult education. We fully recognize that the range of sites is selective and that there are many other important domains that could just as easily have been included, such as adult literacy education. We hope this book inspires others to bring the struggles in these domains into clearer focus.

The second issue was whether to organize the chapters by sites of practice, by the specific analysis of power offered, or by some other principle. The twelve chapters in Parts One, Two, and Three describe enormously rich and complex sites of practice, analyses of power, and strategies for action. The sites range from the micro level of teaching practice in the classroom to the macro level, where global policies for lifelong learning and the discourse around workplace learning are the focus for discussion. The approaches to power range from the politics of identity, to neo-Marxist theory, to postmodern and poststructural analyses of discourse. Some of the chapters include more than one site of practice or more than one analysis of power in practice. Although this variety is exciting and quite productive, its complexity has made the job of organizing the chapters a challenging one, and any principle for doing so is essentially arbitrary. We have chosen to use sites of practice as the organizing principle because of our position that although multiple and interlocking relations of power may be separated in theory, they necessarily converge in the locations where adult education takes place. What sets this book apart from other literature in the field, then, is our locating the discussion of adult education, knowledge, and power "within the particular material circumstances prevailing . . . today" (Harvey, 1993, p. 41).

Overview of the Contents

Chapter One lays out the book's basic idea, that adult education is centrally involved in the struggle for knowledge and power in society. The chapter reviews three different ways that the adult education literature has approached the connections between power and practice in adult education. We conclude by calling for a relational analysis that takes seriously the idea that adult education does not stand outside the unequal relations of power that define the wider systems of society.

The chapters in Part One focus on the struggles for knowledge and power in the sphere of work and the workplace. In Chapter Two, Mojab uses the situation of immigrant women in Canada to illuminate the connections between the global economy, the state, and retraining programs. In Chapter Three, Schied, Carter, and Howell move us from the macro-level forces in the global economy to the workplace, showing how training programs are often used as a form of management control. In Chapter Four, Butler discusses the discourses of work-related lifelong learning in Australia, showing how our language is a vital site of political struggle. In Chapter Five, Rubenson uses the Organization for Economic Cooperation and Development's policies about work and learning to analyze the political and moral role of the state in the forming of policy for lifelong learning.

The chapters in Part Two address the struggles for knowledge and power in institutions of higher education. In Chapter Six, Hall focuses on the relationships between economic globalization, the global civil society, and the graduate preparation of adult educators. In Chapter Seven, Johnson-Bailey shows us the struggles of Black women who return to college as adults in institutions that mirror the racial and gender hierarchies of the wider society. In Chapter Eight, Tisdell writes about the struggles of teachers who are attempting to name and reconstruct the hierarchical power relations in the classroom. In Chapter Nine, Hart also addresses classroom struggles that arise when teachers who possess social privilege try to work as political allies of marginalized learners.

The chapters in Part Three address the struggles for knowledge and power that are embedded in the technologies of practice used by adult educators. In Chapter Ten, Miller focuses on the struggles for knowledge and power in programs that use distance learning technologies in an educational program for black women in an urban British setting. In Chapter Eleven, Brookfield illuminates how the social struggles for material superiority and ideological legitimacy are played out in that most ubiquitous technology, the discussion group. In Chapter Twelve, Wilson shows how the seemingly commonplace decision of selecting a location for a continuing education program is an important site of struggle for the distribution of knowledge and power in adult education. In Chapter Thirteen, Sessions and Cervero show how the political struggles of an urban gay community are played out in the programs offered for HIV-negative gay men by a community agency.

Given the book's many analyses of power in practice, in the final chapter we ask, What now? We explain why the emerging conversation around the struggle for knowledge and power has profound implications for what are considered the foundations of adult education practice. We argue that adult educators' role in practice is best conceived as that of a knowledge and power broker.

Acknowledgments

A project of this scope can be brought to fruition only in collaboration with many other people. First and foremost, we must recognize the authors who joined with us in producing the book. The willingness of these adult educators to ground the discussions in the material realities of their worlds have given a true vitality to this book. This vitality makes the book feel "real" and thus, we hope, will allow other adult educators to join more easily in this emerging conversation on the struggle for knowledge and power in adult education. We have long benefited from the relational analysis of education that Michael Apple has offered, and were delighted that he agreed to provide the inspirational Foreword to the book. We deeply appreciate the breadth of critique and specific suggestions offered by the reviewers of the book manuscript. Their reactions after careful reading helped us to better position the book's content to speak to a wider readership. Finally, Debra Dukes, a graduate student at the University of Georgia, was of immense help in the editorial process and the preparation of the manuscript at its various stages of production.

Athens, Georgia   RONALD M. CERVERO
Ithaca, New York   ARTHUR L. WILSON
September 2000

References

Cervero, R. M., & Wilson, A. L. (1994). *Planning responsibly for adult education: A guide to negotiating power and interests.* San Francisco: Jossey-Bass.

Cervero, R. M., & Wilson, A. L. (Eds.). (1996). *What really matters in adult education program planning: Lessons in negotiating power and interests.* New Directions for Adult and Continuing Education, no. 69. San Francisco: Jossey-Bass.

Harvey, D. (1993). Class relations, social justice and the politics of difference. In M. Keith & S. Pile (Eds.), *Place and the politics of identity* (pp. 41–65). New York: Routledge.

Newman, M. (1999). *Maeler's regard: Images of adult learning.* Sydney: Stewart Victor.

The Authors

Ronald M. Cervero is professor in the Department of Adult Education at the University of Georgia. He received his B.A. degree (1973) in psychology from St. Michael's College (Vermont), his M.A. degree (1975) in the social sciences from the University of Chicago, and his Ph.D. degree (1979) in adult education, also from the University of Chicago.

Cervero has published extensively in adult education, with particular emphasis in the areas of the politics of adult education, program planning, and continuing education for the professions. His book *Effective Continuing Education for Professionals* (1988) received the 1989 Cyril O. Houle World Award for Literature in Adult Education from the American Association for Adult and Continuing Education and the 1990 Frandson Award for Literature in the Field of Adult Education from the National University Continuing Education Association. His other books in this area are *Problems and Prospects in Continuing Professional Education* (1985) and *Visions for the Future of Continuing Professional Education* (1990). His recent books with Arthur L. Wilson offer a political perspective on planning educational programs for adults: *Planning Responsibly for Adult Education: A Guide to Negotiating Power and Interests* (1994) and *What Really Matters in Adult Education Program Planning: Lessons in Negotiating Power and Interests* (1996). His research with Arthur L. Wilson in this area received the 1995 and the 1997 Imogene Okes Award for Research from the American Association for Adult and Continuing Education.

Cervero has served in a variety of leadership positions in adult education. He was on the executive committee for the Adult Education Research Conference (1982, 1983) and was a cofounder of the Midwest Research-to-Practice Conference in Adult and Continuing

Education (1982), a member of the executive committee for the Commission of Professors of Adult Education (1986–1988; 1998–2000), and coeditor of *Adult Education Quarterly* (1988–1993). He has been a visiting faculty member at the University of Calgary, the University of Tennessee, the University of Wisconsin-Madison, the University of British Columbia, and Pennsylvania State University.

Arthur L. Wilson is associate professor in the Department of Education at Cornell University. He received his B.A. degree (1972) in sociology from the University of Virginia, his M.S.Ed. degree (1980) in adult and continuing education from Virginia Polytechnic Institute and State University, and his Ed.D. degree (1991) in adult education from the University of Georgia.

Wilson's major areas of research emanate from his extensive practical experience as an adult educator in ABE and GED classroom teaching, curriculum development and teacher training in both local and statewide literacy staff development, a national program of professional training and certification, and graduate program development in adult education. In his research on adult learning, he has focused on its role in professional practice and continuing professional education. His interest in adult education foundations has produced a number of historical and philosophical articles and chapters; a report from his doctoral dissertation on the epistemological foundations of adult education received the Graduate Student Research Award (1992) given by the North American Adult Education Research Conference. He and Ronald M. Cervero have produced a number of works on adult education program planning and more generally the politics of adult education: *Planning Responsibly for Adult Education: A Guide to Negotiating Power and Interests* (1994) and *What Really Matters in Adult Education Program Planning: Lessons in Negotiating Power and Interests* (1996). Their research on program planning practice received the 1995 and 1997 Imogene Okes Award for Research from the American Association for Adult and Continuing Education.

Wilson served on the executive board of the Virginia Association for Adult and Continuing Education (1986–1988) and received its distinguished service award (1987); he also served as the executive secretary for technical assistance for the Indiana Association of Adult and Continuing Education and the Indiana Community Education Association (1992–1995). He has chaired the Imogene Okes Award for Research committee and was on the executive committee of the Commission of Professors of Adult Education (1997–1999). He received a Kellogg Fellowship (1988–1990) to attend the University of Georgia.

Wilson has extensive editorial experience as assistant editor of the *Virginia ABE Newsletter* (1979–1981), as editor of the *Virginia Association for Adult and Continuing Education Newsletter* (1986–1988), as editorial associate for *Adult Education Quarterly* (1988–1991), and as a consulting editor for *Adult Education Quarterly, International Journal of Lifelong Education, Journal of Adult Basic Education,* and *Canadian Journal for the Study of Adult Education.* He is coeditor of the *Handbook of Adult and Continuing Education: New Edition* and currently coeditor of *Adult Education Quarterly.* He has been a visiting faculty member at Old Dominion University, George Mason University, and the University of Alberta, Canada.

Stephen D. Brookfield holds the title of Distinguished Professor at the University of St. Thomas in Minneapolis, Minnesota. He also serves as a consultant to the adult education doctoral program at National-Louis University in Chicago. Prior to moving to Minnesota, Brookfield spent ten years as a professor of higher and adult education at Teachers College, Columbia University, where he is still adjunct professor.

Brookfield's main research activities have been in the areas of adult learning, teaching, and critical thinking and reflection. He currently serves on the editorial boards of *Adult Education Quarterly* (United States), *Canadian Journal for the Study of Adult Education, Studies in Continuing Education* (Australia), *Studies in the Education of Adults* (United Kingdom), and *International Journal of University Continuing Education.*

He is a three-time winner of the Cyril O. Houle World Award for Literature in Adult Education: in 1986 for his book *Understanding and Facilitating Adult Learning,* in 1989 for *Developing Critical Thinkers,* and in 1996 for *Becoming a Critically Reflective Teacher. Understanding and Facilitating Adult Learning* also won the 1986 Imogene E. Okes Award for Outstanding Research in Adult Education. His other books include *Adult Learners, Adult Education and the Community* (1984), *Self-Directed Learning: From Theory to Practice* (1985),

Learning Democracy (1987), *Training Educators of Adults* (1988), *The Skillful Teacher* (1990), and *Discussion as a Way of Teaching* (1999, with Stephen Preskill).

Elaine Butler is a senior lecturer in education at the University of South Australia, teaching in work studies, work-related education, vocationalism, research and policy studies, and curriculum studies. She holds a diploma in teaching (1979) and a B.Ed. degree (1979) from the University of South Australia, as well as an M.Ed. degree (1995) from the University of Canberra. She is a member of the Australian College of Education and of the Asia-Pacific Centre of Educational Innovation for Development, a UNESCO committee. Fifteen years of working in the finance industry resulted in her politicization and an enduring interest in social justice. She has published a number of chapters, research publications, papers, and reports; she coedited one book and coauthored two forthcoming publications, *Irreconcilable Differences? Women in Business and the Vocational Education and Training System* and *Don't Be Too Polite, Girls! Women, Work and Vocational Education and Training: A Critical Review of the Literature.*

Butler's teaching career includes lecturing at technical and further education colleges in community, vocational, and basic adult social education at the University of Papua New Guinea (Goroka Teachers' College), and in work studies, research, and policy studies at the University of Adelaide. Much of Butler's academic work has investigated women and work, and, more recently, the feminization of work. Her research and teaching focus on the dynamic interrelationships between the changing nature, organization, and distribution of work; work-related learning; and emergent global and local policy logics in this broad field. Of central interest are issues of globalization, knowledge production, and governance in so-called knowledge economies, and in the discourses of lifelong learning. Butler has an active interest in poststructuralism, governmentality, and feminisms, and in the literatures associated with modernity and detraditionalization, place, pedagogies, and embodied and located knowledge practices.

Vicki K. Carter received her Bachelor of Music degree (1967) from Indiana University and her M.Ed. in adult education from Pennsylvania State University. Currently she is an instructional designer as well as a doctoral candidate in the adult education program at Penn State. Her thesis research is based on a critical cultural study of workplace learning.

Budd L. Hall is professor of adult education and community development and chair of the Department of Adult Education, Community Development, and Counseling Psychology at the Ontario Institute for Studies in Education, University of Toronto, Canada. Hall holds a Ph.D. in comparative and international education from the University of California at Los Angeles, an M.Ed. degree from Michigan State University, and a B.A. degree in political science from Michigan State University. He was secretary general of the International Council for Adult Education between 1979 and 1991. He has held academic appointments with the University of Dar es Salaam (Tanzania), the University of Sussex (England), and the University of Montreal. He is currently vice president for North America of the International Council for Adult Education. His academic writing has been in the fields of participatory research and international and comparative adult education. Hall is also a poet.

Mechthild Hart is associate professor at the School for New Learning, DePaul University in Chicago, where she teaches in an interdisciplinary liberal studies program for working adults. She received her Ph.D. (1984) in adult education at Indiana University. The classes she teaches and her research interests are linked to a lifelong commitment to social justice and to educational efforts that are anchored in the desire for individual and social change. Since the publication of her book *Working and Education for Life: Feminist and International Perspectives on Adult Education* (1992), she has expanded her specific interest in forms of life-affirming work and how they shape experiences, ways of knowing, social and individual identity, and learning desires.

Sharon L. Howell received her B.A. from Kalamazoo College and her M.Ed. in adult education from Penn State University. She is currently a doctoral candidate in adult education at Penn State, where her thesis research focused on a case study of workers' perspectives on informal learning in the workplace.

Juanita Johnson-Bailey is an associate professor in the Department of Adult Education and Women's Studies at the University of Georgia. She received her Ed.D. in adult education and her graduate certificate in women's studies from the University of Georgia in June 1994. She held an academic appointment at Georgia College and State University from 1993 to 1995.

Johnson-Bailey's main research areas are race, gender, and power dynamics in the educational setting. She has published articles on power issues in teaching, racism and sexism in higher education, and the experiences of Black reentry college students. She is the author of *Sistahs in College: Making a Way Out of No Way* (2000, Krieger Press) and the coeditor of *Flatfooted Truths: Telling Black Women's Lives* with Patricia Bell-Scott (1998). She is a recipient of the Houle Scholars Grant and a Lilly Teaching Fellows Grant. Johnson-Bailey has served on the steering committee of the Adult Education Research Conference and on the editorial board of *Adult Education Quarterly*. She founded the Adult Education Black Caucus and the Women of Color discussion group, an international on-line listserv and website.

Nod Miller is professor of innovation studies and assistant vice chancellor (lifelong learning) at the University of East London (UEL). She obtained a B.A. in social studies from the University of East Anglia (1970), an M.A. in the sociology of education and mass communication from the University of Leicester (1976), and a Ph.D. from the University of Manchester (1989).

Miller joined UEL in 1995 after seventeen years in the Faculty of Education at the University of Manchester, most recently as head of the Centre for Adult and Higher Education. She describes herself variously as an adult educator, a media sociologist, a communications specialist, a fan of popular culture, an action researcher, a T-group trainer, a feminist, an autobiographer, an experiential learner, an internationalist, and a member of a working-class family. Her research interests include experiential learning, autobiography, interpersonal communication, and media sociology, and she has published widely across these areas. Her edited books include *Working with Experience: Animating Learning* (1996, with David Boud). She has contributed to learning events in Australia, Brazil, Canada,

Finland, Germany, Holland, India, Israel, Nigeria, Thailand, New Zealand, and the United States, as well as in the United Kingdom.

Shahrzad Mojab is assistant professor in the Department of Adult Education, Community Development, and Counselling Psychology, the Ontario Institute for Studies in Education (OISE) at the University of Toronto. She earned her B.A. degree (1977) in English language in Iran; her M.A. degree (1979) with a joint focus in comparative education and in administration, higher and continuing education; and her Ph.D. (1991) in educational policy studies and women's studies from the University of Illinois at Urbana-Champaign. She specializes in educational policy studies with a focus on policies affecting the academic life of marginalized groups in universities and colleges. Before joining OISE, she participated in initiating, developing, and implementing employment and educational equity programs at several Canadian universities. As a member of the Advisory Working Group, she consulted the Ontario minister of multiculturalism and citizenship on antiracism and equity-related policies.

Mojab's areas of research and teaching interest include minority women's access to education; antiracism education; social justice and equality; political economy of adult education; adult education in comparative and global perspectives; women, ethnicity, violence, and learning; feminism and nationalism; and women, globalization, and citizenship. Her publications include articles and book chapters on Islamic feminism, diversity and academic freedom in Canadian and Iranian universities, minority women in academe, feminism and nationalism, adult education and civil society in the Middle East, state-university relations, and women's access to higher education. She is the editor of the forthcoming book *Women of a Stateless Nation: The Kurds* and the coeditor of the forthcoming book *Property and Propriety: The Role of Gender and Class in Imperialism and Nationalism.*

Kjell Rubenson is professor of adult education and codirector of the Centre for Policy Studies of Higher Education and Training at the University of British Columbia. He obtained a Ph.D. in education (1975) from the University of Gothenburg, Sweden. Before settling in Canada in 1987, he held a chair in adult education, first at the University of Stockholm and then at Linkoping University. He has worked broadly in the area of the sociology of adult education and is presently specializing in adult and higher education policies and training with a focus on participation in lifelong learning and the long-term effects of education and training. He has been involved in several large international studies on adult education and training, including the present International Adult Literacy Survey (IALS). He has been a consultant to the OECD and UNESCO on issues related to adult education and training, and has worked with Statistics Canada. His recent publications include *An Analysis of Ten Years of OECD Reviews of National Policies for Education* (1997) and *The Knowledge Society: Public Policy and Private Strategies: A Comparison of Canada and the European Union* (coedited with H. Schuetze; 2000).

Fred M. Schied received his B.A. degree (1991) in history from the University of Illinois-Chicago, where he also did graduate work in European history. He received an M.A. from DePaul University and his D.Ed. in adult education from Northern Illinois University. His primary research interest is in sociocultural perspectives on learning and work. Schied is currently associate professor of education and coprofessor-in-charge of the graduate program in adult education at Penn State University.

Fred M. Schied, Vicki K. Carter, and *Sharon L. Howell* have spent the last four years investigating issues of power, control, and gender as they intersect with learning and management structures in a variety of work sites. This research has produced a variety of papers, articles, and book chapters on feminist perspectives on HRD, critical examinations of HRD and the concept of organizational learning, education and control in quality management approaches, and the origins of HRD.

Kimberly B. Sessions is assistant director of the Emory/Atlanta Center for AIDS Research (CFAR). She earned her B.A. degree (1979) in psychology at the University of the South in Sewanee, Tennessee, and her M.Ed. (1995) and Ed.D. (1998) in adult education at the University of Georgia. Before joining the staff at CFAR, she was an HIV/AIDS medical educator for the Southeast AIDS Training and Education Center for ten years. Sessions's main research activities have concerned factors affecting the acceptance and success of HIV/AIDS education programs, and recruitment and retention issues affecting participation in HIV/AIDS clinical trials.

Elizabeth J. Tisdell is an associate professor in the Department of Adult and Continuing Education at National- Louis University in Chicago. She earned her B.A. degree (1977) in mathematics from the University of Maine, her M.A. degree (1979) in religion from Fordham University, and her Ed.D. degree (1992) in adult education from the University of Georgia. Before joining the faculty at National Louis University, she served as core faculty in the graduate programs in education at Antioch University in Seattle (1994–1998). She also worked at the Georgia Center for Continuing Education and taught in women's studies at the University of Georgia (1992–1994), and worked as a campus minister and adjunct faculty member at Loyola University in New Orleans (1982–1989).

Tisdell's research and scholarship is in the areas of gender, race, and diversity and equity issues in adult education, particularly in adult higher education. Her prior research has been on power relations based on gender, race, and class in adult higher education classrooms, on how faculty deal with diversity issues in the classroom, and on feminist pedagogy. In a similar vein, her current research focuses on how underlying spiritual commitments motivate and influence the educational practices of a multicultural group of women adult educators who are teaching across borders of race, class, gender, and culture for social action and transformation. She is the author of *Creating Inclusive Adult Learning Environments: Insights from Multicultural Education and Feminist Pedagogy* (1995) and numerous articles and book chapters that deal with feminist and multicultural issues in adult education. She is on the editorial review boards of *Adult Education Quarterly* and *Studies in Continuing Education*.

Chapter One

At the Heart of Practice
The Struggle for Knowledge and Power
Ronald M. Cervero, Arthur L. Wilson

The education of adults has played an active part in the ongoing constitution of social, economic, political, and cultural life since the beginning of human history. The recognition of the importance of these activities and their being brought together into a field of educational practice, however, had to wait until the 1920s. As signaled by the creation of the American Association for Adult Education in 1926 and the vision of leaders such as Eduard Lindeman and Alain Locke, adult education was seen as an important means of bringing "democratic participation to adults who throughout their lifespan struggle to participate in social and economic decisions affecting them" (Heaney, 1996, p. 5). Over the past seventy-five years, the many and varied institutions of society, from trade unions to higher education, from local community-based organizations to multinational corporations, have increasingly turned to adult education to fashion a society in terms of their own interests and values. As one observer of the worldwide growth of adult education notes, "The formal structures of adult education reach literally tens of millions of adults throughout the world in a complex and intricate variety of adult education offerings. . . . Aside from the formal channels of media communication, the combined network of adult education structures reach a larger proportion of the world's population than any other single form of communication" (Hall, 1997, p. 18).

It is clear that adult education has moved to a central position in the constitution of social life (Hake, 1999). Although adult education has always been an expression of wider processes of social power, conflict, and change, its widespread use by institutions of the state, the market, and civil society has highlighted the need to understand its relationship to society. We know that adult education has a role in the distribution not only of knowledge but also of social, cultural, and economic power. If adult education did not have these material effects, no one would care very much about it. Would employers have spent $210 billion on education for fifty-nine million adults in 1996 ("Statistical Picture," 1997) if these activities did not have a demonstrable effect on the economic and social life of workplace institutions? Would thousands of campesinos in El Salvador have educated themselves through popular education for a decade in the middle of war and poverty unless they saw its connection to political struggle and social transformation (Hammond, 1998)? Would the policymakers and lawmakers of the U.S. government have made "welfare-to-work" programs central to the new $16.4 billion welfare reform legislation (D'Amico, 1997) without a vision of how this form of adult education connects to wider social relations? Would traditionally black and colored trade unions in postapartheid South Africa come to the planning table with the new, democratic government for the first time in history to make educational policy for workers without understanding how this policy could reshape political relationships in their union and country (Cooper, 1998)? Can the presidents of institutions of higher education in the United States be immune to the wider political-economic changes in society when 45 percent of their students are now over the age of twenty-five (Levine & Cureton, 1998)? Would the President's Commission on Race have recommended a variety of forms of adult education to remedy racial prejudice, privilege, and disparities without understanding that it would have an effect on the redistribution of power in society (President's Initiative on Race, 1998)?

As these examples illustrate, adult education cannot be a neutral activity in the continual struggle for the distribution of knowledge and power in society. This is hardly a new idea, as most people recognize that the policies, practices, and institutions of adult education are caught up in the conflicts and constitution of our economic, cultural, social, and political systems (Cunningham, 2000; Welton, 1995). The important question, then, is not whether adult education is connected to these conflicts and processes, but how and why. These questions call for a relational analysis that takes seriously the idea that adult education does not stand above the unequal relations of power that structure the wider systems in society (Apple, 1990). Rather, as the foregoing examples show, we believe that the institutions and practices of adult education not only are structured by these relations but also play a role in reproducing or changing them. We therefore take as our starting point for answering these questions the assumption that "education represents both a struggle for meaning and a struggle over power relations. Thus, education becomes a central terrain where power and politics operate out of the lived culture of individuals and groups situated in asymmetrical social and political positions" (Mohanty, 1994, p. 147). This relational view requires that we ask that timeless political question about our efforts in adult education: Who benefits? Perpetually tied to this question is the ethical one: Who should benefit? The increasing importance of adult education in the constitution of social, political, economic, and cultural life demands no less.

The remainder of this chapter provides a context for how the book addresses these questions. First, we discuss three ways the adult education literature has approached the connections between power and practice in adult education. In the next section, we explain our understanding of power, politics, and practice in adult education. Finally, we provide the rationale for a better understanding of how the political struggles in the wider society are played out in the particulars of adult education practice.

Three Views on Adult Education, Power, and Practice

Given our position that issues of power are at stake in adult education, it follows that a conception of politics is embedded in any discussion of the field. In this regard, we review three different conceptions of the political in adult education practice. All three conceptions have historical antecedents, as well as current manifestations, in the literature of the field. The first strand of the literature, the "political is personal," focuses on "the adult learner." In this strand, power relations are implicit but nonetheless quite important. The other two conceptions are explicitly about power. The "political is practical" strand focuses on the ability to get things done within existing political relationships. In contrast, the social vision of the "political is structural" strand is to redistribute power.

The Political Is Personal: Romancing the Adult Learner

This strand of the literature has always promoted an optimistic view about adult education as a field. Knowles (1980) explains that adult education "brings together into a discrete social system all the individuals, institutions, and associations concerned with the education of adults and perceives them as working towards common goals of improving the methods and materials of adult learning, extending the opportunities for adults to learn, and advancing the general level of our culture" (p. 25). This optimism stems from the belief that by helping adults learn, adult educators improve the lives of individuals, increase the effectiveness of organizations, and meet the needs of society. The most important element in this view is the relationship between learners and educators. Robertson (1996) synopsizes this relationship in saying that the "most influential images of exemplary adult educators include Belenky's midwife, Brookfield's skillful teacher, Daloz's mentor, Freire's partner, Knowles' andragogue, and Mezirow's emancipatory educator" (p. 41). These images of practice "urge adult educators to develop trusting, caring relationships with adult learners and to give their professional hearts and souls over to helping those learners to experience empowering paradigm shifts. Surely this goal is above reproach" (p. 43).

This romancing of the adult learner leads to a view of practice that is very comforting for adult educators. At the heart of practice is the adult learner, whose needs for learning, once uncovered, can be met through the effective design of educational programs. These learning needs can be about any topic and can be met anywhere or anytime. As *Principles of Good Practice in Continuing Education* states: "A generally accepted purpose of continuing education programs is to help maintain, expand, and improve individual knowledge, skills (performance), and attitude and, by so doing, equally meet the improvement and advancement of individuals, professions, and organizations. Therefore, a primary emphasis in the principles of good practice is on the individual learner" (Council on the Continuing Education Unit, 1984, p. 3). By romancing the individual adult learner, organizations and society are improved because "a society whose central dynamic, change—economic and technological, political, social, cultural, even theological—requires a citizenry that is able to change" (Knowles, 1980, p. 36). The highest professional and moral principle for adult educators, then, is to involve learners in identifying their needs. Key metaphors are those of building on the experience of these potential adult learners; hearing their "voice," which has often been silenced; or giving them access to learning opportunities that historically have been denied.

In this scenario of practice, adult educators become facilitators of learning, who often have to "get around" social and organizational structures to "help" serve these adult learners. This view has produced quite a useful array of strategies and techniques for adult education. As an approach to power and politics, however, this view of adult education has come under extensive criticism (Collins, 1991; Rubenson, 1982). Griffin (1988) identifies the lack of an explicit social vision, arguing that "critical thinking, perspective transformation, and andragogy can all be put to universal purposes, whether these be the reinvigoration of democracy, the struggles of oppressed groups, or the learning needs of managers of international corporations. This is because they lack any kind of social structural reference and are, apparently, of no ideological significance" (p. 178). Cunningham (2000) critiques the focus on the generic learner: "much of the field's rhetoric centers on *the learner,* as if learners are disembodied creatures and as if the social context, the social structures, the social class in which we all exist do not affect the process of education." In essence, issues of power are invisible, and we are left with a view that asks us to believe that the political is personal (Mohanty, 1994). Many agree that the fundamental problem with learner-centeredness as a guiding principle for adult education is that "as a pedagogy it is inherently ambivalent and capable of many significations. There is a need to stop seeing experiential learning . . . as a natural characteristic of the individual learner or as a pedagogical technique, and more in terms of the contexts, socio-cultural and institutional, in which it functions and from which it derives its significations" (Usher,

Bryant, & Johnston, 1997, p. 105). The context for adult education practice is not simply the background in which adult learners are served. Rather, the social location of the trade union, the university, the popular education program, and the corporation provides the significance and meaning for the adult education offered. The trade union and the HRD department offer programs that define workers differently in terms of economic relationships with management and owners of capital. These workers are not generic adult learners, but rather are specific adult learners whose participation can be understood only within the material order of the program's social location. The educational program itself cannot be neutral with respect to the social and economic relations of power in the setting of the corporation, but necessarily carries with it a social vision. Adult education is not practiced on a neutral stage. Rather, it happens in a social location that is defined by a particular social vision in relation to the wider systems of social, economic, and cultural relations of power.

The Political Is Practical: The Ability to Get Things Done

A second strand in the literature defines politics explicitly in contrast to the learner-centered view. This perspective is not philosophically opposed to the learner-centered view of practice, but sees it as incomplete in the real world because of its political naïveté. Politics in this strand focuses on the "how to" and is defined as "the ability to get things done, to mobilize resources, to get and use whatever it is that a person needs for the goals he or she is attempting to meet" (Kanter, 1977, p. 166). It is important to note that this definition of politics as the ability to get things done takes the existing relations of power in the organizational or social setting as acceptable, or at least unchangeable. This approach to politics is commonly found in the literature that discusses adult educators' inability to get things done due to this marginal institutional status. Certainly Burton Clark's book (1958) on the marginality of adult education in the Los Angeles public school system spoke to a central issue for many, if not all, adult educators. His themes continue to this day (Burnham, 1989) as adult educators worry about "turf" issues with other providers, the place of adult education in the "parent" institution in which it is embedded, and the constant tension between the learning agenda of their programs and its intersection with the political-economic agendas of their institutions.

This concern with the everyday hustle-bustle of politics is recognized by most adult educators. Although adult educators are constantly concerned with the practical issues of politics, this strand has only recently gained a foothold in the field's theory and research efforts. As Griffith (1976) found in his review of adult education and politics twenty-five years ago, "Few articles dealing with political acumen and activities of adult educators can be found in the adult education literature" (p. 270). Attention to the politics of practice has increased worldwide, however, as adult education has become a more highly visible activity carried out by institutions of the state, the market, and civil society. As Thomas (1991) explains, the literature of adult education in the West is just now catching up to the rest of the world, where adult education has always been seen as a political enterprise. Much of this literature focuses on political models for decision making in organizations (Yang, Cervero, Valentine, & Benson, 1998) with an emphasis on higher education contexts (Bourgeois & Lienard, 1992; Maclean, 1996). Attention has also been given to issues of competition and collaboration across organizations (Beder, 1984; Stern, 1983) and to the policymaking and legislative activities of the state (Jarvis, 1993).

Although it is true that practicing adult educators, regardless of their ideological stance, must attend to the practical issues of how to operate within existing political relationships, this strand has come under criticism on two counts: (1) its definition of power is narrowly focused along individual lines, and (2) its largely unprincipled attention to the "how to" of politics leaves aside issues of "what for." As Forester (1989) explains about the wider literature on organizational politics, this view "first found great favor for being practical, but then inspired no end of criticism for being unprincipled . . . admonishing us to 'make do'" (p. 32). Although this strand may help adult educators recognize how to negotiate organizational politics, it defines those politics largely in terms of which individuals have power in the organizational setting. Thus it fails to conceptualize power in sociostructural terms, in which the hierarchical relationships of, for example, race, class, and gender are manifested in adult education. Because it lacks an analysis of adult education's relationship to the wider systems of power in society, this view of politics does not usually have an explicit social vision of whose interests should be served by adult education (Collins, 1991). This stands in contrast to the next strand, which offers both sociostructural theories of power in relation to adult education and an explicit social vision regarding the need to change existing relations of power through adult education.

The Political Is Structural: Redistributing Power

The third strand has always been centered on a relational view of education in terms of the wider systems of society, has seen socially structured power relations as advantaging certain groups and disadvantaging other groups in society, and has a clear social commitment to using adult education to redistribute this power (Apple, 1996). Politics in this strand is not so much about the ability to get things done but rather "pertains to the operation, exercise, and distribution of power—and the contest and struggle for power—within the social structure; which shapes human life within a society, having consequences for the interests and life possibilities of its members" (Lankshear, 1987, p. 16). The common cause of adult education in this strand is not the generic adult learner but adult learners who are oppressed by socially structured power relations along economic, racial, cultural, or gendered lines. Proponents of this strand stress the relational view of education, as Mayo (1994, p. 139) explains in comparing two prominent theorists, Freire and Gramsci, who believe that adult education "is not neutral and is very much tied to the hegemonic/counter-hegemonic interests within a given society. . . . Radical adult education initiatives, therefore, underline a commitment to a cause. The common cause in Gramsci's and Freire's writings is the struggle against oppression caused by the exploitation of 'subaltern' groups by dominant, hegemonic ones" (p. 139). As Newman (1994, p. 31) so forcefully argues, we can also put a face on these inequitable relations of power, and can thus identify who the learners should be:

> The problem for adult educators constrained by the ideals of decency, detachment and civic responsibility is that we do live in a world where we have harsh and unpalatable conflicts of interests,

and where we have real and tangible enemies. . . . We have irresponsible and lawless multinationals that put profit before anything else, and whose executives ignore or deny the humanity of the people they employ. We have racists. . . . We have corporate oligarchies, groups of the "elite," people with access to power and privilege who try to restrict the extent to which ordinary people exercise democracy.

There is a strong impetus not only to see education relationally but also to use education to reshape these systems to a more just and equitable life for all people.

The goal of redistributing power through adult education has been a constant theme in the literature of the field (Heaney, 1996). However, there has been a tremendous expansion of literature in the past two decades that articulates a variety of democratically inspired social visions and ways of analyzing power (Cunningham, 2000; Rubenson, 1989; Wangoola & Youngman, 1996). These discussions of power, informed by social theorists as diverse as Anthony Giddens, Antonio Gramsci, bell hooks, Cornel West, Jürgen Habermas, and Michel Foucault, address such issues as empowerment and emancipation (Inglis, 1997), knowledge (Pietrykowski, 1996), and identity (Wilson, 1999). The legacy of Marxism continues to be expressed in the forms of critical theory (Hart, 1990; Welton, 1995) and theories of political economy, particularly in reference to issues of globalization (Walters, 1997; Wangoola & Youngman, 1996) and the state (Torres, 1995). The ways in which systems of power and privilege based on race, class, gender, and sexual orientation are played out in adult education have been the focus of numerous analyses (Hayes & Colin, 1994; Hill, 1995; Johnson-Bailey & Cervero, 2000; Sheared, 1998).

This perspective clearly draws attention to the political and ethical nature of adult education. Its insights show how existing societal relations of power shape adult education activities and offer encouragement to foster dialogue, democracy, individual freedom, and social justice. Yet although it forces our vision outward to the impact of adult education on the wider society, this perspective has been criticized for failing to provide a concrete direction for practice. Apple (1988) clearly agrees with this criticism with regard to the wider field of education: "We have a relatively highly developed body of meta-theory, but a seriously underdeveloped tradition of applied, middle-range work" (p. 200). In terms of adult education, Shirley Walters agrees, arguing that "our understanding of micro educational practices, which are crucial in mediating our macro politics, is not necessarily advancing" (1996, p. 294). Youngman (1996, p. 27) also argues that these micro educational practices are vitally important: "The consideration of social and political theory derives its importance from its usefulness in clarifying the contexts of the practical activity of adult education. Indeed, it is in the content, methods and processes of the teaching and learning situation that the adult educator concretizes abstractions such as democracy and equality."

Power, Politics, and Practice in Adult Education

With three different conceptions of the political as background, we now turn to our understanding of power, politics, and practice in adult education. We propose three starting points that, when linked together, offer a map for understanding the fundamental issues of practice in adult education. These starting points are as follows: (1) there is a reciprocal relationship between power and adult education, (2) adult education is a site of struggle for knowledge and power, and (3) all adult educators practice with a social vision.

There Is a Reciprocal Relationship Between Power and Adult Education

This book is premised on the need to see adult education relationally, which "involves seeing social activity—with education as a particular form of that activity—as tied to the larger arrangement of institutions which apportion resources so that particular groups and classes have historically been helped while others have been less adequately treated" (Apple, 1990, p. 10). This relationship is reciprocal in that the effects go in both directions. In one direction, the social, economic, cultural, political, racial, and gendered power relations that structure all action in the world are played out in adult education. These systems of power are almost always asymmetrical, privileging some people and disadvantaging others. This is true for any policy, program, or practice of adult education regardless of its institutional and social location or the ideological character of its content. This holds true for a national policy on lifelong learning, a continuing medical education class at a university, or an antiracism workshop held for community leaders. In a real sense, the power relations that structure our lives together do not stop at the doors of our classrooms or institutions that provide adult education. In the other direction, our educational efforts always play a role in maintaining or reconstructing these systems of power. Power relations are never static but are continually reproduced or reshaped, thus providing more or fewer life chances for the adults who are affected by a program, policy, or practice of adult education. In sum, power relations both provide the grounds for action in adult education and are also always acted on by adult education (Giddens, 1979; Isaac, 1987).

This premise requires us to recognize that adult learners exist in the structurally defined hierarchies of everyday life and that these differences matter at a most fundamental level. Thus, although adults are an important part of adult education practice, they enter this process marked by their location within larger systems of power and privilege that have shaped their experiences. Like adult learners, adult educators also enter the educational practice as participants in larger systems of power and privilege, and their actions are both enabled and constrained by their place in these systems. Hart, Wilson, & Clark (1990, p. 259) summarize this crucial relationship between power, adult education, and practice: "The new themes which are proposed here . . . refer to the fact that individual learners (as well as educators) are embedded in different social realities, that power manifests itself concretely and specifically, and that educational practices need to take these particularities and differences into account."

Adult Education Is a Site of Struggle for Knowledge and Power

If power relations provide the grounds for action, then politics "is concerned with the *means* of producing, reproducing, consuming, and accumulating material and symbolic resources" (Morrow &

Torres, 1995, p. 464, emphasis added). Once we have defined adult education relationally within the wider society and economy, we must then locate it "on the ground" in the material world. Furthermore, in establishing our premise that power is always being negotiated, we place this book in the tradition of moving away from both determinism and unfettered human action in adult education (Giddens, 1979). Foley articulates this particular way of seeing the significance of adult education when he says that although power is universal, "it is also continually contested, so history may also be seen as a continual struggle by ordinary people to maintain or extend control over their lives" (1993, p. 23). Adult education's particular role in history can be seen as a struggle for knowledge, which is interwoven with the struggle for power. These struggles are the engines that drive and define adult education and are central to practice on the ground.

If these struggles define the politics of adult education, then negotiation is the central metaphor for practice (Cervero & Wilson, 1994, 1998). It is out of these struggles that a particular purpose, content, and audience for adult education are negotiated. This idea of adult education as a struggle for knowledge and power recognizes that there are multiple interests at stake in any adult education activity. Because adult education is about many things, there is almost always conflict among the agendas of the many people who might benefit from the adult education effort. Sometimes these conflicts are between the learning agenda and the political and economic agenda of the institutional provider. At other times the conflicts are between the competing social agendas of the institutional provider. In negotiating these conflicts, those responsible for adult education address that timeless political question about their efforts: Who benefits? As a central dynamic of practice then, our perspective on power in practice sees people acting in struggle as the focus of attention.

All Adult Educators Are Social Activists in Practice

Asking the question, Who benefits? is an important tool for understanding the politics of adult education in any setting. However, out of the struggles that define the politics of practice comes an adult education program, practice, or policy. By their actions, adult educators have answered the ethical question, Who should benefit? Cunningham (1988, p. 142) makes explicit that the fundamental link between politics and ethics occurs in practice when she says, "It is in the politics of practice that the question of ethics is confronted." The political and ethical questions raised in practice are not easy, for what happens when adult educators meet real systems of power and privilege in our classrooms, institutions, and communities? In this world in which adult education happens, what are the political and ethical dilemmas, the contradictions, and the possibilities of action? At the same time that we are asking the political question, Who benefits? we also need to ask the question, Who should benefit from our efforts in adult education?

Because the question of who should benefit is answered in practice, there can be no politically innocent place for adult educators. At the heart of practice, then, we must clearly understand that every adult educator is a social activist, regardless of his or her particular vision of society. We cannot be released from our responsibility for affecting the wider world in which we live. Hall (1997) explains that all adult education can make an impact in fashioning a different world in virtually all settings: "Elements of this shift from the vision of a world which doesn't work to a world which might work better are possible to include in literally any course or programme that can be conceived. It may require some extra effort, it may require the development of a whole new set of tools or ways of working, but it can be done and it is important to try" (p. 18). Hall emphasizes that even though a program may be technical or vocational, or otherwise circumscribed, there is always something an adult educator can do to draw attention to possibilities of change. Youngman (1996, p. 4) amplifies this idea: "Adult educators work in a wide variety of situations, ranging from institutions of the state to organizations of civil society. Their scope for a critical practice varies accordingly. However, it is our contention that spaces can be found in all situations if adult educators are clear about their social goals and how these can be embodied in their day to day activities." We agree with Youngman that all roads to these social goals lead through the politics and ethics of practice, the discussion of which is this book's focus.

Rationale for This Book

The book's three starting points underline the need to understand how the macro-level systems of power define the struggles for knowledge and power in adult education. These points also focus our attention on the negotiations that occur in and about particular adult education programs, practices, and policies. However, an increasing number of adult educators have noted the discrepancy between the need for this new understanding and what is available in the literature. Foley (1993, p. 22) argues, "Currently, a number of writers on adult education are attempting to articulate a more critical approach to the analysis of adult education. . . . This is a welcome development because it challenges adult educators to locate their work more firmly in social analyses and struggles for social justice. A major problem, though, with much supposedly critical adult education theory is that it is often very abstract; it has generally failed to develop analyses of adult learning in particular social contexts." Newman (1999) also expresses his frustration with the abstract level at which issues of power are discussed in adult education. He says that these frustrations "lead [him] to go looking for writers on adult education who will provide detailed case study and so locate their theory in time and place" (p. 217). Inglis (1998) is specific about the need to better understand how power relations operate in people's lives, saying, "The development of a knowledge and understanding of how power operates, of how social, political, and economic life is structured, is central to developing viable strategies and tactics through which existing discourses and institutional structures can be restructured, if not revolutionized" (p. 74).

Recently, some exciting work has begun to examine education as a site of struggle for knowledge and power in both K–12 and adult education settings. For example, Gore (1993) positions her work in this regard: "I emphasize the power relations which operate through the fundamental and specific relation of teacher and student. Previous 'micro' level analyses of classrooms . . . have tended to ignore the constitutive role of power in pedagogy. Radical pedagogies, on the other hand, have tended to focus on the 'macro' level of ideologies and institutions while downplaying the instructional act. My work fits between and responds to these discourses by focusing on the 'micro' functioning of power relations in pedagogy" (p. xiv). There have been similar efforts in adult education. For example, Schied (1993) describes the place of learning and education in the everyday lives of the German working-class community during the nineteenth century. Two illuminating studies have been done in adult literacy education, showing how power relations based on race and gender are played out in the particulars of education for Mexican Americans in the Southwest (Sparks, 1998) and women in North Carolina and Philadelphia (Luttrell, 1993). Darrah's study (1995) of workplace training, Foley's work (1993) on women's community learning centers, and Scott and Schmitt-Boshnick's work (1996) on women's collective community action derive from the researchers' seeing adult education as a site of struggle over knowledge and power.

Because we live in a world where power and knowledge are continually negotiated, adult education offers hope and possibility to many people. In order to realize these possibilities, however, we need to focus attention at the heart of practice to understand how power relations in the wider society are being enacted in the specific locations of adult education. We believe that by bringing greater visibility to the political and ethical choices, contradictions, and consequences of adult education, we can better understand how to create educational programs, practices, and policies that give people more control over their social, cultural, economic, and political lives. To this end, the book does not offer a transcendent "political perspective" but rather engages with the dynamics of our world to gain a greater understanding of its "shifting tectonics of power and the fault lines they generate" (Ó Tuathail, Herod, & Roberts, 1998, p. 2).

References

Apple, M. W. (1988). *Teachers and texts: A political economy of class and gender relations in education*. New York: Routledge.

Apple, M. W. (1990). *Ideology and curriculum* (2nd ed.). New York: Routledge.

Apple, M. W. (1996). Power, meaning, and identity: Critical sociology of education in the United States. *British Journal of Sociology of Education, 17*(2), 125–144.

Beder, H. (Ed.). (1984). *Realizing the potential of interorganizational cooperation.* New Directions for Continuing Education, no. 23. San Francisco: Jossey-Bass.

Bourgeois, E., & Lienard, G. (1992). Developing adult education in universities: A political view. *Higher Education Management, 4,* 80–90.

Burnham, B. (1989). Marginality thirty years later. *Proceedings of the 30th Annual Education Research Conference, 11,* 49–54. Madison: Department of Continuing and Vocational Education, University of Wisconsin, Madison.

Cervero, R. M., & Wilson, A. L. (1994). *Planning responsibly for adult education: A guide to negotiating power and interests.* San Francisco: Jossey-Bass.

Cervero, R. M., & Wilson, A. L. (1998). Working the planning table: The political practice of adult education. *Studies in Continuing Education, 20*(1), 5–21.

Clark, B. R. (1958). *The marginality of adult education.* Chicago: Center for the Study of Liberal Education for Adults.

Collins, M. (1991). *Adult education as vocation: A critical role for the adult educator.* London: Routledge.

Cooper, L. (1998). From "rolling mass action" to "RPL": The changing discourse of experience and learning in the South African labour movement. *Studies in Continuing Education, 20*(2), 143–157.

Council on the Continuing Education Unit. (1984). *Principles of good practice in continuing education.* Silver Spring, MD: Author.

Cunningham, P. M. (1988). The adult educator and social responsibility. In R. Brockett (Ed.), *Ethical issues in adult education* (pp. 133–145). New York: Teachers College Press.

Cunningham, P. M. (2000). Learning and education in the real world: A sociology of adult education. In A. L. Wilson & E. R. Hayes (Eds.), *Handbook of adult and continuing education: New edition* (pp. 573–591). San Francisco: Jossey-Bass.

D'Amico, D. (1997). *Adult education and welfare to work initiatives: A review of research, practice and policy.* Washington, DC: National Institute for Literacy.

Darrah, C. H. (1995). Workplace training, workplace learning: A case study. *Human Organization, 54*(1), 31–41.

Foley, G. (1993). The neighborhood house: Site of struggle, site of learning. *British Journal of Sociology of Education, 14*(1), 21–37.

Forester, J. (1989). *Planning in the face of power.* Berkeley: University of California Press.

Giddens, A. (1979). *Central problems in social theory.* Berkeley: University of California Press.

Gore, J. (1993). *The struggle for pedagogies: Critical and feminist discourses as regimes of truth*. New York: Routledge.

Griffin, C. (1988). Critical thinking and critical theory in adult education. In M. Zukas (Ed.), *Papers from the transatlantic dialogue* (pp. 176–180). Leeds, England: University of Leeds.

Griffith, W. S. (1976). Adult educators and politics. *Adult Education, 26*(4), 270–297.

Hake, B. (1999). Lifelong learning in late modernity: The challenges to society, organizations, and individuals. *Adult Education Quarterly, 49,* 79–90.

Hall, B. L. (1997, July). Transformative learning and democracy: Whose vision, whose planet, whose learning? In B. L. Hall & E. O'Sullivan (Chairs), *Embracing the world: Transformative learning, human-earth relations, democracy, and the quality of life.* Symposium conducted at the 27th annual conference of the Standing Conference for University Teachers and Researchers in the Education of Adults (SCUTREA), London.

Hammond, J. L. (1998). *Fighting to learn: Popular education and the guerrilla war in El Salvador.* New Brunswick, NJ: Rutgers University Press.

Hart, M. (1990). Critical theory and beyond: Further perspectives on emancipatory education. *Adult Education Quarterly, 40,* 125–138.

Hart, M., Wilson, A. L., & Clark, C. (1990). Emancipatory education: Further perspectives on Mezirow's theory of adult learning. In *Proceedings of the 31st Annual Adult Education Research Conference* (pp. 257–262). Athens: University of Georgia.

Hayes, E. R., & Colin, S.A.J., III (Eds.). (1994). *Confronting racism and sexism.* New Directions for Adult and Continuing Education, no. 61. San Francisco: Jossey-Bass.

Heaney, T. (1996). *Adult education for social change: From center stage to the wings and back again.* Columbus, OH: ERIC Clearinghouse on Adult, Career, and Vocational Education.

Hill, R. J. (1995). Gay discourse in adult education: A critical review. *Adult Education Quarterly, 45,* 142–158.

Inglis, T. (1997). Empowerment and emancipation. *Adult Education Quarterly, 48,* 3–17.

Inglis, T. (1998). A critical realist approach to emancipation: A response to Mezirow. *Adult Education Quarterly, 49,* 72–76.

Isaac, J. C. (1987). *Power and Marxist theory: A realist view.* Ithaca, NY: Cornell University Press.

Jarvis, P. (1993). *Adult education and the state: Towards a politics of adult education.* London: Routledge.

Johnson-Bailey, J., & Cervero, R. M. (2000). The invisible politics of race in adult education. In A. L. Wilson & E. R. Hayes (Eds.), *Handbook of adult and continuing education: New edition* (pp. 147–160). San Francisco: Jossey-Bass.

Kanter, R. M. (1977). *Men and women of the corporation.* New York: Basic Books.

Knowles, M. S. (1980). *The modern practice of adult education: From pedagogy to andragogy.* Chicago: Association Press.

Lankshear, C. (1987). *Literacy, schooling, and revolution.* New York: Falmer.

Levine, A., & Cureton, J. S. (1998). What we know about today's college students. *About Campus, 3*(3), 4–7.

Luttrell, W. (1993). "The teachers, they all had their pets": Concepts of gender, knowledge, and power. *Signs: Journal of Women in Culture and Society, 18*(3), 505–546.

Maclean, R. G. (1996). Negotiating between competing interests in planning continuing medical education. In R. M. Cervero & A. L. Wilson (Eds.), *What really matters in adult education program planning: Lessons in negotiating power and interests.* New Directions for Adult and Continuing Education, no. 69. San Francisco: Jossey-Bass.

Mayo, P. (1994). Synthesizing Gramsci and Freire: Possibilities for a theory of radical adult education. *International Journal of Lifelong Education, 13*(2), 125–148.

Mohanty, C. H. (1994). On race and voice: Challenges for liberal education in the 1990s. In H. A. Giroux & P. McLaren (Eds.), *Between borders: Pedagogy and the politics of cultural studies* (pp. 145–166). New York: Routledge.

Morrow, R. A., & Torres, C. A. (1995). *Social theory and education: A critique of theories of social and cultural reproduction.* Albany: State University of New York Press.

Newman, M. (1994). *Defining the enemy: Adult education in social action.* Sydney: Stewart Victor.

Newman, M. (1999). *Maeler's regard: Images of adult learning.* Sydney: Stewart Victor.

Ó Tuathail, G., Herod, A., & Roberts, S. M. (1998). Negotiating unruly problematics. In A. Herod, G. Ó Tuathail, & S. M. Roberts (Eds.), *An unruly world: Globalization, governance, and geography* (pp. 1–24). London: Routledge.

Pietrykowski, B. (1996). Knowledge and power in adult education: Beyond Freire and Habermas. *Adult Education Quarterly, 46,* 82–97.

President's Initiative on Race. (1998). *One America in the twenty-first century: Forging a new future.* Washington, DC: Author.

Robertson, D. L. (1996). Facilitating transformative learning: Attending to the dynamics of the educational helping relationship. *Adult Education Quarterly, 47*, 41–53.

Rubenson, K. (1982). Adult education research: In quest of a map of the territory. *Adult Education Quarterly, 32*, 57–74.

Rubenson, K. (1989). The sociology of adult education. In S. B. Merriam & P. M. Cunningham (Eds.), *Handbook of adult and continuing education* (pp. 51–69). San Francisco: Jossey-Bass.

Schied, F. M. (1993). *Learning in social context: Workers and adult education in nineteenth century Chicago.* De Kalb: LEPS Press, Northern Illinois University.

Scott, S. M., & Schmitt-Boshnick, M. (1996). Collective action by women in community-based program planning. In R. M. Cervero & A. L. Wilson (Eds.), *What really matters in adult education program planning: Lessons in negotiating power and interests.* New Directions for Adult and Continuing Education, no. 69. San Francisco: Jossey-Bass.

Sheared, V. (1998). *Race, gender, and welfare reform.* New York: Garland.

Sparks, B. (1998). The politics of culture and the struggle to get an education. *Adult Education Quarterly, 48*, 245–259.

A statistical picture of employer sponsored training in the United States. (1997, October) [Special Issue: Industry Report 1997]. *Training.*

Stern, M. (1983). *Power and conflict in continuing professional education.* Belmont, CA: Wadsworth.

Thomas, A. (1991). Relationships with political science. In J. M. Peters, P. Jarvis, & Associates, *Adult education: Evolution and achievements in a developing field of study* (pp. 301–321). San Francisco: Jossey-Bass.

Torres, C. A. (1995). State and education revisited: Why educational researchers should think politically about education. In M. W. Apple (Ed.), *Review of research in education* (Vol. 21, pp. 255–321). Washington, DC: American Educational Research Association.

Usher, R., Bryant, I., & Johnston, R. (1997). *Adult education and the postmodern challenge.* London: Routledge.

Walters, S. (1996). Gender and adult education: Training gender-sensitive and feminist adult educators in South Africa—an emerging curriculum. In P. Wangoola & F. Youngman (Eds.), *Towards a transformative political economy of adult education: Theoretical and practical challenges* (pp. 293–319). De Kalb: LEPS Press, Northern Illinois University.

Walters, S. (Ed.). (1997). *Globalization, adult education, and society.* London: Zed Books.

Wangoola, P., & Youngman, F. (Eds.). (1996). *Towards a transformative political economy of adult education: Theoretical and practical challenges.* De Kalb: LEPS Press, Northern Illinois University.

Welton, M. (Ed.). (1995). *In defense of the lifeworld: Critical perspectives on adult learning.* Albany: State University of New York Press.

Wilson, A. L. (1999). Creating identities of dependency: Adult education as a knowledge-power regime. *International Journal of Lifelong Education, 18*(2), 85–93.

Yang, B., Cervero, R. M., Valentine, T., & Benson, J. (1998). Development and validation of an instrument to measure adult educators' power and influence tactics in program planning practice. *Adult Education Quarterly, 48,* 227–244.

Youngman, F. (1996). A transformative political economy of adult education: An introduction. In P. Wangoola & F. Youngman (Eds.), *Towards a transformative political economy of adult education: Theoretical and practical challenges* (pp. 3–30). De Kalb: LEPS Press, Northern Illinois University.

Adult Education
and Work

The chapters in Part One recognize that the economy and the organization of paid work are primary axes for the distribution of material and symbolic power and resources in any society. The role of adult education in the institutions where adults are employed is more important than ever and, increasingly, a site of struggle for knowledge and power.

In Chapter Two, Shahrzad Mojab locates her analysis of training immigrant women in the context of the political struggle between citizens and the market-state bloc. Instead of reducing the training of immigrant women to a problem of educational strategy, she argues that the failure of the policy and practice of retraining must be understood in the context of an imbalance of power between these women and the market-state.

In Chapter Three, Fred M. Schied, Vicki K. Carter, and Sharon L. Howell move from the macro picture of how the economy structures opportunity to the workplace itself as a site of struggle. They examine the many forms of power converging around training programs and show how a specific program was used as a form of management.

In Chapter Four, Elaine Butler takes on the discourses around lifelong work-related learning with the assumption that this language itself is a vital site of political contestation and power struggles. Specifically, she uses Foucault's approach to analyze the official discourses concerning lifelong learning in the workplace.

In Chapter Five, Kjell Rubenson discusses the role of the state in public policy decisions from several competing ideological perspectives. He focuses on the policies about work and learning set forth by the Organization for Economic Cooperation and Development (OECD). He addresses the political and moral logic of these competing positions in relation to equality, the market, and individual freedom.

Chapter Two

The Power of Economic Globalization

Deskilling Immigrant Women Through Training

Shahrzad Mojab

The political and economic upheavals of the 1990s have left their mark on the field of adult education. A major source of change is the globalization and restructuring of the capitalist economy, which make extraordinary demands on education in general and adult education in particular. The changing economy calls for the reorganization of adult education into a training enterprise fully responsive to the requirements of the market. Within the field, developments in social theory, especially theoretical positions carrying the prefix *post-*, challenge traditional approaches and favor ruptures with the past.

Many observers of the Western industrial economies were preoccupied during the last quarter of the twentieth century with making sense of the changes that affected the entire system, nationally and internationally. They were theorizing that what they saw was a transition from the production-based capitalist economy to an

This research was made possible by generous funding from the University of Toronto, Connaught Fund. I would also like to acknowledge the contribution of my research partners Shanaz Kahn, Gity Nasehy, and Rachal Ogbagzy. However, I alone am responsible for the views expressed.

information- or knowledge-based system. According to these theorists, the transition was profound, affecting the entire economic formation as well as social, cultural, and political relations. It is argued, now, that the labor force is changing from one engaged in physical or manual work to one immersed in the production of knowledge and information. A related development is the displacement of physical property by intellectual property. Some cultural theorists argue that modernity was the era of industrial capitalism immersed in the production of commodities, whereas postmodernity is characterized by the proliferation of images (Best & Kellner, 1991).

The transition to a "knowledge economy" occurs in the context of globalization, which is associated with trends such as transnationalization, deindustrialization, and privatization. The institution of the state is actively involved in "restructuring" the economic order, especially the relationship between capital and labor. The workforce is expected to be adaptable, flexible, and able to rapidly change its skill base under conditions of the unceasing movement of capital in search of more profitable opportunities. Restructuring occurring in the midst of a worldwide economic crisis has contributed to the formation of an unstable and fragile job market. According to an analysis by the Centre of Excellence for Research on Immigration and Settlement (1999b), in this market society the era of "a single transition from full-time school to full-time work" is "giving way to the idea of multiple pathways, back and forth, through different life cycles—the concept of lifelong learning." The educational equivalent of an information society is the learning society, one in which education turns into lifelong learning, and the workplace acts as a learning organization.

Although visions about the goals and directions of adult education are diverse and difficult to synthesize, I will focus here on a significant divide among adult educators. This division is over how people view the relationship between education and economy, but it constitutes nothing less than a struggle about the position of human beings in a rapidly changing world still dominated by the market and the state. The problem is not new in the sense that people with conflicting interests have always disagreed on the goals of education. Far from being nonpartisan, disinterested, impartial, or objective, education has always been a site of struggle for the assumption, maintenance, and exercise of power. Today, the tendency of the market, which is enjoying state support in the powerful nation-states of the European Union, North America, and elsewhere, is to strive for the monopolistic control of the goals and directions of education.

The Debate

One of the claims about the new (or postindustrial or knowledge or information) economy relates to the type of workforce on which it draws. A highly skilled labor force undergoing regular skill upgrading is, the argument goes, indispensable for the postindustrial market. This is so to a large extent because, in contrast with material production, the production of information or knowledge demands frequent upgrading, and active and creative worker involvement in the process. At the same time, the changing economy demands a flexible workforce that undergoes continual, "lifelong" training and is capable of shifting from one skill to another (Livingstone, 1999).

This "upgrading" thesis, which focuses on the need of the postindustrial economy for a highly skilled workforce, is rejected by those who argue that "there is little hard evidence that the level of education needed within the actual labor processes has greatly increased" (Livingstone, 1996, p. 83). The continuing unemployment and underemployment in the 1990s was due to job shortages rather than educational deficiencies. According to this view, "the present reality of underemployment is that, while the knowledge of our continually learning species has reached unprecedented levels, our work-related collective knowledge is increasingly being wasted in our workplaces as currently organized" (p. 77).

The debate about the locus of skills in the postindustrial economy is of great practical significance for educators, policymakers, and employers in the private and public sectors. It is equally significant, on the theoretical level, for adult educators and activists interested in democratization, peace, justice, and prosperity in a world threatened by poverty, war, genocide, and ecocide. In what follows, I will join the debate by first looking at the situation of a group of immigrant women, perusing some statistical data, and also reflecting on my own experience. Although the experiences of immigrants and minorities are the focus, I look at the larger context of these experiences. I will then probe into the theoretical controversy of the relationship between education and the economy by focusing on the questions of power, education, and democracy.

The upgrading thesis, which presumes that the postindustrial economy is dependent on highly skilled labor, is one of the underlying assumptions of government policy in Canada (Shields, 1995). Public policy ties the prosperity of Canadians to the enhancement of the skills of the labor force (Human Resources Development Canada, 1994). In 1992, for instance, the minister of employment and immigration initiated a major shift in immigration priorities by introducing Bill C-86 (Avery, 1995). This legislation, which made professional and skilled immigrants one of the preferred target groups, illuminates the relationship between the Business Immigration Program and Canadian economic policy (Wong, 1993). The arrival of some 1.4 million immigrants in Canada during the first half of the 1990s created the highest immigration flow since the 1940s. According to a study based on the data from the censuses of population between 1986 and 1996, newcomers between the ages of twenty-five and forty-four had, on average, higher levels of education than Canadian-born members of the same age group, but they were generally less likely to be employed than their cohorts (Badets & Howatson-Leo, 1999). This trend seems to challenge the upgrading thesis. However, the access of immigrants to the job market is complicated by many factors, such as knowledge of official languages, gender, ethnicity, country of origin, length of stay, and the "health" of the economy.

Statistical data on trends in the development of the economy and workforce require considerable contextualization and interpretation. In order to see what lies behind census figures and other statistical data, I interviewed a group of immigrant women who were participating in language and computer training classes (Mojab, 1999). About 40 percent of the trainees were highly skilled "knowledge workers" with considerable professional experience in their countries of origin. However, instead of a smooth entry into the knowledge-based market, they either remained unemployed or were pressured into nonskilled jobs, which, as one interviewee (a biologist) put it, demanded "the use of their hands rather than their minds." I will argue that the changing economy cannot be essentialized as a new system depending on highly skilled labor. Rather, I argue, this economy continues to skill and deskill the workforce, and shows a strong tendency toward polarizing workers into highly skilled and nonskilled segments.

The Dynamics of Deskilling

The following description (Mills & Simmons, 1995, p. 184) depicts, precisely, my daily experiences at the Ontario Institute of Studies in Education, a graduate school where many courses are taught in the evenings.

> Whenever we leave our office at the end of a particularly full day and beat a hasty retreat through the empty hallways and corridors of the deserted campus buildings, we encounter members of a community who are largely invisible during the day. Like the legendary Owl of Minerva, they only seem to emerge when the shades of night are falling. We are talking, of course, about the evening workforce of cleaners and janitors. . . . It is a community largely made up of women, many of whom are from minority ethnic backgrounds. Some are visible minority women: West Indians, South Asian, Filipinos, Chileans, and other non-European nationalities. Others are from European countries. . . . But within this community of women the only men to occasionally be seen are the supervisors or foremen who periodically come to inspect the work that is done.

I have to add, however, that some members of this evening workforce of cleaners and janitors are real Owls of Minerva, if holding a doctoral degree entitles one to the status of the mythological bird who served the goddess of arts, crafts, and wisdom.

Months after the interviews I had conducted were over, I was truly surprised to see one of the interviewees, the biologist quoted earlier, appear in my office to collect the garbage. I expected to see the person who regularly did the work and did not recognize the new face, although I was sure I had met her. A week passed, and in moments of solitude I reviewed the features of the face and tried to make some associations. At last, on another evening, as I was leaving the building I ran into her again, and suddenly I placed her as one of the interview participants. I said hello, and before I said more, reading the question in my face, she said, "Yes, I was in the group." I told her about my struggle to remember where I had seen her. She said, "I told you that this will be my fate. I'm ashamed; you know I'm a scientist." She continued, "But at least I am a janitor in a university." Then she told me she had registered with a recruiting agency and was called to work as a temporary replacement for the department's regular janitor, who had injured herself while vacuuming.

Like many immigrant women, I too was discouraged from pursuing my knowledge-based skills when I first arrived in Canada while working on my doctoral dissertation in 1986. I was told to abandon my aspirations for teaching in an academic setting. "Before it is too late," I was told, "you had better start looking somewhere else." Even an immigrant, a young doctoral candidate in a Toronto university, told me, "You'll never get a teaching position in a Canadian university." The view is widely shared that getting a position in one's area of expertise demands extraordinary effort, persistence, and determination. Although gratifying, my success conceals the pain of feeling the situation as being one of injustice or inequality. I know several immigrants with doctoral degrees from North American universities who continue to experience deskilling after years of struggle. The situation casts doubts about one's creativity, intelligence, worth, and confidence. A woman in this study attending advanced English as a Second Language (ESL) classes and preparing herself for taking the TOEFL said, "What I learn in English classes are not enough for what I have in mind as my future plan. Our lessons put too much emphasis on restaurants, and food services, which we are told to be a strong market with a strong labor need. I often think maybe they are right."

Stories of individual experiences of the deskilling of immigrants appear in the popular media. A daily paper in Toronto (Quinn, 1999, pp. B1, B5) ran the story of how a woman doctor's dreams, like those of many others in the profession, had gone sour. An obstetrician-gynecologist from China, she failed to find a position matching her skills. Before immigrating, she had her "qualifications assessed and learned that they were equivalent." However, the doctor found that "she was blocked from using her skills once in Canada." After years of delivering babies and providing pre- and postnatal care, she was not able to become a midwife. A university turned down her application for admission in the program because she was "overqualified." The story is the same for hundreds of foreign-trained physicians who are allowed to practice only if they complete the International Medical Graduate program at one of the five Ontario medical schools, pass written and oral exams, and finish a residency training program at a hospital. With only twenty-four residencies available per year, many have to wait for years to practice.

Deskilling Immigrant Women in Canada

It is difficult to understand the relationship between skills and jobs without looking at the dynamics of economic restructuring in the context of the worldwide economic crisis. I also looked at the way globalization shapes the changing economic life of Canada. In trying to understand the situation under study, I also relied on my own experience of living as an immigrant woman in Canada for more than ten years prior to this research. My struggle was to find a job compatible with my training, education, and experience of teaching in a Middle Eastern university. Throughout these years, I worked in a women's center and in the employment equity office of two postsecondary institutions. Outside the academy, I knew about the job histories of many acquaintances with both highly skilled and less skilled backgrounds.

Downsizing, privatization, restructuring, merging, and layoffs were making headline news in the local, national, and international media in the 1990s. In Canada, unemployment rates were in the double or near-double digits throughout much of the decade. Between 1993 and 1996, up to 20 percent of the population was in a low-income situation for at least one year. Individuals who immigrated after 1976 had a "relatively high risk of exposure to low income" (Statistics Canada, 1999). *Low* was defined as income below Statistics Canada's "after tax low income cut-offs" (for example, $23,460 for a family of four in an urban area with a population of 30,000 to 99,999 in 1996). In early 1999, Statistics Canada released figures that cast doubt on the indispensability of high skills in the changing economy. Although new immigrants had better knowledge of English than earlier immigrants, and those in the twenty-five to forty-four age group were better educated than their

Canadian-born cohorts, they were less likely to get jobs (Carey, 1999, p. A8).

My interviews with eighty-six immigrant women in Toronto showed a complex pattern of deskilling. These women were from Afghanistan, Bangladesh, Bosnia, Brazil, Bulgaria, Chile, Colombia, Cuba, El Salvador, Eritrea, the Philippines, Hong Kong, India, Iran, Iraq, Mexico, Morocco, Nicaragua, Nigeria, Pakistan, Peru, Poland, Portugal, Romania, Russia, Somalia, Sri Lanka, Venezuela, and Vietnam. They were participating in adult ESL and computer training programs provided by various community-based organizations in Toronto. The ESL classes were offered at basic, intermediate, and advanced levels. The computer classes were mostly lessons in basic processing or in gaining familiarity with a specific item of processing software.

The immigrant women from Eastern European countries and the former Soviet Union were highly educated. Thirteen out of nineteen were university educated, including one with a doctoral degree in chemistry. These women were distinguished from the others by the fact that most of their degrees were in nontraditional, male-dominated fields of study, such as chemical, mechanical, and electrical engineering. Similarly, twelve out of fifteen Latin American women were university educated. Their degrees, however, were predominantly in the humanities and social sciences. There was more heterogeneity among East Asian, Indian, and African immigrant women. The women from Afghanistan had the lowest level of education, and some were illiterate in their native language.

Overall, prior knowledge of the English language was low among all the participants. Unlike Latin American, East Asian, and African women who had some exposure to English, East European women expressed a great deal of difficulty with learning the language. In more mixed classes (in terms of country of origin), there was a tension between the demand for a more structural and grammatical focus and for more conversation-oriented lessons. The more educated women who aspired either to pursue a degree in Canada or to apply for professional licensing asked for more instruction in written and specialized English.

These women had various reasons for attending ESL and other skill-training classes. Access to the job market was the predominant motivation, followed by the need for socialization and access to social services such as welfare. The East European women identified lack of language proficiency as the main barrier in finding employment, especially in their own field of specialization. Women with a university education also described the difficulties they encountered in the evaluation of their professional degrees. The sense that they had "to start all over again from scratch" was disheartening, they said. Some even indicated that had they known better prior to their migration to Canada, they would have made a different decision. This is consistent with the results of a survey on the issue of the recognition of foreign credentials; one recommendation was as follows: "Those private and public agencies brokering information on foreign credentials should coordinate efforts to enhance the reliability and consistency of information being provided to those migrating to Canada" (National Organization of Immigrant and Visible Minority Women of Canada, 1996, p. 17).

The interviewees indicated that overall their intellectual capacity had been undermined in Canada, and consequently they were seen merely as a potential source of manual labor. One Cuban woman who previously taught physics and astronomy now works as a janitor because her job does not require much communication in English. Because the post-1992 immigration policy favored highly skilled immigrants, there was a close relationship between the level of education and the length of stay in Canada. Thus, the higher the immigrant woman's level of education, the lower the length of her stay in Canada. For example, the majority of women with university degrees from Latin America and Eastern Europe had been in Canada for less than two years.

The number of women with postsecondary education was thirty-five, or 40.6 percent of the eighty-six women interviewed. At the time of interview, twenty-two of the thirty-five (62.8 percent) were unemployed. Of the ten women who had been teachers in their country of origin, three were housewives, three were unemployed, and the rest were in traditional jobs (alteration work, janitorial, postal work, hair dressing, cooking). Four of the five engineers (electrical, computer, civil) were unemployed, and one was a bookkeeper. One of the two lawyers in the group was unemployed, and the other worked as a maintenance manager. Four of the six women who gave information about their university degree instead of their previous professions were unemployed, and the remainder worked as cooks. One woman in the ESL course had stayed in Canada for sixteen years and had been a math teacher in her country of origin. She was employed as a worker in a locksmith business under management and in a work environment where her native tongue was spoken. Her knowledge of the official language was therefore limited.

One of the obstacles to immigrants' entry into the job market is their lack of "Canadian experience." Because the majority of women were newcomers, the market did not value their skills as equal to such experience. Some of the highly skilled women were professionals (lawyers, teachers) who could not readily continue their profession even if they had adequate knowledge of English and their credentials were accredited. This was so in part because the legal and educational systems of Canada and other countries are different. Although the necessary training is available, women are in a disadvantaged position to invest in such rather lengthy and costly reskilling. Although the lack of Canadian experience is a technical problem, it also has racial, ethnic, and class dimensions. There are numerous studies focusing on the intersection of race, gender, class, and immigrant women's access to and participation in the social, economic, and political life of Canadian society (Bakker, 1996; Daenzer, 1993; Flynn, 1998; Giri, 1998; Jamal, 1998; Ng, 1992; Ng & Das Gupta, 1981).

Systemic racism and ethnicism affect immigrants to different degrees. It is likely that immigrants from such countries as the United States, Australia, Britain, or New Zealand would be treated differently from those originating in the Middle East, Africa, Latin America, or Asia. Whatever their national origin, immigrants with financial resources at their disposal will be in a better position to afford the "Canadianization" of their experience or to acquire new skills. Lacking financial resources, including day care service and the cost of transportation, many women in the study experienced considerable difficulty in attending the ESL and computer literacy courses. Under these conditions, if they did find a job it was usually in the informal, service-oriented sector of the economy that profits from the labor of marginalized members of society. In this sector, exploitative relations are prevalent, with low-paying jobs and uncertain opportunities, if any, for personal or professional growth.

The immigrant women in this study expected to find skilled jobs or to acquire skills in one of the best societies among the G7 nations. Ironically, however, they seemed to learn more about the negative impacts of globalization, the "flexible" workforce, and a "jobless" society (or the "end of work") (Rifkin, 1995).

In the decade from 1986 to 1996, education was not a determining factor in accessing the job market. According to one report, Canadian workers are among the best educated in the world. In 1995, 46 percent of men and 48 percent of women in the labor force had a postsecondary certificate or diploma, or a university degree (Centre of Excellence for Research on Immigration and Settlement, 1999a). In the case of the eighty-six immigrant women, the role of skill was mediated by the unequal distribution of power along the lines of gender, class, race, language, ethnicity, national origin, and the state of the economy. Under these circumstances, these highly skilled immigrant women were going through a deskilling process.

The Powers of the Market and the State

The evidence presented here invites controversial and even conflicting readings. My aim in this section is to offer an interpretation of the evidence within the framework of current theoretical and policy concerns about the changing relationships of education and work. I assume that in an advanced industrial capitalist economy, the market is the major factor in the creation and elimination of work, workplaces, and workforces. The role of the state is equally prominent. However, a host of theoretical positions, including neoconservatism, postmodernism, and poststructuralism, posit the "withering away" of the state and the nation-state. Postmodernist positions, much like traditional liberalism, see power as widely diffused in society to the extent that the market and the state lose their centrality (Mooers & Sears, 1992).

I begin by reiterating two conflicting views about the changing relations between education and work outlined in the first section of the chapter. Whereas advocates of the market see in the "education-job gap" a lack of highly trained labor, critics find in that gap evidence of ways the economy regularly underemploys its skilled workforce. Livingstone (1999) points to six basic enduring dimensions of underemployment: "(1) the talent use gap; (2) structural unemployment; (3) involuntary reduced employment; (4) the credential gap; (5) the performance gap; and (6) subjective underemployment" (p. 55). In spite of this systemic underemployment, both the market and the state call for more and multiple skilling of the workforce, an agenda that tends to increase rather than decrease the current levels of underemployment.

If indeed the supply of skilled workers is abundant, it is important from a policy perspective to understand the conditions that generate its waste. Is it a question of improper policymaking? Is it a problem of supply and demand? Is it a question of mismanagement of human resources? Is it a limitation of educational practice? It is plausible to claim that many factors are at work. I argue, however, that the waste of a skilled labor force, much like the waste of natural resources, is endemic to the dynamics of a capitalist economy. If this is the case, educational reform alone cannot address the problems of deskilling, underemployment, or unemployment.

Capitalism is a powerful mode of production that simultaneously overproduces and underconsumes, creates and destroys jobs, and skills and deskills the labor force. These conflicting tendencies constitute a norm rather than a deviation. They are not effects of policy but, rather, its causes, although it is often difficult to separate cause and effect. The conflict and coexistence of deskilling and skilling may be more appropriately located in the driving force of the system, that is, the maximization of profit, which is pursued in a production system characterized by "anarchy." Under conditions of anarchy, goods and services are produced by individual firms in an unorganized market where the order of the day is uncertainty, competition, and risk. Although each economic enterprise, its workforce and workplace, is carefully organized, it enters into unpredictable relations with other participants in the unorganized domestic or national market.

The globalization of the economy, with its international division of labor and markets, further intensifies the anarchy, making each economic undertaking as well as the whole "national" economy susceptible to the uncertainty of the world system. Stock markets throughout the world quickly respond to the health problems of Yeltsin or the collapse of a banking enterprise in Japan. Feeling threatened by "the crisis of global capitalism" in 1998, George Soros (1997, p. 79) warned that "the global capitalist system, which has been responsible for the remarkable prosperity of this country [the United States] in the last decade, is coming apart at its seams. . . . It is time to recognize that financial markets are inherently unstable. Imposing market discipline means imposing instability, and how much instability can society take?"

The United Nations *Human Development Report 1998* (United Nations Human Development Programme, 1998) provides a grim picture of a world economy that wastes, at an alarming rate, both human and natural resources. According to this report, "Well over a billion people are deprived of basic consumption needs. Of the 4.4 billion people in developing countries, nearly three-fifths lack basic sanitation. Almost a third have no access to clean water. A quarter do not have adequate housing. A fifth have no access to modern health services. A fifth of children do not attend school to grade 5. About a fifth do not have enough dietary energy and protein. . . . Worldwide, 2 billion people are anemic, including 55 million in industrial countries." The situation is also alarming in the "rich nations," where more than 100 million suffer from underconsumption and human deprivation. Also, "[n]early 200 million people are not expected to survive to age 60. More than 100 million are homeless. And at least 37 million are without jobs, often experiencing a state of social exclusion" (pp. 2–3). Referring to liberal economist John Kenneth Galbraith, who had warned forty years ago about "private affluence amid public squalor," the report notes that "far from narrowing, the contrasts have grown, and to them are added private and environmental squalor" (p. 11). Galbraith has repeatedly warned in recent years that the "market is unreliable," and about "the continuing flaws, inequities, and cruelties in the market system" (1998, p. 20). According to information provided by World Year, Inc., in the United States between 11 and 12 million were hungry, and 23 to 24 million were "food insecure" in 1998. The poor numbered 35.6 million, or 13.3 percent of all Americans; the number of homeless was about 2 million ("Hunger, Poverty, and Homelessness," 1999).

One of the "cruelties" of the market system is the increase in preventable death of women and the recruiting of millions of

young girls into the prostitution business, which is reconceptual-
ized in economic terms as "sex trade." Statistics from the 1997
United Nations Population Fund annual report indicate that

> More than 585,000 women around the world die needlessly each
> year from pregnancy-related causes. About 70,000 women die each
> year, and countless more suffer infections and other health conse-
> quences, from unsafe abortions. . . . Two million girls aged between
> 5 and 15 are recruited into the "commercial sex market" every year.
> Improving the quality of women's health services would cost $17
> billion a year by the year 2000, less than the world currently spends
> each week on armaments. Many countries have been forced to cut
> health spending because of "Structural Adjustment" programs, a
> euphemism for the inflation-busting austerity measures favoured by
> international lending institutions. Inadequate health services and
> lack of respect for women's rights have also led to a rise in rape,
> exploitation and sexually related diseases such as AIDS. ["U.N.
> Report," 1997, p. A3]

Estimates of women in the "sex trade" throughout the world
were "tens of millions" in the 1990s (Flowers, 1998, pp. 39–40).
Many of these women, especially those in Asia, are believed to be
"indentured slaves." The government in Thailand, actively involved
in the business, is called "the consummate international pimp."
Prostitution is also big business in the West. In Germany, there are
two hundred thousand female prostitutes, many recruited from
Latin America and Eastern Europe. In Canada, tens of thousands
of teenage girls are being recruited into street prostitution. Child
slavery is widely practiced in countries such as India and Pakistan.

Using Human Development Index criteria such as life ex-
pectancy, education, and income, the UN report ranked 174 countries and placed Canada, for the fifth consecutive year, at the top
of the list, followed by France, Norway, the United States, and Ice-
land. It noted, however, that the "United States, with the highest
average income of the countries ranked, has the highest population share experiencing human poverty" (United Nations Human
Development Programme, 1998, p. 3). The situation is not much
better in Canada; a detailed study documents "the growing gap"
between the rich and the poor. The writers of this study empha-
sized that "no longer can we take pride in having the UN Human

Development Index designate Canada as the 'number one country to live in' when . . . large parts of the population do not share in this affluence" (Anderson & Kitchen, 1998, p. vii).

The spread of poverty, briefly outlined earlier, not to mention ethnic cleansing, genocide (in Rwanda and Iraq), two major wars waged by the Western alliance, and continuing ecocide cannot be adequately understood without addressing the highly unequal division of power on the local, national, and international levels. Among the innumerable actors in this drama, the institutions of the market and the state—rather than civil society—stand out as the most powerful actors. It is quite clear that nonstate and nonmarket actors, the majority of the people, continue to demand decent living conditions and a peaceful life. How do education in general and adult education in particular respond to the challenges of unemployment, poverty, hunger, war, ecocide, violence, and other problems that continue to haunt us?

The Challenge to Adult Education

It is not easy to synthesize the response of the field of adult education to the changing world situation, coming as it does from diverse sources. I will therefore look at the way various activists in the academy, government, the market, and civil society have asserted their positions at the major international gathering of adult educators, the International Conference on Adult Education (CONFINTEA), sponsored by UNESCO.

Like the previous conferences (held in 1949, 1960, and 1972), CONFINTEA IV (held in 1985), according to one observer, continued to look at adult education as "mainly remedial and serving largely economic needs. One important function—'the reduction of inequalities'—was then seen solely as 'due to imperfections in the educational system'" (Fordham, 1998, p. 112). Adult education was seen, at best, as vocational training serving primarily economic goals. By the time the most recent conference was convened in 1997, the narrowly conceived term *adult education* had been challenged, and reworked by some as *adult learning* and *lifelong learning*. Although these conceptualizations continue to be debated, CONFINTEA V introduced a more comprehensive vision by emphasizing, among other things, the following:

1. Only human-centred development and a participatory society based on the full respect of human rights will lead to sustainable and equitable development. The informed and effective participation of men and women in every sphere of life is needed if humanity is to survive and to meet the challenges of the future.

2. Adult education thus becomes more than a right; it is a key to the twenty-first century. It is both a consequence of active citizenship and a condition for full participation in society. It is a powerful concept for fostering ecologically sustainable development, for promoting democracy, justice, gender equity, and scientific, social and economic development, and for building a world in which violent conflict is replaced by dialogue and a culture of peace based on justice. [UNESCO, 1997, p. 1]

In these and other visions inscribed in the Hamburg Declaration on Adult Learning, we see a departure from a market-based, job-centered education. A major achievement of the 1985 declaration was the assertion of "the right to learn" of all adults, but it failed, in its work and follow-up action, to live up to this ideal (Fordham, 1998, p. 112). The 1997 declaration provides a more democratic or, according to some, more "ambitious" vision by tying the question of learning and learners to citizenship, participation, justice, gender equality, peace, economic development, civil society, indigenous peoples, and minorities (King, 1998). Adult educators should not assess these ideals as unrealistic, maximalist, or ambitious. The citizens of the world deserve and are capable of achieving much more. There are, however, serious constraints on the realization of these goals. There are various constraints on incorporating these ideas into curricula, textbooks, term papers, classroom discussions, conferences, dissertations, workshops, or research projects. The main impediment is, however, the demands of the market. The democratic vision does not allow adult education to be used as a force to discipline the workforce into the reserve army of the market. Even if the state recognizes all citizens' right to learn, the unequal distribution of power based on cleavages of class, gender, ethnicity, and national origin does not allow everyone to exercise the right.

If the institution of the state in much of the developing world is a major obstacle to democratization, its powers, both coercive and persuasive, have been replaced in Western democracies by the hegemony of the market. Speaking about the transition of power from the state to the market in the West, Ellen Wood (1995, p. 254) has noted, "No ancient despot could have hoped to penetrate the personal lives of his subjects—their life chances, choices, preferences, opinions and relationships—in the same comprehensive and minute detail, not only in the workplace but in every corner of their lives." Not only is there such a historically significant transfer of power, but the state promotes the market as the lifeline of the citizenry. Generally, this union of the state and the market has not been adequately appreciated in social and educational theory. However, a good example of the connection between the state and the market can be found in Susser's study (1997) of the way the U.S. government serves market interests by reforming welfare laws.

It must be clear by now that education is only one factor, although an important one, in the promotion of prosperity, justice, equality, democracy, and peace. As a citizen-centered project of social change, adult education has to invigorate its ties with social movements, without which it fails to achieve its goals. Hunger, poverty, and war cannot be constrained without continual and radical democratization of the economic, political, and social order. However, the two transformations, educational and economic, do not happen independently. The democratization of the economic order presupposes the conscious action of a majority that refuses to uphold the market as the ultimate regulator of economic, political, and social power. At the same time, to resist the monopoly of power by the market-state bloc requires an education that views human beings as citizens rather than as profit-seeking individuals.

References

Anderson, J., & Kitchen, B. (1998). Preface. In A. Yalnizyan, *The growing gap: A report on the growing inequality between the rich and the poor in Canada* (p. vii). Toronto: Centre for Social Justice.

Avery, D. H. (1995). *Reluctant host: Canada's response to immigrant workers, 1896–1994.* Toronto: McLelland and Stewart.

Badets, J., & Howatson-Leo, L. (1999). Recent immigrants in the workforce. *Canadian Social Trends, 52,* 16–22.

Bakker, I. (Ed.). (1996). *Rethinking restructuring: Gender and change in Canada.* Toronto: University of Toronto Press.

Best, S., & Kellner, D. (1991). *Postmodern theory: Critical investigations*. New York: Guilford Press.

Carey, E. (1999, March 12). Immigrants faced tough job search in 1990s: Statscan, less likely to get work than those who came in 80s. *The Toronto Star*, p. A8.

Centre of Excellence for Research on Immigration and Settlement. (1999a, May 2). *The changing labour market in Canada* [On-line]. Available: www.ceris.schoolnet.ca

Centre of Excellence for Research on Immigration and Settlement. (1999b, May 2). *School and work* [On-line]. Available: www.ceris.schoolnet.ca

Daenzer, P. (1993). *Regulating class privilege: Immigrant servants in Canada, 1940–1990*. Toronto: Canadian Scholar Press.

Flowers, R. B. (1998). *The prostitution of women and girls*. Jefferson, NC: McFarland.

Flynn, K. (1998). Proletarianization, professionalization, and Caribbean immigrant nurses. *Canadian Woman Studies Journal, 18*(1), 57–60.

Fordham, P. (1998). Redefining the field? A personal view of CONFINTEA V. *International Yearbook of Adult Education, 26*, 112–117.

Galbraith, J. K. (1998). *The socially concerned today*. Toronto: University of Toronto Press.

Giri, N. M. (1998). South Asian women physicians' working experiences in Canada. *Canadian Woman Studies Journal, 18*(1), 61–64.

Human Resources Development Canada. (1994). *Report of the advisory group on working time and the distribution of work*. Ottawa: Ministry of Supply and Services.

Hunger, poverty, and homelessness in the U.S. (1999, May 31). [On-line]. Available: www.worldhungeryear.org/hpinfo-us.htm

Jamal, A. (1998). Situating South Asian immigrant women in the Canadian/global economy. *Canadian Woman Studies Journal, 18*(1), 26–33.

King, L. (1998). Indigenous peoples and minorities: Adult education perspectives following CONFINTEA V. *International Yearbook of Adult Education, 26*, 141–148.

Livingstone, D. W. (1996). Wasted education and withered work: Reversing the "postindustrial" education-jobs optic. In T. Dunk, S. McBride, & R. W. Nelsen (Eds.), *The training trap: Ideology, training and the labour market* (pp. 52–96). Halifax, NS: Fernwood.

Livingstone, D. W. (1999). *The education-jobs gap: Underemployment or economic democracy*. Boulder, CO: Westview Press.

Mills, A. J., & Simmons, T. (1995). *Reading organizational theory: A critical approach*. Toronto: Garamond Press.

Mojab, S. (1999). De-skilling immigrant women. *Canadian Woman Studies Journal, 19*(3), 123–128.

Mooers, C., & Sears, A. (1992). The "new social movements" and the withering away of state theory. In W. Carroll (Ed.), *Organizing dissent: Contemporary social movements in theory and practice* (pp. 52–68). Toronto: Garamond Press.

National Organization of Immigrant and Visible Minority Women of Canada. (1996). *A survey of immigrant and visible minority women and issue of recognition of foreign credentials.* Ottawa: Author.

Ng, R. (1992). Managing female immigration: A case of institutional sexism and racism. *Canadian Woman Studies Journal, 12*(3), 20–23.

Ng, R., & Das Gupta, T. (1981). Nation builders? The captive labour force of non-English speaking immigrant women. *Canadian Woman Studies Journal, 3*(1), 83–89.

Quinn, J. (1999, March 10). Doctor's dreams go sour in Canada. *The Toronto Star,* pp. B1, B5.

Rifkin, J. (1995). *The end of work: The decline of the global labor market and the dawn of the post-market era.* Los Angeles: Tarcher.

Shields, J. (1995). Post-Fordism, work flexibility and training. *Socialist Studies Bulletin, 41,* 31–60.

Soros, G. (1997, December 7). The crisis of global capitalism: Prosperity in peril. *Newsweek* (Canadian edition), pp. 78–84.

Statistics Canada. (1999, March 25). Survey of labour and income dynamics: Encountering low income. *The Daily* [On-line]. Available: www.statcan.ca

Susser, I. (1997). The flexible woman: Regendering labor in the informational society. *Critique of Anthropology, 17*(4), 389–402.

U.N. report slams high maternal death rate. (1997, May 28). *The Toronto Star,* p. A3.

UNESCO. (1997). *The Hamburg declaration: The agenda for the future.* Hamburg, Germany: Author.

United Nations Human Development Programme. (1998). *Human development report 1998* [On-line]. Available: www.undp.org/hdro/98.htm

Wong, L. L. (1993). Immigration as capital accumulation: The impact of business immigration to Canada. *International Migration, 31*(1), 171–187.

Wood, E. M. (1995). *Democracy against capitalism: Renewing historical materialism.* Cambridge, England: Cambridge University Press.

Chapter Three

Silent Power

HRD and the Management of Learning in the Workplace

Fred M. Schied, Vicki K. Carter, Sharon L. Howell

Looking at a specific set of circumstances in a detailed fashion is a way to understand how theory relates to everyday life. Studying a situation in the framework of theories of power and from a critical perspective is also an opportunity to explore issues involved in the benefits and purposes of workplace education. In this chapter we intend to explore the many forms of power converging around specific human resource development (HRD) functions of training and development, allowing us an opportunity to explore and expose the existence and ramifications of power.

Like most educators working in other settings, HRD professionals seldom analyze or even acknowledge the existence and consequences of power. In those rare cases where power is discussed, it is seen as operating in situations where conflict is clearly observable. However, power operates at other levels, where conflict is more hidden. At one level, power can be used to suppress issues and prevent them from coming up for decision making. At still another level, power can be mobilized not only to stop conflict or to suppress issues from arising but to prevent any questioning of prevailing dominant ideas and practices. This conception of power sees it as moving from "louder," more overt forms of control to more hidden and quite "silent" forms of control (Fletcher, 1992; Hardy, 1985). Our analysis occurs within this conception of power.

The case we describe in this chapter examines how power, as manifested through HRD, moved from more covert, silent forms to more overt, louder forms when the legitimacy of HRD as a neutral process began to be challenged.

This particular case emerged from our ongoing study, now in its fourth year, of the impact of HRD practices on frontline workers and trainers at several different work sites (Schied, Carter, Preston, & Howell, 1998). Throughout our study, the theme of silent power ran through almost all of the educational processes connected to formal workplace learning programs. For this chapter we have chosen to focus on one case involving one individual so that we can begin to understand the operation of power at a micro level. The case emerged within the confines of an HRD program at a large nonprofit organization. All the training spoke strongly to the idea that organizational forms of ideological, hegemonic, and discursive power, essentially silent kinds of power, function to shape self-disciplined workers who control not only their minds and bodies but also their hearts and souls. The incident resulted in the exercise of coercive and disciplinary powers—louder forms of power—by management through human resource management (HRM) and HRD practices.

This situation also provides a unique opportunity for analysis. It is rare to find situations that can be examined without considering the many forms of oppression that are usually involved in any work situation. In this unusual example, the theoretical analysis is made simpler because the concerns that would be raised about issues of race, class, age, and gender are not present in this case. All the people involved were white, and every major player, specifically Stewart, his supervisor, and the HRD instructor, were all middle class, middle aged, and male.

Learning Discipline: The Case of Stewart

Stewart had worked for the past eight years as a networking and microcomputer specialist in a department of about sixty people located within a large nonprofit organization. Stewart had sole responsibility for maintaining the hardware and networking software for this large group, participated in several interdepartmental and organization-wide committees, and was a Total Quality

Management (TQM) team facilitator for two different groups. One of the TQM teams had been charged by the department to make recommendations for staff recognition and rewards. The department had high visibility within the larger organization, dealing daily with its customer base on very complicated issues and procedures. The perception outside the organization was that customer service was not as good as it could be. Many workers in the department felt it was a high-stress environment with serious morale problems, hence the team addressing recognition and rewards. In addition to his roles of team leader and technology expert, Stewart often voiced his own concerns to his supervisor and his directors about the problems faced by the department. He also passed along general comments made by other staff members, who frequently confided in him. Stewart did experience some personal discord with office leadership along with the problems he perceived to be common across the department. Over the years, he had been promised a change of office space, leadership and promotion opportunities, and salary adjustments, among other things. Not only did these items fail to materialize, but also many of the changes in the office that did occur were in direct conflict with the recommendations of Stewart's recognition and rewards TQM team. Consequently, although he enjoyed his work, Stewart and many of his coworkers believed office processes exhibited little of the democratic and participatory characteristics that were openly espoused at staff meetings and through the rhetoric of departmental leadership.

As part of ongoing staff development activities, departmental staff were asked to attend a customer service training workshop arranged through the organization's HRD group. The training was focused specifically on the department, and the only outsider present was the instructor. Early in the training session, Stewart asked the instructor to clarify the specific purpose of the program, because the impression he and other staff members had was that it would be a hands-on workshop about customer service. Instead, the training was geared toward changing the climate of existing workplaces. During the program, a video was shown that brought out, among other things, questions of trust among staff, leadership, and management; it exposed for analysis the idea that in many organizations, employee trust of management and leadership could be an issue. The instructor asked the participants to outline what they felt were important points in the video segment, and no one responded. Eventually Stewart pointed out that his notes indicated that one of the basic issues raised by the video was trust and that because of his previous interactions with his own departmental leadership, he understood why trust was included as a topic. He then matter-of-factly stated that he personally did not trust departmental management. Stewart then moved on to other items on his outline.

A few days after the workshop, Stewart was called into his supervisor's office and given a memo titled "Behavioral Turnaround." In the memo, and in the meeting with his supervisor, Stewart was told that his behavior had been atrocious and had incited others to be negative. He was told to immediately eliminate his negative attitude, interact positively with all staff members, and openly support all activities related to office leadership. In addition, Stewart was no longer extended the "trusted privilege" of participating in external endeavors where positive representation of the department was paramount. He was told it was unacceptable in a public group to make the statement that he did, that his comments were completely out of line and served no constructive purpose. Finally, the memo stated that behaviors and attitudes exhibiting anything less than talking positively about and to management and providing "cheerleading" in their support would result in termination proceedings. Stewart asked his supervisor to clarify the standards of performance to which he was required to adhere, but failed to obtain any specifics. Stewart then asked what measures would be used to evaluate his performance or nonperformance; the response was that his supervisor "would know."

Stewart immediately called the HRD group instructor to apologize for his atrocious behavior. The instructor, however, was unable to identify which of the participants in the workshop Stewart was, indicating that he could not recall or distinguish Stewart from the other members of the workshop. The instructor did remember that during the session several individuals had expressed concerns and frustrations with their work environment.

Stewart then reviewed his copy of the human resources policies and procedures and determined that he could file a grievance based on the way the situation had been handled and the ambiguous criteria contained in the "Behavioral Turnaround" memo.

After Stewart filed a grievance, his supervisor tore up the "Behavioral Turnaround" memo.

Several days later, Stewart was again called into a meeting with his supervisor and the director of the department. This time he was presented with another memo that described his negative and generally unsupportive attitude, discussed his failure to project a positive image within the department, and delineated standards of performance. The memo stated that correcting his behavior was his responsibility, and it reiterated the points made in the earlier memo. Along with the earlier guidelines Stewart was required to comply with, the second memo required that Stewart attend the next available HRD group courses on intergroup relations and assertiveness. Stewart was given six months to change his behavior, or the termination process would be finalized.

In order to understand how this case fits into the larger context of HRD and the uses of power, we first need to take a closer look at HRD, placing this form of workplace education in a social and historical context.

Contextualizing Human Resource Development: The Basis of Power

HRD was defined by Nadler and Nadler (1989) as learning experiences—specifically training, education, and development—organized and provided by employers during certain periods of time in order to encourage the improvement of employees' performance, the personal growth of employees, or both. HRD programs are often produced internally, as was the case involving Stewart. Programs are also brought in from external sources and modified according to the perceived needs and goals of the organization funding the program. Programmatically, HRD opportunities are usually composed of specific behavioral objectives outlined by a company or institution, and they always help the institution achieve its goals and objectives. Sometimes these goals and objectives are consonant with the personal goals of the employee, but many times they are not. Rothwell and Sredl (1992, p. 190) described their views about the functions of HRD staff: "HRD professionals are frequently responsible for facilitating the socialization of individuals into work settings. As individuals are socialized, they conform to a body of articulated or unarticulated ethical standards and norms of behavior. HRD professionals are also asked frequently by their employers to train others on . . . corporate codes of conduct and implement change that will bring employee behavior into compliance with legal, regulatory and other mandated requirements."

Because its domain is circumscribed by the workplace, HRD bears a strong relationship to adult education and shares many of adult education's issues and concerns. One of the characteristics of adult education is that it is usually voluntary, and learners select the experiences and construct expectations for themselves. In contrast, adults involved in HRD programs are often not there voluntarily, as was the case with Stewart. Furthermore, even though employees may choose to participate in an HRD program, the content and expectations are, in essence, those of the providing or sponsoring organization. In fact, as Wartenberg (1992) pointed out in describing the situatedness of power, "the presence of power relationships causes human beings to make choices that determine the sorts of skills and abilities they will develop" (p. 100).

HRD appears to be relatively unaware of its own historical and socioeconomic basis and of the endemic conflict of priorities and values between employee and employer. Therein lies a profound contradiction for HRD practice and theory. Although sources disagree about the historical origin of training and development, one handbook traces the history as far back as 3500 B.C. (Miller, 1987). Schied (1995) has posited that modern HRD, the most common template for workplace education, ensued from conflict over control of work and the workplace during and shortly after World War II.

HRD postulates human capital theory as an effective basis for facilitating learning in the workplace. Human capital theory connects investment in training and development with a rate of return from individual workers who are taught new skills, increasing their productivity. It is questionable whether education has a direct link to productivity, a question that in turn leads to doubt about human capital theory in general (Baptiste, 1994; Rubenson, 1992). HRD does, however, provide management with a means of exercising significant measures of control that clash with HRD's claims of assisting in developing a productive and empowered workforce. Cunningham (1993) has critiqued how workplace adult educators speak about "human resources, not people, certainly not workers" (p. 13) and has observed that instead of locating themselves in adult education history and acknowledging how the nature of work is socially constructed, HRD professionals ignore the roots of adult education, which is historically "aligned with the political and social movements that challenge the assumptions of the present" (p. 24). As Cunningham (1993) said, these experts now "unabashedly side with management to develop human capital and to make workers responsible for production from which the managerial class profits first and foremost" (p. 24). Much of contemporary adult education has become conflated with training and with acquiring certain competencies, behaviors, and attitudes purported to support the requirements of capitalism.

In addition to suffering from a near absence of a sociopolitical and historical standpoint, HRD professionals also lack an adequate analysis of the power inherent in their practice. The presence of such power was evident in the situation experienced by Stewart. In this instance, the social control of Stewart was conspicuous, as seen through examination of the specifics set forth in his new behavioral requirements. In this case, the exercise of power resulted in noticeable subjugation of an employee who had spoken out, but more often these outcomes take the form of passive victims. In our studies, when HRD professionals were asked about their association with power, they were affronted. These HRD instructors and professionals felt they worked hard to enable and actualize their "clients" and make day-to-day work life better. They expressed a great deal of agitation when confronted with the idea that they were participating in forms of power and control over those very same employees. One instructor was extremely defensive about being "accused of participating in a form of domination and mind control." Nevertheless, education—HRD included—and organizational discourse, symbols, and archetypes are not just words and culture, but are also tools and weapons used consistently to keep workers "productive" and enacting the correct social and organizational philosophy (Cherryholmes, 1988; Fiske, 1993). In essence, as Usher and Edwards (1994, p. 50) wrote, "regulation works through empowerment."

Townley (1993, 1994) has argued that HRM and HRD units function as production "black boxes" and constitute methods for inputting employees (selecting, training, evaluating, and remunerating) in order to output the requisite amount of labor. Townley described HRM as prescriptive, reductive, and instrumental—a set of goal-attaining tools positioned inside the interior of organizations—and as an orchestrating, cataloguing, and measuring discipline involving space, time, tasks, movement, behavior, and interactions. For example, HRD programs such as Employee Orientation and Introduction to the Company work by constituting the human subject through socialization and induction methods. Later in an employee's career, training and development for social, interpersonal, and listening skills reinforce and constitute ideology, tying these behaviors to "appropriate" employee identities. Health programs and employee assistance programs (EAPs) are other ways workers are "helped" to adopt certain types of accommodating workplace attitudes or postures (Weiss, 1986).

Limited Perspectives: The Discourse of Power in HRD

Rothwell and Sredl (1992) described power as "simply the capacity to effect (or affect) organizational outcomes" (p. 212). Although the authors stated that the subject of power had been "widely ignored in HRD," they felt the topic was an "ethical issue of greatest concern to those in the role of organization change agent" (p. 212). Yet out of eleven HRD roles delineated by the authors, the change agent position was the only one connected with power issues. Rothwell and Sredl stated that power was now getting more attention in the field because HRD professionals have "historically been outmatched by their more politically savvy counterparts in operating management," who often made ill-conceived decisions about HRD because "they lack[ed] the insight into human performance that could have been provided by HRD professionals" (p. 212). This point of view is an interesting one; it describes what is in essence a turf issue for a field that, according to the code of ethics of the American Society for Training and Development, purports to "recognize the rights and dignities of each individual and develop human potential" (p. 198). In spite of Rothwell and Sredl's questioning ethical dilemmas, harmful practices, and moral issues involving individuals and organizations vis-à-vis power, the authors exemplify the field's simplified, underanalyzed, and limited perspectives on the effects and relations of power in which people both participate and are positioned.

In general, HRD can be characterized as not recognizing the power inherent in its institutional functions. For example, HRD practitioners typically do not have an awareness of nor understand how human and organizational development practices use corporate ideology to teach workers to discipline themselves. HRD program offerings are significantly skewed to organizational goals and values, even when they appear to be for the individual's growth and development; consider such programs as *Dress for Success, Resume Building, Career Management Strategies,* the wonderfully euphemistic *Career Plateauing,* and *Moving On,* which all benefit the institution offering these courses. Interestingly, in Stewart's HRD organization, most programs carried a financial charge to the employee or to the employee's department, including courses required for employees to do their jobs. For example, educational offerings on how to use the organization's required business and record-keeping systems required employees to pay for courses. Of almost three hundred courses listed in one HRD bulletin, the TQM category had the most courses listed. Only computer-related courses, many of which were duplicates necessary to accommodate differences in IBM and Mac platforms, had more. All the TQM courses were free. A curriculum weighted heavily with no-cost HRD-delivered TQM courses supports the contention of many who believe that implementation of quality programs in the workplace and in schools, similar to many other management techniques, is less a management philosophy and more a form of management control over its workforce (Dennis, 1995; Parker & Slaughter, 1994; Rinehart, Huxley, & Robertson, 1997).

Just as in professional associations that require ongoing education, employee training and development help maintain discipline. Increasing numbers of employees can be monitored, particularly electronically through information systems, listening in on telephone transactions, or through camera surveillance. For those employees who are not easily monitored, self-regulation and acceptance of institutional ideology are especially useful and important. Discourse is manipulated by groups interested in sustaining or creating certain structures, and management exercises a symbolic violence through its power to impose and legitimize meanings by concealing the power relations that are the basis of this force. To understand whether organizations are transforming or restricting, liberating or dominating, HRD practitioners must analyze the organizational power relations in which they participate and which they help create. HRD often fails to acknowledge its complicity in deploying management and corporate power; and in not theorizing its own forms of ideology and discourse, HRD cannot really uncover its contradictory situatedness between human agency and transformation and organizational dominance and rhetoric (Fiske, 1993; Townley, 1993, 1994).

HRD as a Function of Managerial Power

Power in organizations has traditionally been defined, albeit somewhat cynically, as either the ability to get others to do what you want or get them to do something they would otherwise not do (Weber, 1978). Clearly, for Weber, as well as for Marx, power, legitimized in organizational structures, was tantamount to domination, and attempts to challenge this domination were forms of resistance. Since those rather cynical and unidirectional conceptions of power were developed, the study of how power is distributed and used in organizations and how that power is related to hierarchical structure has become more sophisticated. Yet curiously, despite the ever more sophisticated and critical understanding of the role of power in organizations, Weber's conceptualization still provides a basis to begin the investigation of power and its relationship to workforce discipline. The rest of this section will attempt to lay the groundwork for understanding how educational practices in organizations, often (though not exclusively) under the rubric of HRD, can become processes of domination and a means to manufacture consent.

Hardy and Clegg (1996) have pointed out that within the managerial literature, the issue of power has been subsumed into a struggle between two groups whereby one side is forced to use power to overcome the opposition of the other side. Inherent in this definition is the notion of politics being an illegitimate and fundamentally dysfunctional process aimed at thwarting initiatives that are intended to benefit the entire organization. Thus Mintzberg (1983), a leading management theorist, defines politics this way: "Distilled to its essence, therefore, politics refers to individual or group behavior that is informal, ostensibly parochial, typically divisive and above all, in the technical sense, illegitimate" (p. 172). However, as Hardy and Clegg (1996) point out, such definitions "ignore the question: in *whose* eyes is power illegitimate, unsanctioned, or dysfunctional?" (p. 629). Hardy and Clegg go on to argue that managerial interests are treated as if they were synonymous with organizational interests. Ignored by the management literature, of course, is that managers, just like any other group, would seek to serve their own vested interests.

Existing organizational structures and management systems are not neutral or apolitical. Indeed, these structures and systems have developed over time in specific historical and social situations. In other words, there is nothing "natural" or inherently logical or inevitable about turning humans into resources that need to be developed. Yet virtually all of the HRD literature depoliticizes organizational life and obscures the working of power in organizations. For example, HRD practitioners and organizational developers typically see efforts to change organizational leadership, culture, or structure as neutral and objective. Seeing their efforts as neutral and objective obscures the workings of power that management uses to dominate workers. By failing to get beneath the surface and examine the workings of power outside of a predetermined structure defined and legitimated by upper management, HRD practitioners, through their seemingly neutral activities, actually enhance management's efforts to produce self-disciplining workers.

From a critical perspective, the central question of understanding domination becomes one of understanding the apparent lack of conflict in organizations. For if, as Weber argued, power equals domination, then why has there not been more resistance to this domination in organizations? However, as numerous studies have pointed out, conflict might exist even if it is not directly observable (Gaventa, 1980). In fact, power is also manifested in structural ways. Thus the nonpowerful are excluded from decision-making processes through the establishment of procedures and routines that deflect issues. In our study, for example, we found that such supposedly participatory management processes as ISO 9000 and TQM, procedures that supposedly relied on the decision-making ability of frontline workers, were really processes by which managers at corporate headquarters were able to exercise invisible power by controlling the ways in which workers' knowledge could be channeled so as to use it for managerial benefit (Schied, Carter, Preston, & Howell, 1998).

In a key work on power, Lukes (1974) has argued that there is another form of power, what we have called silent power. Lukes attempts to explain why inaction on the part of workers is another form in which organizational power manifests. He argues that people often become complicit in their own oppression, in effect helping to sustain it. Thus power can be used to shape "perceptions, cognitions, and preferences in such a way that [workers] accept their role in the existing order of things, either because they can see or imagine no alternative to it, or because they view it as natural and unchangeable, or because they value it as divinely preordained and beneficial" (Lukes, 1974, p. 24). From this perspective, the ability to define reality becomes the key to organizational power. If management is able to define what behaviors are not only appropriate but also natural and unchangeable, then any questioning of those definitions becomes impossible.

It is important to note that different forms of power, such as the silent and louder forms described in this chapter as well as many other forms, are not mutually exclusive, but are expressed in varying proportions at various times. Indeed, it is in terms of this movement among the levels of power that the case of Stewart needs to be understood.

The Case of Stewart Revisited: Understanding Power

The case of Stewart makes explicit the means of control and the ideologies of management because these mechanisms were deployed when departmental leadership was crippled because silent forms of institutional power relations had gone awry. When psychological self-monitoring power fails, other kinds of power may be activated (Fiske, 1993). In an intimidating manner, the department used HRD and then HRM processes and procedures to reapply rigorous and aggressive control measures not dependent on quieter hegemonic forms such as loyalty and self-discipline. The department decided to institute these measures in order to recover its prior organizational reality, which until that point had sustained particular political objectives and secured specific employee identities.

One intent of the HRD courses offered to Stewart and his department was to constitute the subject by inculcating staff with appropriate rules, habits, and clear ideas of expected norms. Through workplace education this inculcation could occur with various degrees of individual engagement and participation. In Stewart's case, however, the status of the individual and the human right to express individuality, to have agency, and all that constitutes agency were erased as part of these reapplication processes. Although it was risky for management to reveal its power in this way, it did so in order to publicly show that unity of departmental leadership and departmental employees was in everyone's best interests.

When the department failed to quietly and properly inculcate organizational norms and values into Stewart, it resorted to intimidation through disciplinary and coercive power. In spite of the "empowering efforts" of HRD programs and management ideology, "many employees feel not empowered, but intimidated. Fear is the bluntest of management tools" ("For Now," 1993, p. 13). In a manner that recalls Foucault's notion of the panopticon as a symbol of surveillance, Stewart needed to behave as though he was being watched at all times. Threatened with dismissal, Stewart was required to submit himself for "correction" through more training and development. Stewart's reaction to this type of power had been minimal resistance rather than violence or despair and apathy, which often stem from what Fiske (1993, p. 142) called "imperializing gone too far." Through Stewart's small acts of resistance, he was attempting to create a "locale," a bottom-up localizing power contesting management's "stationed" imperializing power. Usually management and institutional leadership, with the help of training and development, effectively marginalized resistant and oppositional knowledge. In this case, Stewart's management, through HRD and HRM policies and procedures, effectively stopped him from producing a locale by positioning him in their workplace system of relations. Stewart became the unnormalized Other who now lived under constant monitoring and threat and who needed to be resocialized before being reinserted into the system of norms. Stewart was not the typical stationed body, but rather a stationed heart and soul whose ill-managed emotions had to be more finely tuned. And in Stewart's situation, even though severe punishment was involved, the department also adhered to the "principle of correct training rather than that of vengeful punishment" (Fiske, 1993, p. 73) by requiring even more training and development.

Stewart's situation paralleled Hochschild's research (1983) on the "managed heart," whereby organizational forms of power resulted in expectations not only of physical and mental work but also of "emotional labor." This sort of labor, demanding a coordination of mind and feeling, "draws on a source of self that we honor as deep and integral to our individuality" (p. 7). Stewart was expected and in fact forced to accept leadership's statements and directions without question and without comment. Any disagreement had to be suppressed with predefined behavior in evidence at all times. The boundaries of control were enlarged so that heart and spirit were involved in an obvious and public form. Stewart's values were to be inculcated in order that body and soul could be viewed as departmental commodities existing as means to reach instrumental institutional missions and goals.

Similar to the fake smiles and accommodating demeanor of many customer service employees, Stewart's feelings and expressions were outlined and monitored by his supervisor. This commanding of feelings and emotions was a blatant example of controlling culture by asking for and actually enforcing a theatrical performance. Power of this kind obviously stifles creativity and energy, turning enthusiastic and sincere employees into malleable robots. In contrast to creating an atmosphere of productivity, quality, and teamwork, it may actually endanger the performance of an organization by silencing employee critique, recommendations, or comments about institutional issues and problems. Mumby (1988) succinctly described how ideological power plays out when he said "power operates ideologically when it is used to impose a certain form of organizational rationality on members, while simultaneously restricting the articulation of contradictory or competing rationales" (p. 51).

Conclusion: Challenging HRD

The story of Stewart presented the opportunity to focus attention on the role of HRD as a source of power, in both its louder and more silent manifestations. The HRD training received by Stewart and his coworkers presented and supported the organizational and managerial points of view; in this particular case the goal was to adjust and alter the work environment of Stewart's department. When Stewart did not articulate the corporate ideology in the first HRD class, his supervisors took the actions they felt were necessary to avoid further damage to the people and structures around him. Part of Stewart's "punishment" was to be returned to HRD classes for sessions on assertiveness and intergroup communication. The more silent forms of institutional power having failed, punishment by continuing education exemplified how much management counted on HRD experts and professionals to act as therapists, resocializing deviant individuals into the objective reality of a symbolic organizational universe.

Education, because of its humanistic stance, would benefit from understanding Marshall's observation (1989) about power being exercised in a search of controllable and governable people. Marshall wrote, "if it is more humane, it is more subtle; if it is less overt and involves less violence to bring power into play, it may be more dangerous because of its insidious silence" (p. 109). In other words, what appears to be relatively safe and peaceful as long as conformance and compliance or even silence is in evidence changes in the presence of vocal resistance. At that point, and Stewart's situation was a good example, acquiescence can be commanded.

Yet the question still remains: What can critical adult educators concerned with workplace learning do? How can issues of power be challenged? Clearly, the academic and intellectual origins of HRD need to be continually and systematically questioned. Workplace educators are often trained in adult education programs, and the field of HRD is often closely aligned with adult education. This presents critical adult educators with a dilemma. Whereas in the past progressive adult education has had close ties with the workplace, in more recent times the workplace has, with some notable exceptions, been left mostly to those espousing a human capital approach. We would argue that the philosophical basis of HRD is vulnerable to deep social critique and that such critique needs to occur where HRD professionals are trained—graduate programs in adult education. Moreover, we agree with Cunningham (1998), who has forcefully highlighted the questions that would form the basis for a challenge to the social purposes of HRD. She states, "Economic activity is basic to any society—the question is the nature of that economic activity. Should economic activity be eco-logically sound? Should gender discrimination in the workplace be addressed? Should corporations be socially responsible? Should workers share the benefits from their labor? Should 'mother work' be acknowledged? Should work be redefined in ways to suppress greed?" (p. 5).

Yet we also understand that there is more at stake than mount-ing a sustained intellectual critique. For as Canadian labor educa-tor D'Arcy Martin (1998) has stated: "Training is not just about jobs. In society, training is conducted . . . to equip people to be active cit-izens and advocates" (p. 133). We argue that at a national (and international) level, corporate control and power manifested through HRD programs can be effectively challenged only by a committed and active labor movement. Parker and Slaughter (1994) have pointed out that for many unions the job training issue has moved to the center of union negotiation strategy, and unions have begun to recognize that training is about changing worker relations and power. Training must be based on worker-centered approaches that have at their center a vision of workplace democ-racy. Progressive adult educators need to establish alliances with unions, many of which have developed engaged and highly creative approaches to workplace education (La Luz, 1997; Parker & Slaugh-ter, 1994; Saganski, 1995). Such programs form a link, both intel-lectually and pragmatically, in challenging the power of HRD.

However, in a case such as Stewart's where unionization, at least in the immediate future, is unlikely, other forms of resistance may be possible. Our research concluded that Stewart's experience was not an isolated example. Other attempts at maintaining a "locale" outside the seemingly totalizing management system occurred. These locales need to be connected. Initial efforts would, of course, be small and occur at the ground level. Nevertheless, they may serve to protect workers from some of the egregious HRD policies and begin to develop solidarity among workers. For exam-ple, workers at Stewart's organization could begin to challenge the costing structure of HRD courses, using the management rhetoric of empowerment to question the basis of the fee structure. In addi-tion, efforts could be made to assure that discussions in the HRD classroom remain confidential. Although these efforts are neces-sarily small in scope, they can serve as a beginning to challenge such management slogans as "teamwork" and "empowerment" and replace them with solidarity-building values, such as dignity, respect, and fairness.

References

Baptiste, I. (1994). *Educating politically: In pursuit of social equality.* Unpublished doctoral dissertation, Northern Illinois University, De Kalb, IL.

Cherryholmes, C. (1988). *Power and criticism: Poststructural investigations in education.* New York: Teachers College Press.

Cunningham, P. M. (1993). The politics of worker's education: Preparing workers to sleep with the enemy. *Adult Learning, 5*(1), 13–14, 24.

Cunningham, P. M. (1998, March). *Race, class, gender and the practice of adult education in the U.S.A.* Paper presented at Buffalo State University [On-line]. Available: http://www.snybuf.edu/~lllcntr/alsympo.htm

Dennis, D. (1995). *Brave new reductionism: TQM as ethnocentrism.* Education Policy Analysis Archives *3*(9) [On-line]. Available: http://info.asu.edu/asu-cwis/eppa

Fiske, J. (1993). *Power plays, power works.* London: Verso.

Fletcher, J. K. (1992). A poststructuralist perspective on the third dimension of power. *Journal of Organization Change Management, 5*(1), 81–88.

For now. (1993, July 17). *The Economist, 328*(7820), 13–14.

Gaventa, J. (1980). *Power and powerlessness: Quiescence and rebellion in an Appalachian valley.* Oxford, England: Clarendon Press.

Hardy, C. (1985). The nature of unobtrusive power. *Journal of Management Studies, 22*(4), 384–399.

Hardy, C., & Clegg, S. R. (1996). Some dare call it power. In S. R. Clegg, C. Hardy, & W. R. Nord (Eds.), *Handbook of organization studies* (pp. 622–641). Thousand Oaks, CA: Sage.

Hochschild, A. (1983). *The managed heart.* Berkeley: University of California Press.

La Luz, J. (1997). Education for worker empowerment. In S. Fraser & J. B. Freeman (Eds.), *Audacious democracy: Labor, intellectuals, and the social reconstruction of America* (pp. 85–93). Boston: Houghton Mifflin.

Lukes, S. (1974). *Power: A radical view.* Old Tappan, NJ: Macmillan.

Marshall, J. (1989). Foucault and education. *Australian Journal of Education, 33,* 99–113.

Martin, D. (1998). A decade on the training rollercoaster: A unionist's view. In S. M. Scott, B. Spencer, & A. M. Thomas (Eds.), *Learning for life: Readings in adult education* (pp. 153–163). Toronto: Thompson.

Miller, V. A. (1987). The history of training. In R. L. Craig (Ed.), *The training and development handbook* (pp. 3–14). New York: McGraw-Hill.

Mintzberg, H. (1983). *Power in and around organizations.* Englewood Cliffs, NJ: Prentice Hall.

Mumby, D. (1988). *Communication and power in organizations: Discourse, ideology, and domination.* Norwood, NJ: Ablex.

Nadler, L., & Nadler, Z. (1989). *Developing human resources: Concepts and a model* (3rd ed.). San Francisco: Jossey-Bass.

Parker, M., & Slaughter, J. (1994). *Working smart: A union guide to participation programs and reengineering.* Detroit: Labor Notes.

Rinehart, J., Huxley, C., & Robertson, D. (1997). *Just another car factory? Lean production and its discontents.* Ithaca, NY: ILR Press.

Rothwell, W., & Sredl, H. (1992). *The ASTD reference guide to professional human resource development roles and competencies* (2nd ed.). Amherst, MA: HRD Press.

Rubenson, K. (1992). Human resource development: A historical perspective. In L. E. Burton (Ed.), *Developing resourceful humans* (pp. 3–30). London: Routledge.

Saganski, G. (1995). A worker-centered approach to education and training. In S. Babson (Ed.), *Lean work: Empowerment and exploitation in the global auto industry* (pp. 326–339). Detroit: Wayne State University.

Schied, F. M. (1995). How did humans become resources anyway? HRD and the politics of learning in the workplace. In *Proceedings of the 36th Annual Adult Education Research Conference* (pp. 287–292). Edmonton: University of Alberta.

Schied, F. M., Carter, V. K., Preston, J. A., & Howell, S. L. (1998). Complicity and control in the workplace: A critical case study of TQM, learning, and the management of knowledge. *International Journal of Lifelong Learning, 17*(3), 157–172.

Townley, B. (1993). Foucault, power/knowledge, and its relevance for human resource management. *Academy of Management Review, 18*(3), 518–545.

Townley, B. (1994). *Reframing human resource management: Power, ethics and the subject at work.* Thousand Oaks, CA: Sage.

Usher, R., & Edwards, R. (1994). *Postmodernism and education.* London: Routledge.

Wartenberg, T. (1992). Situated social power. In T. Wartenberg (Ed.), *Rethinking power* (pp. 79–101). Albany: State University of New York Press.

Weber, M. (1978). *Economy and society: An outline of interpretive sociology* (2 vols., G. Roth & C. Wittich, Eds.). Berkeley: University of California Press.

Weiss, R. (1986). *Managerial ideology and the social control of deviance in organizations.* New York: Praeger.

Chapter Four

The Power of Discourse

Work-Related Learning in the "Learning Age"

Elaine Butler

Learning, it seems, is serious business—very serious business indeed. The following two statements from leaders of government and business illustrate the point: "Education is the best economic policy we have" (Tony Blair, quoted in "Introduction," Department for Education and Employment, 1998); and "Humanware—the human element—will be the core of everything in the future" (Minolta Europe GmbH director Akio Miyabayashi, quoted in O'Donnell & Garavan, 1997, p. 1).

What are we to make of these statements? The notion of "making meaning" is an integral part of education, especially adult education, where educators and learners come together—for a plethora of reasons and motivated in myriad ways—to engage in a diversity of pedagogic activities, seeking to extend knowledge, to enhance or clarify understandings, to challenge or to change, to learn new skills. Within the broad field of adult education, work-related learning rep-

My thanks to colleagues at the Research Centre for Vocational Education and Training, University of Technology, Sydney, for the opportunity to discuss some of these ideas in a seminar presentation, "Global Logics of Vocationalism, Work and Work-Related Learning: Where Next for Australia?" in May 1999.

resents a specific location of educational activity. Work-related learning, however, does not have a single history that leads inexorably to an uncontested set of intentions. Rather, it has many histories, all of which represent both personal and political efforts to determine what work-related learning should be. These diverse and often conflicting efforts inevitably shape not only specific work-related learning intentions and practices but the overall constitution of our everyday lives as well.

This chapter seeks to make visible the role of discourse(s) in shaping power relations in work-related learning. In keeping with this goal, the chapter investigates the politics of power, especially as power operates in and through dense discursive networks in contemporary global transformations of work, knowledge, pedagogic discourses, and worker-learners. Haraway (1997) advises that "where to begin and where to be based are the fundamental questions in a world in which power is about whose metaphor brings worlds together" (p. 39). The point is to learn to remember that we might have been otherwise, and yet might be, as a matter of embodied fact. One way to consider how we might otherwise be is to examine what work-related learning means. To examine work-related learning, I will use this chapter to question the meaning of the discourses and discursive practices of the workplace; the meaning of the sites in which learning occurs; and the meaning of the desires, practices, achievements, and dilemmas of practitioners-teachers-learners-workers in the workplace. I contend that if we pay attention to the interplay of global-local discourses of power enacted through our taken-for-granted locations, ascriptions, and everyday pedagogic practices, the leaky boundaries between macro- and micropolitical practices become apparent, and so open to continual contestation and re-formation.

Drawing boundaries for any consideration of the contemporary condition of work-related adult education is no easy task, given the constant flux and contestations in the worlds of work and of education, globally and in specific locations, be they nation-states, regions, communities, workplaces, or homes. Both education and work merge into each and all of these sites, as they do into how we know ourselves. Furthermore, there is a continual barrage of information, hype, and opinions about work, education, and training (and, increasingly, about education and training for work) in both the print-based and electronic media.

Learning for and about work is social, political, economic, and cultural. It is public and private. It moves between and across zones of time and place. It crosses so-called sectors of education (formal-informal, compulsory-postcompulsory, institutionalized-community). Work-related learning is everywhere and, perhaps, also nowhere. In this chapter, I trace some of the contours and fissures of this terrain. My interest responds to the query, What is going on here? Why? And what might some of the implications be? In other words, my endeavor is both to make meaning of contemporary shifts in work-related learning and to investigate how meaning is being made here, by whom, and why.

Thinking about meaning means thinking about practices of power. To think about power, I use Foucauldian notions of the omnipresence of power: "not because it has the privilege of consolidating everything under its invincible unity, but because it is produced from one moment to the next, at every point, or rather in every relation from one point to another. Power is everywhere, not because it embraces everything, but because it comes from everywhere" (Foucault, 1981, p. 93); that as a "network of power relations ends by forming a dense web that passes through apparatuses and institutions, without being exactly localised in them, so too the swarm of points of resistance traverses social stratifications and individual unities" (Foucault, 1981, p. 97).

Thinking about power means thinking about politics, knowledges and pedagogies, locations and identities. Thus the chapter will consider whether, in these destabilized times, education and educators can seek (yet again) to insert a new pedagogic politics of difference. Drawing on Haraway (1997), I agree that "the point is to make a difference in the world, to cast our lot for some ways of life and not others. To do that, one must be in the action, be finite and dirty, not transcendent and clean. Knowledge-making technologies, including crafting subject positions and ways of inhabiting such positions, must be made relentlessly visible and open to critical intervention" (p. 36). For the purposes of this chapter, I shall not rehearse at length the usual literatures, descriptions, and arguments relating to adult education, work, or "new times" (see Butler, 1998,

1999, and Edwards, 1997, for review and references). Instead, and in keeping with the theme of this book, I use Haraway's term *knowledge-making technologies* as a device to co-locate and politicize both the knowledge-making practices that are at the heart of pedagogical moments when adults (and children) learn work, and the discursive "truth games" (Foucault, 1988a) that I contend are providing a (not so new) political rationality.

To assist in this endeavor, I call on a broad variety of literatures that pursue questions relating to the "problematics of rule—Foucault's 'conduct of conduct' through ideas associated with governmentality" (Rose, 1996, pp. 41–42). It is my hope that this approach will display—and so make open to critical intervention—a partial view of the struggles around knowledges, meaning making, identity formations, and material-cultural resources that are being played out in and through the ever-fragmenting field of education, and especially that of work-related learning.

Locating Work-Related Learning

This section introduces the discourses around work and work-related learning and shows the need to problematize these terms.

Work

Despite the vast amount of theorizing on the topic of work, the word *work* remains perhaps one of the most underproblematized terms in popular and political use. As Grint (1998) advises, "whether any particular activity is experienced as work . . . is intimately related to the temporal, spatial and cultural conditions in existence. . . . We should consider the past and present definitions of work as symbols of cultures and especially as mirrors of power: if what counts as work is glorified or despised or gender-related, then the language and practice of work allows us to read embodied fragments of wider social power" (p. 6). Despite the multiplicity of approaches to understanding and experiencing work, the contemporary framing of work in work-related education discourses and texts tends to both interpret and so re-present work in its capitalist garb: as paid work in the labor market/force, as the production or consumption of commodities—resources, goods, services, ideas, artifacts, knowledge/information, and, arguably, people.

Certainly, as many authors (Bauman 1998a, 1998b; Beck, 1992; Grint, 1998) agree, in industrial and postindustrial times, paid work is *the* organizing principle, privileged over all other activities and acting as the pivotal axis around which self, family, society, and state revolve. Notions of work are now firmly located in the opaque, no-questions-asked canon of globalization. As Bauman (1998a) decries, "globalization is on everybody's lips; a fad word fast turning into a shibboleth, a magic incantation, a pass-key meant to unlock the gates to all present and future mysteries. For some, globalization is what we are bound to do if we wish to be happy; for others global-ization is the cause of our unhappiness. For everybody, though, globalization is the intractable fate of the world, an irreversible process. . . . We are all being globalized" (p. 1).

Accompanying this mantra are the feelings of disease, of dis-order, and of constant change in the everyday lives of people, whether at work or not. Global patterns can be traced in the chang-ing nature of work itself—in its organization and distribution, in the complex restructuring of both production and of workforces, and in the deepening patterns of relationships between core and periphery, advantage and disadvantage—as well as in myriad emer-gent vocabularies and managerial technologies. Castells (1998) sit-uates these changes in what he describes as *informational capitalism,* which is, in his view, "a hardened form of capitalism in its goals . . . incomparably more flexible than any of its predecessors in its means. [It relies] . . . on innovation-induced productivity and glob-alization-oriented competitiveness to generate wealth, and to ap-propriate it selectively. It is, more than ever, embedded in culture and tooled by technology. But, at this time, both culture and tech-nology depend on the ability of knowledge and information to act upon knowledge and information, in a recurrent network of glob-ally connected exchanges" (pp. 338–339). To satisfy the needs of this evolving form of capitalism and work, older governance tech-nologies such as the instilling of a work ethic are no longer suf-ficient. Rather, a new order is required. This new order is moving away from producing producers to producing flexible worker-consumers (Bauman, 1998a, 1998b), from finding meaning *in* work to creating meaning *through* work.

Work-Related Learning

The last decade has witnessed a quiet revolution—of continual colonization and commodification of learning to serve national and global economic competitiveness, in times that are framed in terms of risk, crisis, and uncertainty. During this period, social, cultural, and economic institutions have experienced marked destabilization and change, often associated with the retreat of many Western governments from modernist welfare states to so-called postindustrial societies. Invoking a new form of human capitalism, the global policy community now promotes the concept of the learning age, represented as a univocal construction of global logic.

The discursive framing for this transformation is that of the pervasive rhetoric of lifelong learning, designed to simultaneously seduce and command compliant disembodied citizen-learner-workers to willingly accept responsibility for the ongoing development of their personal exploitable capacities. Central to this discursive framing are notions of a "learning" or "information" age (Department for Education and Employment, 1998), "learning societies" (Castells, 1996; Edwards, 1997), "learning" or knowledge economies (Marceau, Manley, & Sicklen, 1997), learning communities, learning organizations, and "smart" or "skills" states. In Australia, for example, the state of Victoria markets itself as the "skills" state, while Queensland is intending to represent itself as the "smart" state. All of these notions shape and are supported by pedagogical discourses of work and work-related learning under the twin banners of globalization and (info)technologization. Work-related learning (and learners) now perform center stage: "Today's and tomorrow's workers must never stop learning: learning is not just for adults . . . it is lifelong" (Australian National Training Authority, 1999, p. 1).

Embedded in this imperative to "never stop learning" are discursive and material-symbolic shifts from social to economic, from collective to individual, from rights to choice or to "user pays," from employment to employability or job readiness, from *unemployed* to *job seeker,* from social citizenship to active contributor to global-national productive culture. Moreover, this imperative for lifelong learning privileges and promotes what Yeatman (1994) (drawing on the work of Lyotard) describes as a metadiscourse for contemporary neoliberal public policy. This neoliberal policy metadiscourse attempts to shift the economic and political responsibilities for providing social welfare from the state to individuals. Policy imperatives for lifelong learning thus help facilitate a shift from the state's providing work-related education to individuals' managing of their own learning. In this neoliberal policy context, "performativity," defined as the maximization of effort and outcome (Lyotard, 1979), is best viewed as a cybernetic systemic "model" that in turn serves "meta-production" (Deleuze, 1995, p. 181). Rather than the state being a guarantor of progress, it is transformed into a "manager of destiny" (Donzelot, 1991a, p. 176).

In understanding the meaning of neoliberal policy discourse about work-related learning, the concept of performativity provides important insights into how the meaning of work-related learning is being changed to produce certain relations of power and to support a specific globalized economic agenda. As argued by Lyotard (1979) two decades ago now, in these times of legitimation crises, "decision makers attempt to manage . . . clouds of sociality according to their input/output matrices, following a logic which implies that their elements are commensurable and that the whole is determinable. They allocate our lives for the growth of power. In matters of social justice and scientific truth alike, the legitimation of that power is based on optimizing the system's performance-efficiency" (p. xxiv). Performativity enhances the competitive abilities of the state through increased efficiency, economy, and effectiveness, while at the same time borrowing "its cultural and structural integrity from . . . earlier phases of the modern state's existence" (Yeatman, 1994, p. 112). Performativity is thus a form of governance, which refers "to any strategy, tactic, process, procedure or programme for controlling, regulating, shaping, mastering or exercising authority over others in a nation, organization, or locality" (Rose, 1999, pp. 16–17). As Lyotard (1979) explains it, "the true goal of the system . . . is the optimization of the global relationship between input and output—in other words, performativity" (p. 1). Within a managerialist-functional rhetoric based on managing the relationships between input and output, institutions such as education are "emptied . . . [of] substantive politicized content, . . . [with] executive decision making . . . undertaken in relation to a series of disciplinary instruments" (Yeatman, 1994,

p. 112). Performativity then is linked to the corporatized or "audit" state (Rose, 1996, p. 55).

Learning work is pivotal in the shifts I have sketched here, with performative outcomes-based learning or training linked to ever-increasing demands for flexibility, productivity, innovation, and endless generation and exploitation of new knowledges. The (local or global) enterprise, most often in the modernist guise of industry, occupies privileged corporate stakeholder status, and as such is both reified and positioned as expert about and key decision maker in and for education. Workplaces, whether Fordist or post-Fordist, large or small, manufacturing or service(s) oriented, are increasingly sought out as the preferred pedagogical sites for learning work. In these workplaces, where workers work-learn-train, an increasingly symbiotic relationship between work and learning work is emerging, with each transforming the other. Concurrently, the role of educators is also rapidly transforming (Seddon, 1998). Paradoxically, as education moves center stage, educators-as-workers also learn the lessons of globalizing labor in their own work sites. Education workers now continually transgress the boundaries between education and training as they redefine themselves as trainers and engage in ever-hybridizing, mutating pedagogical practices.

Despite the focus on learning, the concept of trainability (visible in Donzelot's exposé [1991b] of perpetual training) continues to be vigorously promoted, with depoliticized, prepackaged vocationally oriented education now reaching into all spheres of education and training policy and practice, connecting macro policy/power dynamics with micropractices. Bernstein (1996) contends that the concept of trainability carries with it an understanding of an "actor to be appropriately formed and re-formed according to technological, organizational and market contingencies . . . [with] the ability to be taught, the ability to respond effectively to concurrent, subsequent, intermittent pedagogics" (p. 72). In what he terms a pedagogized future, learning is indeed a new form of labor (Zuboff, 1988). Indeed, according to Bernstein, the ability to be trained (to learn work) "is crucial to the survival of the actor, the economy and presumably the society" (1996, p. 73).

Although it is well understood that both labor and learning are sites of political contestation and power struggles (and have been since industrialization), little or no acknowledgment of spaces for contestability is apparent in the seductive official rhetoric about lifelong learning for or at work. For example, as discussed earlier, work as a concept is rarely, if ever, problematized. It is assumed that paid work is and should be the central defining feature of our modern-postmodern market-oriented lives and that continual learning or training will be embraced by all. Similarly, and not surprisingly, official texts are silent on issues of power. Whose metaphors are these calls to lifelong work-oriented learning? And what is their purpose? According to Rose (1999), an analysis of political power is possible through the analytics of governmentality, if one begins "by asking what authorities of various sorts wanted to happen, in relation to problems defined how, in pursuit of what objectives, through what strategies and techniques" (p. 20).

Governmentality, Control, and Meaning Making

Foucauldian notions of governmentality are based on Foucault's identification of four technologies: production, sign systems, power, and the self. Foucault (1988b, p. 18) describes these technologies as follows:

> As a context, we must understand that there are four major types of these "technologies," each a matrix of personal reason: (1) technologies of production, which permit us to produce, transform, or manipulate things; (2) technologies of sign systems, which permit us to use signs, meanings, symbols, or signification; (3) technologies of power, which determine the conduct of individuals and submit them to certain ends or domination, an objectivizing of the subject; (4) technologies of the self, which permit individuals to effect their own means or with the help of others a certain number of operations on their own bodies and souls, thought, conduct, and way of being, so as to transform themselves in order to attain a state of happiness, purity, wisdom, perfection, or immortality.

As Foucault (1988b) explains, "these four types of technologies hardly ever function separately, although each one of them is associated with a certain type of domination. Each implies certain modes of training and modification of individuals, not only in the obvious sense of acquiring certain skills but also in the sense of acquiring certain attitudes" (pp. 18–19). Rose (1996) takes this idea of governmentality further when, in his discussions of political rationality, he suggests that governmentalities can, for the purposes of analysis, be thought of as intellectual technologies or techniques that have the capacity to render "reality thinkable in such a way that it is amenable to political programming" (p. 42).

Political programming of course refers to the development of governmental policy. These technologies of power are useful for understanding how the meaning of lifelong learning is being redefined in policy and practice as work-related learning. As Rose (1996) has argued, the power of the state results from "the translation of political programs articulated in rather general terms" (p. 43) into actual practice in specific places. What I am suggesting is that through a mapping of discourses of lifelong learning and narratives promoting globally competitive free market futures (especially in those nations that privilege neoliberal or advanced-liberal forms of governance; see Butler [in press] for related literature), it *is* possible to locate authorities of various sorts and to understand what they want to have happen, who is posing the problems, and what the objectives and their ambitions are. It *is* possible to locate a "centre of calculation" (Rose, 1996; 1999, pp. 210–211) and to see whose metaphors are bringing worlds together. The similarity (despite local divergences) of rhetoric about and approaches to lifelong learning generally and to vocational and work-related learning in Organization for Economic Cooperation and Development (OECD) countries (Coffield, 1998, 1999; Holford, Griffin, & Jarvis, 1998) provides a compelling overview of knowledge-making technologies, calling into play Lyotard's performative clouds of sociality, Foucault's governmental technologies, the networked translations discussed by Rose (1996)—all modern operations of power/knowledge (Rose, 1999).

Although it could be argued that this mapping of power/knowledge operations represents a Western view of the world, it should also be remembered that these translations mutate further into new forms of colonization when, in the case of lifelong learning, (globalizing) education is packaged, priced, and marketed, both through aid programs and through the metaphor of entre-preneurial internationalization, by organizations and agencies of education and by educators themselves. Indeed, the OECD (1998) proclaims that "fostering entrepreneurship is central to the func-tioning of market economies. . . . Many, but not all, of the behav-iors associated with entrepreneurship can be taught" (pp. 1–2). It is also timely to remember that, in this era of footloose capital, mobile labor, and off-shore production, increasingly it is workers from so-called less industrialized or developed countries who, as cheap, unregulated, dis-organized laboring bodies, are the very point of production in the ever-perpetuating cycles of produc-tion/consumption/technologies of desire. De Certeau (1984, p. 31) explains this idea as follows: "In reality, a rationalised, expan-sionist, centralised, spectacular and clamorous production is con-fronted by an entirely different kind of production, called 'consumption' and characterised by its ruses, its fragmentation, (the result of circumstances), its poaching, its clandestine nature, its tireless but quiet activity, in short by its quasi-invisibility, since it shows itself not in its own products (where would you place them?) but in an art of using those imposed on it." Such perpetuating cycles shape our lives.

Taylor, Rizvi, Lingard, and Henry (1997) identify the global policy community as a highly influential site in the development of transnational education policy. I argue that this site is indeed a center of calculation, reinforced by the networks of association be-tween the OECD and other supranational organizations, such as the European Union, UNESCO, the International Labour Orga-nization, the World Bank, the International Monetary Fund, and indeed the consortium of the world's richest nations known as the G7, which adopted a strategy (Cologne Charter, 1999) in relation to lifelong learning and training in June 1999.

Secretary General Johnston (1998) of the OECD makes that consortium's position relating to lifelong learning quite clear, stat-ing that OECD's economic rationale is based on two key factors: the threshold of skills required by employers in knowledge-based economies, and the impact of technological developments on skills, work organization and distribution, and rapidly shifting mar-ket conditions. As Johnston stated, "lifelong learning does not mean 'recurrent' training, but *a constant relationship with education,* starting with an emphasis on 'learning to learn.' . . . Of the historical constituents of economic growth—land, labour and capital— *human capital has emerged as the most important resource.* Resource poor societies have developed it to engineer impressive comparative advantages. The foundation on which human capital is built must be education" (p. 1, emphasis added).

Given the overlap of membership, the international-global geographies that are their playing fields, the highly influential think-tank suprapolicy and supragovernmental roles assigned to or assumed by the aforementioned bodies individually and collectively, and their various vested interests in global economic free market competitiveness, it is hardly surprising that the rhetoric displayed in narratives emanating from such bodies is perceived as global logic. For example, the OECD describes itself thus: "The Organisation for Economic Co-operation and Development has been called a think tank, monitoring agency, rich man's club, an unacademic university. It has elements of all, but none of these characteristics captures the essence of the OECD. The OECD groups 29 member countries in an organization that, most importantly, provides governments a setting in which to discuss, develop and perfect economic and social policy. They compare experiences, seek answers to common problems and work to coordinate domestic and international policies that increasingly in today's globalized world must form a web of even practice across nations" (Organization for Economic Cooperation and Development, 1999, p. 1). The OECD is thus a club of like-minded countries (albeit a quite rich although not exclusive club: OECD countries produce two-thirds of the world's goods and services, but membership is limited only by a country's commitment to a market economy and a pluralistic democracy). As indicated in their self-description, OECD aims to form "a web of even practice across nations." This globalized logic is translated into the micropolitics of state and local approaches to education in the transformation of institutions of education (Butler, in press; Raggatt & Williams, 1999), policy formulation and implementation (Boshier, 1998; Griffin, 1998; Taylor, Rizvi, Lingard, & Henry, 1997), and the pedagogical arrangements and practices that position and shape both educators and learners in specific relations and locations.

Together, then, these globalizing visions and local translations coalesce in the formation of what is being described as the globalization of governmentality (Herod, Ó Tuathail, & Roberts, 1998). Within this globalizing of governmentality, a new metanarrative (Roberts, 1998) around lifelong learning is being developed and deployed by economic policymakers that accommodates, supports, and promotes technocapitalism in the old guise of the inevitability of progress. Jessop's notion (1999) of metagovernance—the "governance of government and governance"—is useful here, especially given the OECD's ambition for a global web of even practice. Jessop suggests that "turbulent environments pose different governance problems from those that are relatively stable. . . . Governance mechanisms must provide a framework in which relevant actors can reach agreement over (albeit possibly differential) spatial and temporal horizons of actors vis-à-vis their environment" (p. 4).

In less than fifteen years and as predicted by Lyotard in 1979, education has been commodified and repackaged as a tradable positional good. Quasieducation markets have been created (Marginson, 1997), and education, from primary schooling to universities and community education, has been vocationalized to link directly with ever-changing worlds of work and requirements of capitalism in the production of enterprising, entrepreneurial, change-oriented worker-learners (Butler, 1998). Moreover, these workers and would-be workers are assigned differentiated futures according to their trainability and the needs of capital (Bauman, 1998a; Castells, 1998; Hake, 1998; Hart, 1992; Kell, 1996; Stevenson, 1998) and according to their workplaces (Butler, 1999; Carter, Howell, & Schied, 1999; Garrick & Solomon, 1997).

Is this then the future that Deleuze (1995) foreshadowed when he extended Foucault's notions of disciplinary societies to control-oriented societies? Or is it the future foreseen in Lyotard's prophecy (1979) of context control? According to Deleuze's interpretation, we have moved from the spaces of enclosure (family, school, barracks, factory, prison) that composed Foucault's disciplinary societies. With the changes accompanying late modernity, boundaries are leaky, nonpermanent, in a state of constant renegotiation and flux. Drawing on Virilio's analyses of "ultra-rapid forms of floating control," Deleuze (1995) suggests that whereas in disciplinary societies "one was always starting again," in "societies of control one is never finished with anything" (p. 179)—an apt description indeed of lifelong work-related learning.

In Deleuze's discussion (1995) about the embedded modulation of the corporation and the education system, the corporation replaces the factory, and perpetual training replaces education. Should we consider the accompanying shift to regimes of performance indicators and measurement throughout education, the shift from learner assessment to system accountability, the shift to self-managing and self-governing schools, and the ever-increasing top-down insertion of vocational education into schools accompanied by "traineeships, work place based learning, training packages and competency based forms of knowing/doing as evidence of the introduction of the corporation at all levels of education" (Deleuze, 1995, p. 180)? I believe it is hard not to do so.

This corporate system, according to Deleuze, has new ways of "handling money, profits and humans that no longer pass through the old factory form" (1995, p. 4). Footloose fast capital, e-commerce, venture capital, virtual workplaces, continual restructuring, nonstandard employment, flexible specialization, just-in-time production, lean production, mobile workforces, telecottages, wired workers—the lexicon of capital/humans/work is in a state of constant flux. All performances associated with the lexicon contribute to knowledge-making technologies—Deleuzian higher-order capitalism of metaproduction, intellectual capital/communication flows, and market conquests. These metaproductions, capital and communication flows, and market conquests are demonstrations of Lyotard's notion of tradable flows of money-like knowledges (1979)—disembodied knowledges that define workers, that require capturing, packaging, and managing, and that engender new technologies of accounting around intellectual capital.

What then does this new corporate system mean for adult education? What does it suggest about pedagogies? How do technologies of governmentality and knowledge-making shape meaning and identities? Are these meanings and identities all as new as they seem? Are we, in Deleuzian terms, at the beginning of something? Or can we, in keeping with Grint's idea of a "history helix" (1998, pp. 320–323), dis-locate ourselves from the constraints of Western unilinear notions of time, place, and progress to think about things differently?

Pedagogic Discourses, Knowledge-Making Technologies, and Practices of Power

When educators think about pedagogy[1] and pedagogical practices, we usually tend to think about our teaching, learning, and meaning-making practices from personalized, relational, and situated perspectives. Given the networks of relationality around work and learning work, of macro- and micropractices of power, our understandings can benefit from a multidirectional, multilayered analysis of what work-related learning means. Although I generally subscribe to a Foucauldian understanding of discourse to frame this chapter, Bernstein's idea of pedagogic discourses (1996) is useful in pushing my understandings about pedagogical practices and thus offers an opportunity to think about knowledge-making practices in a context of global economic and social change. Bernstein suggests that pedagogic discourse can be thought of as "a principle for the circulation and reordering of discourses," whereby a discourse can be relocated from its original site to a pedagogical site and, in the recontextualizing, "selectively appropriates, relocates, refocuses and relates other discourses to constitute its own order" (p. 47).

Bernstein (1996) goes further in suggesting that pedagogic discourses selectively create imaginary subjects—pedagogic identities—while they also act as sites for the ongoing "construction, distribution, reproduction and change" of such identities that are embedded in the notion of a (moral, knowledge, and locational) "career," and so are open to never-ending practices of trainability (1996, pp. 47, 80). Trainability, then, is the crafting of subject positions through knowledge-making technologies—positions that offer the lures of meaning making and of the self as a work(er) engaged in lifelong learning, one who acts in a *constant relationship with education*. It is also in this crafting that the ability to "profit from continuous pedagogic re-formations and so cope with new requirements of 'work' and 'life'" (Bernstein, 1996, p. 73) is framed in terms of mutual benefit and obligation.

An interrogation of the policies and practices of vocational education and training in Australia at the end of the twentieth century well illustrates Bernstein's propositions. Work-related education is now pervasive, transforming a myriad of sites into pedagogical spaces. Not only has education been vocationalized in schools, and to a large degree in universities, but a pedagogic basis for short-term, ever-changing working futures is well embedded in social understandings. Education and training policies are, by default, youth policy, despite well-researched challenges that discount popular notions of pathways from school to work, between training and work, and indeed links between training and job creation or availability (Dwyer, 1997; Dwyer & Wyn, 1998; Spierings, 1999). Similarly, it is claimed that European social policy is, to a large degree, work-related policy (Rose, 1999).

In these policies, then, work-related pedagogic sites are indeed everywhere. The message is clear: to have a meaningful personal and national future depends on the capacity to project one's self *meaningfully* (Bernstein, 1996, p. 73). The idea of making meaning through work is not new. In his treatise "Pleasure in Work," Donzelot (1991b) provides a compelling analysis of forms of (global-local) governance in France in the late 1960s. The technology designed to transform understandings of work, workers, family, and state in those times of crisis was that of *formation permanente*—continued retraining—to "set free" the productive capacity of workers and, in so doing, to reduce costs (economic and social) associated with productivity for both enterprises and the (pedagogic) state (p. 279). Similarly, the notion of the pedagogic state is not new (Hunter, 1996). We should not be surprised at either the (re)emergence or the reach of the contemporary project of lifelong work-related learning, given its situatedness in times of hot-linked networks. What is new is that it is indeed everywhere and nowhere; daily life becomes a series of pedagogical spaces for globally oriented work-related learning—sites for the crafting of subject positions that "world" workers for local performative displays of labor.

Work-related learning, through the knowledge-making technologies it employs, comprises a myriad of "little" pedagogies or pedagogic techniques that are articulated in novel ways (Rose, 1999). It collapses the bipolar positions visible in Donzelot's account: public-private, family-work, production-consumption. Like a hologram, knowledge-making technologies actively mirror and project shifting multidimensional visions and suggestive meanings of, for, and by citizen-worker-learners. Knowledge-making technologies also incorporate unknowing and unlearning (Beck, 1998).

As Bauman (1998a) also expounds, new work-related pedagogies entail forgetting as much as learning: "the pressure today is to dismantle the habits of permanent, round-the-clock, steady and regular work; what else may the slogan of flexible labour mean? . . . Labour can conceivably become truly 'flexible' only if present and prospective employees lose trained habits of day-in-day-out work, daily shifts, a permanent workplace and steady workmates' company; only if they do not become habituated to any job, and most certainly only if they abstain from (or are prevented from) developing vocational attitudes to any job currently performed and give up the morbid inclination to fantasize about job-ownership rights and responsibilities" (p. 112).

How do we make meaning of this scenario? What does it say about power? Castells (1998, pp. 346–347) advises,

> Globalization of capital, multilateralization of power institutions, and decentralization of authority to regional and local governments introduce a new geometry of power, perhaps inducing a new form of state. . . . In an informational society, [power] *becomes inscribed, at a fundamental level, in the cultural codes through which people and institutions represent life and make decisions, including political decisions.* In a sense, power, while real, becomes immaterial. It is real because wherever and whenever it consolidates, it provides, for a time, individuals and organizations to enforce their decisions, regardless of consensus. But it is immaterial because such a capacity derives from the ability to frame life experience under categories that predispose to a given behavior and can then be presented as to favor a given leadership.

Certainly it can be argued that the new discourses of lifelong work-related learning and discursive pedagogical practices around such learning both *are* and *act as* political rationalities (Rose, 1999). They encapsulate, translate, transmit, and transform through their embedded/embodied codes of morality, epistemologies, and languages, admirably demonstrating networks of relations of power. This power is not "power over," however. Despite the many interventionist techniques and the persuasive narratives about globalization, the needs for skill formation and lifelong learning translated and displayed through a plethora of networks of governance (actors, organizations, buildings, geographic-social localities, legislations, courses, bodies) are examples of acts of resistance.

Vocational education in Australia, despite massive institutional renorming (Butler, in press) and national reforms, is described as a "mass of contradictions" looking to "re-market" itself in terms of recalcitrant citizens who value qualifications but not necessarily learning (Osmond, 1999, p. 9). The most recent Australian response designed to order this ungrateful and unruly world of work-related (vocational) education and training is to engage public relations experts to transform values through technologies of culture and persuasion—to create a national "learning culture" (Australian National Training Authority, 1999). The clearly stated aim of this move is to inculcate a national and individuated desire "to love learning as much as we love the bush, the beach or the cricket" (Osmond, 1999, p. 9). Not surprisingly, Australia is not alone in this strategizing—plans to establish a culture considered conducive for a "learning age" are well under way in Britain (Fryer, 1998). Despite its position of privilege (as key stakeholder, driver, *and* leader of Australia's national vocational education and training system), industry is also proving somewhat reluctant, and indeed continues to fragment into multiple enterprise sites, making regulation and audit increasingly problematic, especially in light of the incentives available in a user choice system (Schofield, 1999).

Perhaps those with little or no apparent real choice or perceived power are (present and future) worker-learners and, increasingly, educators and trainers with a passion for engaging in teaching-learning (rather than training) relations with their students. Like power, however, choice is illusory in the scope of work-related education in times of pedagogic appropriation and reappropriation and the creation of not-so-imaginary subjects— "pedagogic identities" (Bernstein, 1996, p. 80). As educators, we have choices to make and work to do.

Pedagogic Practices of Freedom

Narratives and, for that matter, metaphors, do what they do. They might well do otherwise, as Haraway (1997) reminds us. Two decades ago, Lyotard (1979), in his discussions about knowledge games, offered wise advice in his claim that narratives "define what has the right to be said and done in that culture in question, and, since they are themselves a part of that culture, they are legitimated by the simple fact that they do what they do" (p. 23). As educators, we are located both within and without truth games through our knowledge-making practices. We cannot be out of the action, nor can we declare ourselves victims of power beyond reach. We have choices to make about the knowledge-making practices we engage in, the technologies we employ, the subject positions we craft, and the way we inhabit those positions. We have choices to make about the kind of futures we craft through our pedagogical relations and translations.

Adult education, and especially that of work-related education, offers limitless potentialities and dangerous opportunities. There are many ways of remembering histories and shaping futures, none of them prescribed and none impervious to acts of power and freedom. How do we think and talk and learn and teach about work? Are we learning workers? Do we consider our worker-learner-students to be knowledge workers, humanware, generic workers, or human terminals? Are we, as educators, educator-networkers, not "centres of calculation" ourselves, linking with countless other global-local "centres," calculating and enacting? Are we continually re-counting, doing, and so naturalizing the very narratives and metaphors we rail against? As educators, we can shift focus, cross boundaries, move locations, offer alternative perspectives, challenge, and provide opportunities to support learning about many ways to read, know, and be in the world. As ever, we have choices to make.

Note

1. My choice of the term *pedagogy* here is deliberate. While acknowledging that *andragogy* is a term used by many writers in relation to adult education, I do not believe that the category of age warrants a shift from the many ways in which pedagogy has been theorized, and its potential for inclusive, participatory, and reflexive practices. I acknowledge my many conversations with colleague and friend Sue Shore about this topic.

References

Australian National Training Authority (1999). Why lifelong learning? In *Marketing skills and learning* [On-line]. Available: http://www.anta. gov.au/lifelong/why/Default.asp

Bauman, Z. (1998a). *Globalization: The human consequences.* Cambridge, England: Policy Press.

Bauman, Z. (1998b). *Work, consumerism and the new poor.* Buckingham, England: Open University Press.

Beck, U. (1992). *Risk society: Towards a new modernity.* Thousand Oaks, CA: Sage.

Beck, U. (1998). *Democracy without enemies* (M. Ritter, Trans.). Cambridge, England: Policy Press.

Bernstein, B. (1996). *Pedagogy, symbolic control and identity. Theory, research and critique.* London: Taylor & Francis.

Boshier, R. (1998). Edgar Faure after twenty-five years: Down but not out. In J. Holford, C. Griffin, & P. Jarvis (Eds.), *International perspectives on lifelong learning* (pp. 3–20). London: Kogan Page.

Butler, E. (1998). Persuasive discourses: Learning and the production of working subjects in a post-industrial era. In J. Holford, C. Griffin, & P. Jarvis (Eds.), *International perspectives on lifelong learning* (pp. 69–80). London: Kogan Page.

Butler, E. (1999). Technologising equity: The politics and practices of work-place learning. In D. Boud & J. Garrick (Eds.), *Understanding learning at work* (pp. 132–150). London: Routledge.

Butler, E. (in press). Knowing now, learning futures: The politics and knowledge practices of vocational education and training. *International Journal of Lifelong Education.*

Carter, V. K., Howell, S. L., & Schied, F. M. (1999). *Shaping self-disciplined workers: A study of silent power in HRD.* Paper presented at the 40th American Education Research Conference [On-line]. Available: http://www.edst.ubc.ca/aerc/1999/99carter.htm

Castells, M. (1996). *The information age: Economy, society, culture: Vol. 1. The rise of the network society.* Oxford, England: Blackwell.

Castells, M. (1998). *The information age: Economy, society, and culture: Vol. 3. End of millennium.* Oxford, England: Blackwell.

Coffield, F. (Ed). (1998). *Learning at work.* Bristol, England: Policy Press.

Coffield, F. (Ed). (1999). *Why's the beer always stronger up north? Studies of lifelong learning in Europe.* Bristol, England: Policy Press.

The Cologne Charter. (1999, June). [On-line]. Available: http://www.unesco.org/education/efa/newsjune1999/g8charter.htm

de Certeau, M. (1984). *The practice of everyday life.* Berkeley: University of California Press.

Deleuze, G. (1995). *Negotiations 1972–1990* (M. Joughin, Trans.). New York: Columbia University Press.

Department for Education and Employment. (1998). The learning age: A renaissance for the new Britain [On-line report]. Available: http://www.lifelonglearning.co.uk/greenpaper/index.htm

Donzelot, J. (1991a). The mobilization of society. In G. Burchell, C. Gordon,

& P. Miller (Eds.), *The Foucault effect: Studies in governmentality* (pp. 169–180). Chicago: University of Chicago Press.

Donzelot, J. (1991b). Pleasure in work. In G. Burchell, C. Gordon, & P. Miller (Eds.), *The Foucault effect: Studies in governmentality* (pp. 251–280). Chicago: University of Chicago Press.

Dwyer, P. J. (1997). Outside the educational mainstream: Foreclosed options in youth policy. *Discourse: Studies in the Cultural Politics of Education, 18*(1), 71–85.

Dwyer, P. J., & Wyn, J. (1998). Beyond the linear models: Pathways and outcomes of 1991 Victorian exit students. In F. Ferrier & D. Anderson (Eds.), *Different drums, one beat? Economic and social goals in education and training* (pp. 76–87). Leabrook, Australia: National Centre for Vocational Education Research (NCVER).

Edwards, R. (1997). *Changing places: Flexibility, lifelong learning and a learning society*. London: Routledge.

Foucault, M. (1981). *The history of sexuality* (Vol. 1). London: Penguin.

Foucault, M. (1988a). The political technology of individuals. In L. H. Martin, H. Gutman, & P. H. Hutton (Eds.), *Technologies of the self: A seminar with Michel Foucault* (pp. 145–162). Amherst: University of Massachusetts Press.

Foucault, M. (1988b). Technologies of the self. In L. H. Martin, H. Gutman, & P. H. Hutton (Eds.), *Technologies of the self: A seminar with Michel Foucault* (pp. 16–49). Amherst: University of Massachusetts Press.

Fryer, R. H. (Chair). (1998). *Creating learning cultures: Next steps in achieving the learning age*. Second report of the National Advisory Group for Continuing Education and Lifelong Learning [On-line]. Available: http://www.lifelonglearning.co.uk

Garrick, J., & Solomon, N. (1997). Technologies of compliance in training. *Studies in Continuing Education, 19*(1), 71–81.

Griffin, C. (1998). Public rhetoric and public policy: Analysing the difference for lifelong learning. In J. Holford, C. Griffin, & P. Jarvis (Eds.), *International perspectives on lifelong learning* (pp. 21–31). London: Kogan Page.

Grint, K. (1998). *The sociology of work* (2nd ed.). London: Policy Press.

Hake, B. (1998). Lifelong learning and the European Union. In J. Holford, C. Griffin, & P. Jarvis (Eds.), *International perspectives on lifelong learning* (pp. 32–43). London: Kogan Page.

Haraway, D. J. (1997). *Modest_Witness@Second Millennium.FemaleMan_Meets OncoMouse: Feminism and technoscience*. London: Routledge.

Hart, M. (1992). *Working and educating for life*. London: Routledge.

Herod, A., Ó Tuathail, G., & Roberts, S. M. (1998). *An unruly world: Globalization, governance and geography*. London: Routledge.

Holford, J., Griffin, C., & Jarvis, P. (Eds.). (1998). *International perspectives on lifelong learning*. London: Kogan Page.

Hunter, I. (1996). Assembling the school. In A. Barry, T. Osborne, & N. Rose (Eds.), *Foucault and political reason* (pp. 143–166). London: UCL Press.

Jessop, B. (1999). The dynamics of partnership and governance failure [On-line paper]. Available: http://www.lancaster.ac.uk/sociology/soc015rj.html

Johnston, D. (1998, October/November). Lifelong learning for all. *The OECD Observer, 24*, 1.

Kell, P. (1996). Creating a disposable workforce: New inequalities in work, education and training. *Education Australia, 34*, 6–8.

Lyotard, J. F. (1979). *The postmodern condition: A report on knowledge*. Minneapolis: University of Minnesota.

Marceau, J., Manley, K., & Sicklen, D. (1997). *The high road or the low road? Alternatives for Australia's future. A report on Australia's industrial structure for the Australian Business Foundation Ltd*. North Sydney: Australian Business Foundation.

Marginson, S. (1997). *Markets in education*. St. Leonards, Australia: Allen & Unwin.

O'Donnell, D., & Garavan, T. N. (1997). New perspectives on skill, learning and training: A viewpoint. *Journal of European Industrial Training, 21*(4), 1.

Organization for Economic Cooperation and Development. (1998). Fostering entrepreneurship. *OECD Policy Brief,* no. 9 [On-line report]. Available: http://www.oecd.org/publications/Pol_brief/9809_pol.htm

Organization for Economic Cooperation and Development. (1999). *About OECD. What is OECD?* [On-line report]. Available: http://www.oecd.org/about/general/index.htm

Osmond, W. (1999, July 25–27). Seminar ponders remarketing VET. *Campus Review,* p. 9.

Raggatt, P., & Williams, S. (1999). *Government, markets and vocational qualifications: An anatomy of policy*. London: Falmer Press.

Roberts, P. (1998). Rereading Lyotard: Knowledge, commodification and higher education. *Electronic Journal of Sociology, 3,* 3.

Rose, N. (1996). Governing advanced liberal democracies. In A. Barry, T. Osborne, & N. Rose (Eds.), *Foucault and political reason* (pp. 37–64). London: UCL Press.

Rose, N. (1999). *Powers of freedom: Reframing political thought*. Cambridge, England: Cambridge University Press.

Schofield, K. (1999). *Independent investigation into the quality of training in*

Queensland's traineeship system. Report prepared for the Vocational Education, Training and Employment Commission (VETEC). Brisbane: Department of Employment, Training and Industrial Relations, Queensland.

Seddon, T. (1998). Teachers for the learning society. *Fine Print, 21*(4), 3–7.

Spierings, J. (Ed.). (1999). *Australia's young adults: The deepening divide.* Ultimo, Australia: Dusseldorp Skills Forum.

Stevenson, J. (1998, December). Vocational knowledges for uncertain futures. *Unicorn, 24*(3), 51–59.

Taylor, S., Rizvi, F., Lingard, B., & Henry, M. (1997). *Educational policy and the politics of change.* London: Routledge.

Yeatman, A. (1994). *Postmodern revisionings of the political.* New York: Routledge.

Zuboff, S. (1988). *In the age of the smart machine: The future of work and power.* New York: Basic Books.

Chapter Five

The Power of the State
Connecting Lifelong Learning Policy and Educational Practice
Kjell Rubenson

Adult education developed into a recognized area of practice and research in the 1950s. Those in the field have complained about its marginal status ever since. Now, however, as a result of dramatic changes in the economic sphere, adult learning is taking center stage in public policy discussions, and interest in the topic has never been higher. National policy documents refer to lifelong learning and the need to develop a learning culture, as do reports from such intergovernmental organizations as the Organization for Economic Cooperation and Development (OECD), the European Union, and UNESCO.

Now that lifelong learning is becoming more broadly socially accepted, adult education practitioners face the challenge of maintaining the field's basic principles of justice, equity, and democracy. There is a danger of accepting slogans about the evolving "learning society" too readily and uncritically without carefully examining the underlying political economy driving the developments. For example, despite the gradual rise in levels of educational attainment in North America, a large number of North Americans still find themselves at the tail end of the skills distribution. And although higher-skilled workers will share in the knowledge economy's wealth, they still face frequent job changes, high turnover, and the need for continuing access to education and training. For the many others tied to dormant economic sectors, dead-end jobs with low pay and poor benefits offer few opportunities for acquiring new skills or qualifications. Skills and educational qualifications are powerful factors in determining access to the wealth created by the knowledge economy. Formal schooling and adult education and training (AET) can thus be considered necessary elements in any strategy for improving the life chances of disadvantaged populations. Hence an important issue is the extent to which AET is reaching such populations.

Looked at from this perspective, recent results concerning participation in structured adult education are disturbing. Despite a rhetoric of lifelong learning for all (Organization for Economic Cooperation and Development, 1996) little has happened in terms of extending adult education to disadvantaged groups. Results from the International Adult Literacy Survey (IALS) indicate a noticeable relationship between social background, educational attainment, and adult education participation in all twelve countries in the study (Organization for Economic Cooperation and Development, 1997). It is particularly interesting that this relationship is stronger in some countries than in others. In the United States, university graduates were sixteen times more likely to participate in some form of AET than people with primary school as the highest credential. The comparative ratio in New Zealand was twenty-two times. In some countries—for example, the Netherlands (five times) and Sweden (six times)—the difference was less pronounced. In Sweden this relatively favorable ratio can be explained, in part, by a large publicly funded voluntary sector and earmarked funding for recruitment of groups with low readiness to participate. Similarly, in the Netherlands in recent years there have been attempts to strengthen the adult education sector and find new ways of combining public and private initiatives. The IALS suggests that public policy can be somewhat effective in moderating inequality in adult education participation.

These findings point to the relationship between the state and its citizens. For example, they suggest questions about what notions of democracy should inform state intervention into AET (Rothstein, 1998). Yet the concept of the state is rarely discussed and analyzed in the adult education literature. As Carnoy (1990) points out, there are crucial differences between what adult education attempts to do and what it can do in different sociopolitical structures. He states, "Ultimately, these differences depend heavily on the possibilities and limits of the state, since it is the state that defines adult education and is the principal beneficiary of its effective implementation. These possibilities and limits of the state are, then, a key issue in understanding the form and content of adult education" (p. x). Against this background, the present chapter will focus on the links between the state and adult education practices. In 1996, ministers of education from the OECD countries made a commitment to pursue and implement a broad policy for making lifelong learning a reality for all in their respective countries (Organization for Economic Cooperation and Development, 1996). The purpose of this chapter is to show how the realization of lifelong learning for all depends, in part, on differences in underlying, often implicit, theories of the state.

Competing Perspectives on the State

Competing theories of the state express pronounced views on the appropriateness of state intervention in different spheres of life. Dunleavy and O'Leary (1987) point out the strong disagreements about what are appropriate activities for the state to engage in. Those who see the state as the best guarantor of the common good view it as a mechanism for realizing the public will. Others, more skeptical, point to the state's capacity to be manipulated and used for oppressive purposes. This group looks for constitutional devices to make the state accountable, to achieve institutional pluralism, and to divide and fragment its organizations and capacities. Some advocate a minimal state whose only role is to intervene when private markets are unable to provide a particular benefit.

The difference between the political left and right is commonly presented as the difference between being for or against state intervention, respectively. Dunleavy and O'Leary (1987) show that the main dividing line is one of being for or against state intervention in certain areas, rather than in absolute terms. Thus the new right in Europe and the United States strongly favors, on the one hand, heavy state intervention in the legal and moral sector, increased spending on law and order, and structures to ensure accountability in the education system. On the other hand, they insist that the economic sector should be free of intervention and left to market forces. Conversely, social democrats have been in favor of state intervention in the economic sphere but see less need for the state to be active in the legal and moral sphere. Antithetical views on the nature of power underlie these different theories of the state.

Pluralism and Adult Education Practice

Pluralism is closely connected to liberal political philosophy and has strongly influenced the American view of the state. Pluralism's core value is a rejection of absolute, unified, and uncontrolled state power. Following Tocqueville, pluralists emphasize the importance of civil society and the need for a well-developed system of voluntary associations to counteract state monism. Pluralists see the influence of interest groups on policymaking as essential. The size of an interest group reflects its electoral importance as well as its ability to mobilize. In pluralism, evaluation of interest groups on the basis of membership, size, and rate of mobilization is seen as legitimate from a democratic perspective. Claims that a small number of interest groups wield undue influence over government are refuted with the argument that, given ongoing political change, new groups will constantly mobilize and gain political leverage. According to Dunleavy and O'Leary (1987), "The system is permeable, capable of being penetrated by any group, which can build up its size, mobilize its members, and motivate them to express strong feelings" (p. 37).

Pluralists depart from the assumption that the state is neutral. They regard the state bureaucracy as capable of acting in the best interests of the public. Critics of the pluralist school refute this image of the state as mediator, balancer, and harmonizer of interests. But pluralists see bureaucracy as basically without preference. Rather, it is representative of society in terms of class, race, gender, ethnicity, religion, and sexual orientation. Policymaking is regarded as a rational undertaking whereby all options can be evaluated and the best chosen.

The social and economic crises facing Western industrialized countries in the late 1960s gave rise to severe criticism of the pluralist position from both the right and the left. Neopluralism developed as a response to new right and neo-Marxist positions on the state, as well as to the ecological rejections of modernity that came from the environmentalists. One strand of this neopluralist thinking is based on an unorthodox economics focused on the behavior of large corporations (Galbraith, 1974). Dunleavy and O'Leary (1987) classify unorthodox economists as strictly Keynesian in their macroeconomic approach. Neopluralists accept the criticism that pluralism understated the interconnections between the economy and politics. In contrast to traditional pluralists, they agree that business interests influence public policy more strongly than other social interests do. Neopluralists recognize the tension between the formal political equality of the liberal state and the inherent inequality of power in a democratic capitalist system. But neopluralists remain attached to the notion that liberal democracies remain basically, if inadequately, directed toward the satisfaction of the public will.

Carnoy and Levin (1985) analyze schooling and work in the democratic state and show that the concept of meritocracy is central to the pluralist view of education. The evaluation of individuals according to objective and universal criteria is linked not only to the allocation of resources but also to whose opinion is heard and valued. In this respect, the schools take on the function of allocating power in society. Unequal distributions of wealth and power can be justified on the grounds of unequal distributions of knowledge and abilities. However, as Carnoy and Levin point out, this description of education implicitly rationalizes inequality. Lenski (1966, p. 15) agrees: "Social inequality is thus an unconsciously evolved device by which societies insure that the most important positions are conscientiously filled by the most qualified persons." Paquette (1998) argues that although meritocratic tenets are central to traditional pluralist ideas of democracy, this vision of equity hides difficult underlying questions of what will count as valued knowledge and how skills and knowledge will be evaluated.

Turning to adult education and the differences in participation I presented in the introduction, an acceptance of the meritocratic position has far-reaching consequences for how leaders of the state interpret results and what actions, if any, they recommend. First, inequalities would be seen as the result not of underlying structural differences but rather of imperfections in the present system that could be partly addressed by good planning and incremental reforms. Although inequalities might be noted, they generally would not lead to any far-reaching state intervention to radically alter the consequences of a system based on self-selection. Thus the present demand for adult education, as well as the structure of how adult education is supplied, would be seen as reflecting economic differentiation and serving society in a relatively efficient and equitable way, albeit not without problems.

This interpretation neglects the fact that such a "system" of adult education implicitly takes for granted that the adult is a conscious, self-directed individual. This individual possesses vital instruments to make use of the available adult education possibilities. Further, this interpretation accepts the likelihood that a system based on recruitment by self-selection widens, rather than narrows, the educational and cultural gaps in society. A pluralist perspective might see these widening gaps as inevitable and acceptable as long as selection is based on achievement. Equity thus becomes an issue of removing barriers to adult education participation for those who want to take part but are for various reasons prohibited from doing so.

Amartya Sen's concept of basic capability equality (1982) offers a different point of entry. It refers to the need to take into account differences in those abilities that are crucial for citizens to function in society. From this perspective, Nussbaum (1990) discusses the fact that people living under difficult conditions tend to come to accept their fate, as they are unable to imagine any reasonable alternative. She argues that it is the duty of the state, with due respect to individual rights, to see to it that citizens are in a position to make well-considered choices. With regard to adult education, this would imply a policy strategy directed as much at creating a demand among groups on the periphery of the learning society as at responding further to demands from those already practicing lifelong learning.

The New Right, Public Choice Theory, and Adult Education Practice

The pluralist position on the state dominated the policy agenda after World War II until it was challenged by new right attacks on Keynesian orthodoxy and the welfare state. Pierson (1998) summarizes the new right's objections to the welfare state:

- It is uneconomic, displacing the necessary disciplines and incentives of the marketplace.
- It is unproductive, encouraging the unproductive public bureaucracy while hindering the productive private sector of the economy.
- It is inefficient, due to its monopoly on provision.
- It is ineffective; despite vast resources, it has not eliminated poverty and deprivation.
- It is despotic, a denial of freedom of choice. Also, its heavy progressive tax regime is a form of confiscation.

Inspired by Adam Smith's liberalism, champions of the neoliberal (new right) agenda insist that the role of government must be restricted to ensure healthy competitive free markets (Friedman, 1962). Hayek (as cited in Pierson, 1998) sees the welfare state as undermining the spontaneous order produced by the market and, therefore, as inconsistent with the principles of a free and just society, and a challenge to everything the liberal capitalist ideal represents.

Public choice theory frequently informs the economic and political analyses of scholars who embrace the values of the new right. Public choice theory is rooted in classical economics and game theory; this thinking is brought to bear on the study of collective, social, or nonmarket decision making. A fundamental assumption is that people are rational actors who maximize their benefits and minimize costs. In other words, individual actions are directed by a narrow rational egoism. Explanations of society are framed in terms of aggregations of individuals. Bureaucrats are seen as budget-maximizers who seek increased resources to improve their power and prestige rather than to promote the good of their ministry or department. The theory is based on the assumption that the state will always try to exploit citizens.

With its neoliberal outlook on the role of the state, the new right continues to have a profound impact on the practice of adult education in Western capitalist societies. The ideological shift is taking place in an era when global capitalism is having profound effects on the nature of work as well as on economic and social policies (Thurow, 1997). A state preoccupied with fiscal prudence will accept only minor responsibility for the provision of adult education. In several countries, particularly the United Kingdom, the budget for general adult education has been drastically cut.

The revolutionaries of the right do not restrict themselves to cutting public expenditure but, in accordance with their basic values, emphasize as well the creation of quasimarkets in the educational sector. Marginson (1997) refers to a range of mechanisms used to align economic, social, and personal conduct with sociopolitical objectives. The fundamental strategy for the state is to govern the choices of autonomous citizens in their capacities as consumers, parents, employees, managers, and investors. The same is true for educational institutions; publicly funded bodies are transformed into self-regulating and partly self-financing market organizations. Increasingly, competition is enhanced by transferring public funds to private sector educational providers. Accountability regimes are altered, and it has become common to use market norms to establish systems of accountability. The new governance structure regulating the relationship between the public educational system and the state can best be described as an emerging evaluative state. Thus Dale (1997) stresses that the influence of the neoliberal era on the relationship between education and the state cannot fully be understood by reference to shifts away from state control toward privatization and decentralization. Although education remains a public issue, its coordination has shifted from being the sole responsibility of the state to a range of forms of governance. Instead of carrying out the work itself, the state increasingly determines where education will be done and by whom, and how it will be evaluated.

Returning to the issue of participation in adult education, in this model unequal participation will not be seen as a problem for government. As Gordon (as cited in Marginson, 1997, p. 83) argues, the idea of life as "the enterprise of oneself" means that each person can be regarded as continuously employed in that enterprise. Consequently it is the responsibility of persons to make adequate provision for the creation and preservation of their own human capital. Investment in learning and its financing are individual responsibilities. Differences in participation patterns strengthen the role of lifelong learning in the competition for social resources. An ideology that sees no role for the state in promoting adult education as a public good leaves participation to market forces.

It can be argued that the dominant discourse of what has been called the second generation of lifelong learning (Rubenson, 1997) partly reflects this position. When the idea of lifelong learning, first labeled as lifelong education, appeared on the policy scene at the end of the 1960s, its proponents claimed it would promote a better society and quality of life and would allow people to adapt to and control change. Individuals were expected to work toward achieving the central goals of democracy, and analysis focused on how a system of lifelong learning could reduce rather than increase educational gaps in society. This position had little influence on adult education policy and soon disappeared. Lifelong learning appeared again in the 1980s, this time situated within an "economistic" worldview and embedded in an ideology that favored the market and de-emphasized the role of the state. It stressed the neoliberal policy direction and fostered the entrepreneurial spirit and competencies among learners. By stressing that learning occurs not only in traditional educational settings, this model promotes the idea of individual responsibility and downplays the role of the state. In its promotion of lifelong learning, often as an argument against traditional schooling, adult education is unintentionally reinforcing the neoliberal discourse on lifelong learning.

Marxism, Neo-Marxism, and Adult Education Practice

Like those of the new right, Marxist analyses are critical of the pluralist concept of a neutral state working in consensus toward the common good of all citizens. Whereas the new right sees the state as hindering the development of competitive markets, Marxists claim that it is impossible to reconcile a capitalist system with a truly democratic state. They see the state as a set of administrative, policing, and military organizations, coordinated by an executive authority. This structure includes government at all levels, the state apparatuses (military, police, judiciary, and civil service), and a set of ideological and cultural apparatuses, such as education, religion, and the media. Governments, as the executive authority, coordinate the coercive parts (state apparatuses) and the persuasive parts (the ideological and cultural apparatuses). Because Marxist theories of the capitalist state place this structure in a society that is divided by class, the focus is on the relation between class power and state power. In classical Marxism, the state is seen as directly controlled by the capitalist class and acting to serve its purposes. The capitalists' control of the economy gives them control over the state apparatus and what it does. According to this view, the role of the administration is to make policy in line with the interests of the capitalist class.

Neo-Marxists, critical of the instrumental position of classical Marxism, suggest that the state has a relative autonomy and is not directly controlled by the capitalist classes. One of the leading scholars within this tradition, Claus Offe (1984), argues that the democratic capitalist state is an institutionalized form of political power that operates to achieve and guarantee the collective interests of all members of a class society dominated by capital. According to Poulantzas (1978), the autonomy of the state allows it to adopt measures serving the subordinate classes if these are found to be politically unavoidable or necessary for promoting the long-term interests of capital. Offe's point is that state institutions, although not directly controlled by the interests of the capitalist class, will, through their dependence on capital accumulation, generate policies that tend to guarantee and enhance these very interests. The state must appear class-neutral to preserve the long-term interests of the capitalist class. This appearance can be maintained only because of the relative autonomy of the structure. The state therefore simultaneously represents the interests of the ruling class but appears to represent the interests of all (Poulantzas, 1978).

In this context, Gramsci's work (Adamson, 1980; Boggs, 1976; Gramsci, 1971, 1975) is of interest because of the contrast he draws between two forms of political control, namely, *domination* (direct physical coercion) and *hegemony* (ideological control and consent). The establishment of control through a moral or cultural influence, rather than by physical coercion or political power, is the basis of Gramsci's concept of hegemony. The focus is on the production and reproduction of cultural hegemony. Cultural hegemony is the ideology that disseminates the consciousness of the ruling class, and organizes the consensus of the population to the existing social order. It is in this sense that one can talk about the rule of ideas. The ideas are translated into structures and activities as well as values, attitudes, beliefs, and morality that support the established order and the interests of the dominant class. To the extent that hegemony is internalized, it becomes the "common sense" of a society. In Marxist terms, hegemony is the base of the false consciousness of the working class, and, according to Williams (1975, p. 183), the importance of Gramsci's work lies in his exploration of ways to break the bourgeois hegemony over workers' minds.

From a Gramscian perspective, the role of education and adult education becomes central in the hegemonic struggle. In his essay "Ideology and Ideological State Apparatuses," Althusser (1971) suggests schooling as the most important source for the reproduction of capitalist society. It is through the school that one comes to accept as "real" one's class identity and thereby one's relation to the mode of production. Although the school is seen as relatively autonomous from the economy, it is part of the state apparatus and through this it transmits the ruling ideology. According to Althusser, it is through instruction, social interaction, and other school experiences that ideological and class positions are transmitted. Torres (1990) recognizes that the school tends to reproduce the division of social labor and contributes to the production and socialization of knowledge and values of hegemonic culture. However, he argues that the expansion of education, with the growing incorporation of the popular sectors into the educational apparatus, also generates advances in the democratic processes in society. Echoing Gramsci, Torres points to the fact that the educational system and education in general appear as a privileged instrument for the socialization of a hegemonic culture. In this sense the control of consciousness becomes as much an area for struggle as the control of productive forces.

The neo-Marxist perspective can shed some light on present developments in adult education practices. Following Offe, we can understand the present economization of adult education as a response to the changes taking place in the economy. These are becoming a threat not only to capital accumulation but also to social harmony. The 1970s witnessed vastly increasing public deficits and increased unemployment. The economic context that evolved in the 1980s has been shaped by a series of changes in the international political economy: free trade agreements, the rise of newly industrialized countries, changing financial institutions, and the profound impact of developments in information technologies

(Pierson, 1998). It is in this context that the knowledge economy or, more broadly stated, the learning society is evolving. A policy report from the OECD notes a perception that national differences in economic performance can be attributed to varying degrees of educational effectiveness (Organization for Economic Cooperation and Development, 1989). The generation of skills has become a major issue, and government documents talk about skills as the main "ammunition" in the global economic competition (Statistics Canada, 1999). By focusing on skills and training issues, governments are seen as responding to demands raised by business, media, and citizens. This will help them maintain their electoral support while at the same time enhancing the value of labor through education and training policies.

Although the neo-Marxist literature stresses that the school should be seen as relatively autonomous from the economy, it is apparent that recent economic developments have forced the state to connect the two spheres more closely. The Organization for Economic Cooperation and Development (1989, p. 17) notes that as the human factor assumes preeminence as a factor of production, *education is becoming less distinct from the economy*. With relevance becoming the key concept driving government policies regarding AET, the interests of business have been privileged. The business sector is given the lead role in defining what competencies and skills the educational system will produce (see, for example, the Conference Board of Canada's list of employability skills). Consequently, structural changes (advisory boards, governance structures, funding regulations, cooperative education, and so on) are put in place to ensure that the interests of business are being heard and addressed by educational institutions. The argument is that strengthening the interests of business ensures that the system produces flexible and adaptable learners. Moreover, business involvement will help institutions make the changes necessary to become flexible organizations that are responsive to the new conditions. From a Gramscian perspective, broad societal acceptance of the economic imperative driving adult education can be understood in terms of the hegemonic dominance this idea has achieved in today's society. As stated earlier, the rule of ideas is translated into structures and activities as well as values, attitudes, beliefs, and morality, and becomes the "common sense" of society.

The hegemonic force of the economization of adult education is reflected in the adults' relationship to learning. Thus it is not surprising that studies on adults' learning behavior confirm an influence perhaps best characterized as "the long arm of the job." This shift has radically altered the landscape of adult education since the 1970s (Bélanger & Tuijnman, 1997; Rubenson, 1996). The increase in job-related adult education explains much of the rise in total participation rates in the last two decades. According to participation data collected in connection with the International Adult Literacy Survey, 38 percent of Americans participated in adult education for job-related reasons, but only 5 percent participated for reasons related to personal interest (Houtkoop & Ooserbeek, 1997). Further, only 14 percent of older adults in the United States (those fifty-six to sixty-five years of age) took part in organized learning activities for reasons not related to their job (Organization for Economic Cooperation and Development, 1997, p. 101).

So far, we have argued that adult education practice to a large extent is part of the dominating economic paradigm. However, Gramsci also alerts us to the potential of adult education practice as an instrument in the counterhegemonic struggle. Torres (1990) notes how some forms of popular education can play an important role in the struggle for hegemony. Rubenson (1989) refers to the role of adult education as an integral part of social movements' broader struggle to heighten individual consciousness and commitment to dreams and goals for social change and social justice.

Power Resources Theory and Adult Education Practice

Power resources theory, embedded in social democratic reformist philosophy, is probably the least well known in adult education literature. Nevertheless, it has a lot to offer to those reformers who do not feel at home in either the pluralist or the neo-Marxist camp. It is based on an assumption that in advanced capitalist societies, a division exists between the exercise of economic power and the exercise of political power, that is, between markets and politics. In the economic sphere, the main power resource is control over capital assets, and the principal beneficiary is the capitalist class. This is not the case in the political sphere, where power comes from the strength of numbers mobilized through the democratic process (Korpi, 1983), and thus favors large collectivities, such as organized labor. Power resources theory (PRT) agrees with neo-Marxists that the capitalist class is by far the most powerful actor in society, due to its control of the means of production. But it argues that labor has potential access to political resources that "can allow it to implement social reform and alter distributional inequalities to a significant degree" (Olsen & O'Conner, 1998, p. 8). Thus Korpi (1998, p. 54) suggests "that the extent of bias in functioning of the state can vary considerably as a reflection of the distribution of power resources in these societies and thus that politics can be expected to matter for the distributive processes in society." Korpi (1983) sees institutionalized power struggle between markets and politics reflected in the development of citizenship and the welfare state. He maintains that the difference in power resources in a society between major collectives or classes, particularly between capital and organized labor, regulates the distribution of life chances, social consciousness, and conflicts in the labor market. Similarly, changes in power tend to be reflected in changes in social institutions and their modus operandi. The stronger the labor movement, the more developed the welfare state will become. Thus, power resources theorists have shown that poverty gaps are smallest and benefits more generous in countries with well-mobilized labor.

These theorists also suggest that public policy on funding regimes and the nature of social programs can be understood in terms of various forms of welfare state regimes (Esping-Andersen, 1989). The liberal welfare state, with its means-tested assistance and modest universal transfers, caters mainly to a clientele of low-income dependents. This type of state would see adult education mainly as a way of getting people off welfare. Participation would mainly be left to market forces; entitlements are strict and often associated with stigma. According to Esping-Andersen, rather than tolerate a dualism between state and market and between working class and middle class, the social democratic welfare state promotes an equality of the highest standard, not an equality of minimal needs.

PRT provides an analytical framework for looking at vital policy issues related to the funding and provision of adult education. In a market-driven system, it is obvious that advantaged groups will strongly influence patterns of provision. However, there is also evidence to suggest that even organizations with pronounced ambitions to reach disadvantaged groups actually supply adult education that corresponds best to the demands of the advantaged (Nordhaug, 1991). This is a result of the failure of existing funding regimes to compensate for the increased costs involved in recruiting the underprivileged. In a time when government policies seek to increase efficiency through the adoption of outcomes-based funding and a more market-oriented approach, there is a growing likelihood that the organization will pursue those easiest to recruit and most likely to succeed (McIntyre, Brown, & Ferrier, 1996). Swedish adult education policies over the last twenty-five years shed some light on the influence of funding regime on recruitment effects. Experience has shown that general policies are not effective when it comes to recruiting disadvantaged groups, because traditionally strong groups consume the resources. Instead, it is earmarked funding for targeted strategies, such as outreach, special study aid, and so on that have been effective (Rubenson, 1996).

Returning to the International Adult Literacy Survey and the results on participation in adult education, PRT suggests that the different levels of inequality observed can be explained in terms of the prevailing welfare state regime. Thus, countries like Sweden with a social democratic welfare regime are using the participation pattern of the middle class to arrive at public policy intervention, whereas the Anglo-Saxon liberal welfare state bases its intervention on a minimalist approach. Thus, differences in adult education participation and literacy levels may be better explained by the nature of the welfare state regime than by what happens in the school system. I have argued that the Swedish situation in adult education can be understood in this broader context (Rubenson, 1994). My analysis attempts to show how the strength of organized labor, with its close ties to the ruling party, forced the state to develop far-reaching distributive policies in adult education. Although PRT has been applied mostly to analyses of the capacity of organized labor to influence the political agenda, it is not to be understood as a "one-factor" theory but can applied to study the influence of different social movements and their political power.

Feminist Criticism of State Theories

One of the most notable recent developments in the discussions around power and state has been the increased attention to gender and, to a certain extent, race by feminist scholars critical of mainstream state theories. The critics can be grouped into two broad camps. The first is that of postmodern feminist scholars who outright reject the enlightenment tradition and "grand" or "meta" narratives like liberalism or Marxism. Building on such philosophers as Foucault and Derrida, these feminist writers (Butler & Scott, 1990; Mouffe, 1993) present a poststructuralist understanding of power that is skeptical of the very notion of the state as presented in the foregoing discussion. The other camp consists of feminist scholars working within a certain state tradition but who are critical of the lack of gender awareness, as will be discussed.

A central observation common to both camps is that the traditional state theories do not adequately account for the situation of women in the welfare state and that during the welfare state era there has occurred a feminization of poverty (Goldberg & Kremen, 1990). Pierson (1998, p. 71) reports that in 1995 more than half of all families in the United States were female headed, up from a little over a third in 1970. As Pierson notes, available welfare statistics show that the situation is particularly difficult for elderly women and suggests that the situation of single and elderly women cannot be explained simply by inadequate levels of benefits. Instead, their situation should be understood in terms of the formal inequality of welfare rights for men and women and the consequences of women's role in unpaid domestic labor. Consequently, state theory in general, and the working of the welfare state in particular, needs to be broadened to include not only the monetarized economy but also production and reproduction within the domestic sphere. In this respect it is interesting to note how the various contributions in *Rethinking Restructuring: Gender and Change in Canada* (Bakker, 1996) reveal the contradictory effects of economic globalization on work, whereby gender becomes more important in some spheres and less important in others. This situation is very different from the era of postwar Keynesian macropolitics, which rested on a conception of the household as a single unit supported by a male breadwinner and a woman working at home. The changed situation today makes clear the need to consider gender in theorizing the state (Bakker, 1996). Similarly, Connelly and MacDonald (1996) are critical of the literature for its failure to recognize the gendered nature of economic restructuring.

As Bakker (1996, p. 8) states, it is not that gender is always the most important factor but that a politicoeconomic framework should incorporate the interaction of gender with other agents. However, there is an intense debate within feminist theory about how this incorporation should be achieved. Particularly at issue is the relationship between patriarchy and socioeconomic class. Hartmann (1979) has been critical of those feminist scholars who just subsume women's issues within Marxist analysis. To her, Marx's categories are gender blind, and she proposes that patriarchy and capitalism ought to be regarded as two separate but integrated systems (see also Mutari & Boushey, 1997; Ng, 1985). Smith (1985) is critical of Hartmann's conclusion that patriarchy predates capitalism, and she cannot envisage a mode of production that excludes the organization of gender relations. Thus gender relations are "an integral constituent of the social organisation of class" (p. 3). Regardless of these kinds of differences, most feminist scholars would share Burstyn's view (1985, p. 82) that "insofar as Marxist theory per se has a useful role to play in the longer and larger process of social transformation, Marxist men must begin to engage as seriously with feminist political theory as feminists have done with Marxist political theory." Consequently, in Marxist state theory a gender perspective needs to be injected into the analysis of how the state acts to administer and enforce the interests and needs of the capitalist class.

The gender and class debate is also a central topic among power resources theorists. Recognizing the major contribution these scholars have made to the understanding of the state in general, and welfare state regimes in particular, O'Connor (1998) is critical of their lack of a gender perspective. Traditionally, comparative studies on welfare regimes have focused on how the mobilization of power resources by social classes affects the modification of market inequalities and the definition of class and citizenship. O'Connor warns that a gender-sensitive comparative analysis cannot be achieved by just looking at gender or adding gender to the power resources framework. Instead, some key concepts—such as class, citizenship, and power mobilization—should be reexamined and broadened. She points out that by integrating gender into the analysis, we can question taken-for-granted assumptions about the meaning of citizenship and the exercise of citizenship rights. Further, theorists who restrict their analyses to working-class political mobilization have thereby ignored the influence of nonparty groups. This is specifically true of new social movements, such as the feminist movements. O'Connor maintains that a widening of what constitutes formally recognized political space and action allows for the fact that participation in the political system occurs not only through traditional loci of power but also through bureaucracies, client representative groups, and social movements.

Conclusion

A critical reader might ask why so much attention is given to different understandings of the state in a time of rapid globalization, as seen in deregulation of international markets and greater international mobility for capital freed from strict control from nation-states. The changes represent a challenge to national equity policies irrespective of the varying political aspirations of national governments. Pierson (1998) maintains that whereas there are those who believe that nation states are increasingly losing their powers, others doubt that there really is a new phenomenon of globalization, and Pierson believes that the truth seems to be somewhere in between. Howlett and Ramesh (1995) suggest that there is a tendency in the literature to exaggerate the effects of international economic forces on nations. They state that militarily powerful states and those with large economies have a high capability to protect citizens from foreign pressures. In their view, international economic institutions do not cause a general erosion of states' policy capabilities, as is often suggested in the literature; rather, these policy capabilities vary by policy sector. They are stronger at the macro level, affecting fiscal and monetary tools, whereas there is ample opportunity to negotiate in microeconomic matters and, I would suggest, in education.

The differences in adult education policies and practices that have been observed among liberal democratic countries (Bélanger & Tuijnman, 1997) speak to the importance to adult education of addressing the state and the distribution of power. As stressed in the introduction to this chapter, in a time when lifelong learning is emerging as one of the key public policy issues, we have to ask what understanding of democracy should inform state intervention into AET. Our understanding of adult education practice will be helped not only by subscribing to a normative position on what lifelong learning ought to be but also by critically examining how the learning society is evolving. Reintroducing the role of state into the discussion will help us combine the empirical with the normative and arrive at a constructive theory on lifelong learning. Further, I suggest that the power resources approach provides a fruitful tool for adult education researchers in their attempt to conceptualize the role of power.

References

Adamson, W. L. (1980). *Hegemony and revolution: A study of Antonio Gramsci's political and cultural theory.* Berkeley: University of California Press.

Althusser, L. (1971). Ideology and the ideological state apparatuses. In L. Althusser (Ed.), *Philosophy and other essays* (pp. 121–173). London: New Left Books.

Bakker, I. (1996). Introduction. In I. Bakker (Ed.), *Rethinking restructuring: Gender and change in Canada* (pp. 3–25). Toronto: University of Toronto Press.

Bélanger, P., & Tuijnman, A. (Eds.). (1997). *New patterns of adult learning: A six-country comparative study.* New York: Pergamon Press.

Boggs, C. (1976). *Gramsci's Marxism.* London: Pluto Press.

Burstyn, V. (1985). Masculine dominance and the state. In V. Burstyn & D. E. Smith (Eds.), *Women, class, family and the state* (pp. 45–89). Toronto: Garamond Press.

Butler, J., & Scott, J. (Eds.). (1990). *Feminists theorize the political.* London: Routledge.

Carnoy, M. (1990). Foreword: How should we study adult education? In C. A. Torres (Ed.), *The politics of nonformal education in Latin America* (pp. ix–xv). New York: Praeger.

Carnoy, M., & Levin, H. M. (1985). *Schooling and work in the democratic state.* Stanford, CA: Stanford University Press.

Connelly, P. M., & MacDonald, M. (1996). The labour market, the state and the reorganization of work: Policy impacts. In I. Bakker (Ed.), *Rethinking restructuring: Gender and change in Canada* (pp. 82–91). Toronto: Toronto University Press.

Dale, R. (1997). The state and the governance of education: An analysis of the restructuring of the state-education relationship. In A. H. Halsey, B. Lauder, P. Brown, & A. S. Wells (Eds.), *Education: Culture, economy, society* (pp. 273–282). Oxford, England: Oxford University Press.

Dunleavy, P., & O'Leary, B. (1987). *Theories of the state.* Old Tappan, NJ: Macmillan.

Esping-Andersen, G. (1989). The three political economies of the welfare state. *Canadian Review of Sociology and Anthropology, 26,* 10–36.

Friedman, M. (1962). *Capitalism and freedom.* Chicago: University of Chicago Press.

Galbraith, J. K. (1974). *Economics and the public purpose.* Harmondsworth, England: Penguin.

Goldberg, G. S., & Kremen, E. (Eds.). (1990). *The feminization of poverty: Only in America?* London: Praeger.

Gramsci, A. (1971). *Selections from the prison notebooks* (Q. Hoare & G. N. Smith, Eds. and Trans.). London: Lawrence and Wishart.

Gramsci, A. (1975). *Letters from prison* (L. Lawner, Trans.). New York: HarperCollins.

Hartmann, H. (1979). The unhappy marriage of Marxism and feminism: Towards a more progressive union. *Capital and Class, 8*(1), 1–33.

Houtkoop, W., & Ooserbeek, H. (1997). Demand and supply of adult education and training. In P. Bélanger & A. Tuijnman (Eds.), *New patterns of adult learning: A six-country comparative study* (pp. 17–38). Oxford, England: Pergamon Press.

Howlett, M., & Ramesh, M. (1995). *Studying public policy.* Oxford, England: Oxford University Press.

Korpi, W. (1983). *The democratic class struggle.* London: Routledge.

Korpi, W. (1998). Power resources approach vs. action and conflict: On causal and intentional explanations in the study of power. In J. S. O'Connor & G. M. Olsen (Eds.), *Power resources theory and the welfare state* (pp. 37–69). Toronto: University of Toronto Press.

Lenski, G. (1966). *Power and privilege: A theory of social stratification.* New York: McGraw-Hill.

Marginson, S. (1997). *Markets in education.* St. Leonards, Australia: Allen & Unwin.

McIntyre, J., Brown, A., & Ferrier, F. (1996). *The economics of ACE delivery.* Sydney: BACE.

Mouffe, C. (1993). *The return of the political.* London: Verso.

Mutari, E., & Boushey, H. (1997). Introduction: The development of feminist political economy. In H. Mutari, H. Boushey, & W. Fraher (Eds.), *Gender and political economy* (pp. 3–17). New York: Sharpe.

Ng, R. (1985). Introduction. In V. Burstyn & D. E. Smith (Eds.), *Women, class, family and state* (pp. vii–ix). Toronto: Garamond Press.

Nordhaug, D. (1991). *The shadow educational system: Adult resource development.* Oslo: Universitetsforlaget.

Nussbaum, M. (1990). Aristotelian social democracy. In R. B. Douglass, G. M. Mara, & H. S. Richardson (Eds.), *Liberalism and the good* (pp. 203–252). New York: Routledge.

O'Connor, J. S. (1998). Gender, class and citizenship in the comparative analysis of welfare state regimes: Theoretical and methodological issues. In J. S. O'Connor & G. M. Olsen (Eds.), *Power resources theory and the welfare state* (pp. 209–228). Toronto: University of Toronto Press.

Offe, C. (1984). *Contradictions of the welfare state.* London: Heinemann.

Olsen, G. M., & O'Conner, C. J. (1998). Understanding the welfare state: Power resources theory and its critics. In J. S. O'Connor & G. M. Olsen (Eds.), *Power resources theory and the welfare state* (pp. 3–33). Toronto: University of Toronto Press.

Organization for Economic Cooperation and Development. (1989). *Education and the economy in a changing society.* Paris: Author.

Organization for Economic Cooperation and Development. (1996). *Lifelong learning for all.* Paris: Author.

Organization for Economic Cooperation and Development. (1997). *Literacy skills for the knowledge society.* Paris: Author.

Paquette, J. (1998). Equity in educational policy: A priority in transformation or in trouble. *Journal of Educational Policy, 13*(4), 41–61.

Pierson, C. (1998). *Beyond the welfare state.* University Park: Pennsylvania State University Press.

Poulantzas, N. (1978). *State, power, socialism.* London: New Left Books.

Rothstein, B. (1998). *Just institutions matter: The moral and political logic of the welfare state.* Cambridge, England: Cambridge University Press.

Rubenson, K. (1989). The sociology of adult education. In S. B. Merriam & P. M. Cunningham (Eds.), *Handbook of adult and continuing education* (pp. 51–69). San Francisco: Jossey-Bass.

Rubenson, K. (1994). Adult education policy in Sweden, 1967–1991. *Policy Studies Review, 13*(3/4), 367–390.

Rubenson, K. (1996). The role of popular adult education: Reflections in connection to an analysis of surveys on living conditions, 1975 to 1993. In Parliamentary Commission on Popular Adult Education (Ed.), *Three studies on popular adult education.* Stockholm: Fritzes.

Rubenson, K. (1997). *Adult education and training: The poor cousin—an analysis of reviews of national policies for education.* Paris: Organization for Economic Cooperation and Development.

Sen, A. (1982). *Choice, welfare and measurement.* Cambridge, MA: MIT Press.

Smith, D. (1985). Women, class, and family. In V. Burstyn & D. E. Smith (Eds.), *Women, class, family, and the state* (pp. 1–44). Toronto: Garamond Press.

Statistics Canada. (1999). *Learning a living: An analysis of the 1997 Adult Education and Training Survey.* Ottawa: Statistics Canada.

Thurow, L. (1997). *The future of capitalism: How today's economic forces shape tomorrow's world.* St. Leonards, Australia: Allen & Unwin.

Torres, C. A. (1990). *The politics of nonformal education in Latin America.* New York: Praeger.

Williams, G. (1975). *Proletarian order.* London: Pluto Press.

Adult Education in Colleges and Universities

The chapters in Part Two recognize that higher education has increasingly become a site of education for adults in undergraduate degree programs, continuing education, and the preparation of adult educators in graduate education. Given the central role that knowledge and credentialing play in the distribution of power in society, colleges and universities are a linchpin in the constitution of culture, society, and the economy.

In Chapter Six, Budd L. Hall analyzes the interconnections between globalization, global civil society, and the preparation of adult educators in the university. He grounds his theoretical perspective of "globalization from below" in his daily practices and those of his department, which prepare people for leadership roles in adult education.

In Chapter Seven, Juanita Johnson-Bailey turns our attention to Black women who have returned to college to receive their degrees. She discusses their particular struggles for knowledge in classrooms and institutions that mirror the hierarchies of daily life for these women.

The last chapters in Part Two focus on teaching and learning processes, giving specific attention to how asymmetrical power relations are played out in higher education classrooms. In Chapter Eight, Elizabeth J. Tisdell uses a frame of feminist poststructuralist theory to discuss the special challenges she has faced when teaching for social change. She shares how this form of teaching requires an explicit attempt to name and reconstruct existing power relations in the classroom. In Chapter Nine, Mechthild Hart places the legitimacy of subjugated voices and knowledges of marginalized people at the center of her analysis as she considers the political-ethical ground for teaching and learning as a political ally. Using her own teaching as an example, she discusses the importance of teachers developing a mestiza consciousness.

Chapter Six

The Politics of Globalization
Transformative Practice in
Adult Education Graduate Programs
Budd L. Hall

It strikes me that at the end of this decade, this century, and this millennium, the free market economists of our day very much resemble the skeptical geographers of fourteenth-century Europe who were beginning to have their doubts about whether or not the world was indeed flat. I believe that the globalization gurus of our times share the narrowness of vision of the flat-earth geographers of earlier times. For the fourteenth-century geographers, there was much anecdotal evidence from fishers and travelers to the effect that the world was different from the way they explained it, but as no one had ever returned from sailing around the earth, the dominant opinions held sway. The growing uncertainties of the global financial markets have brought free trade economists, the flat-earth scientists of our story, to the edge of their metaphorical flat earth. They have heard the anecdotes from beyond the edge, but they are not yet ready to declare that there is another form for the world, that there is another story about economy, people, and the rest of nature to explore. An important observation was made to me by my Cree colleague, Laara Fitznor, who specializes in aboriginal education at my university. She pointed out that aboriginal peoples in North America had always known of the earth's roundness, having learned the creation metaphor of an earth shaped like the back of a turtle. Hence, Turtle Island was the name for what the European American settlers came to call North America.

This chapter looks at what we mean by globalization, what some observers of the current health of economic globalization have said, and what some of the responses have been within the global adult education community at the UNESCO level. It will also look at some of the ways that my own practice as a faculty member and chair of the adult education department at the University of Toronto is shaped in response to the ways that global power shapes our current world.

On a global scale, the University of Toronto is rich. We have thirteen full-time faculty members in our adult education program and ten part-time faculty members. We have about five hundred master's and doctoral students in the program at any given time and also make important contributions to the preservice teacher education programs. My adult education practice is expressed most visibly in my teaching and research practice and through work with my colleagues in shaping an adult education program that seeks to maintain a balance between our diverse visions of the world as faculty members and the needs of our students.

What Do We Mean by Globalization?

Globalization is being experienced in a very wide variety of forms and practices. The most commonly understood form of globalization relates to economic structures—business and production. But there are several other forms or dimensions of globalization also worthy of mention: the state, communications, movements of people, sales of arms, violence and crime, resistance, and the rise of global forms of civil society.

Each day, according to the United Nations Development Programme (1999), more than 1.5 trillion dollars changes hands in financial transactions totally apart from funds needed for global trade purposes. These transactions have to do with currency speculation by private and public banks, with investments of all kinds through the computerized stock markets of the world, and with bond undertakings at both private and state levels. The political leadership in most parts of the world has joined the call for each of us to play our part in the competitive global market. Products are assembled everywhere and sold everywhere, crossing borders sometimes scores of times before finding an ultimate place of rest or sale. And the movement of durable goods does not stop with sale. Within days, weeks, or years, most of the goods currently produced will be discarded, and our goods then rejoin the global search for another resting place. If we live in the cities, we send our waste to the rural areas. If our waste is poisonous or toxic, we send it to the furthest reaches of our countries or, failing that, to the poorest parts of the world, where countries fight over the right to become a dumping ground for the waste of the rich. Jobs, health and safety conditions, environmental regulations, human rights, and immigration policies are thrown out as deregulation on a global level strips national legislation of its force.

The state itself has taken on global forms. The richest states of Europe now work together in a powerful economic union where the restrictions and limitations of individual governments are giving way to regional forms of state control. In Asia, no serious economic decisions are made by a single state government without direct or indirect talks with governments of such trading partners as Japan, China, Indonesia, Taiwan, South Korea, Australia, New Zealand, and, increasingly, Thailand and Malaysia. The United Nations system and related regional banking and development agencies are a further layer of an internationalized state function. These multilateral bodies have more power and influence in the medium-size and smaller states, and such institutions as the International Monetary Fund and the World Bank take on nearly full control of the economies of the least powerful states.

Crime and violence are also disturbing features of our globalizing world. The complex combination of drug use in rich countries and weak economies in poor countries creates patterns of international activity that take advantage of all the modern means of communication and money transfer. All over the world, people are caught in vicious patterns of cruelty and violence that spill over into each and every one of our homes (Carlsson & Ramphal, 1995). Entrenched poverty, the increasing gap between the rich and the poor, and the flight of people for economic and security reasons are but a few features of the globalization of violence and crime.

A related form of globalization occurs in the arms trade. Although the overall world expenditures on the military have declined since the 1989 accords between the reformed Soviet Union and the United States, the arms trade itself has taken on a new life, particularly in the form of low-cost ways to kill. The United States in particular has accelerated its sales from roughly $9 billion in 1987 to over $22 billion in 1992. In that same period, the former Soviet Union has decreased arms transfers from $30 billion to $2.8 billion. According to war historian John Keegan, those "who have died in war since 1945 have, for the most part, been killed by cheap, mass-produced weapons and small-calibre ammunition, costing little more than the transistor radios and batteries which flooded the world during the same period" (quoted in Carlsson & Ramphal, 1995, p. 130). And among the low-cost weapons that cross our borders each day are land mines that can be produced for several dollars each and can kill or maim a person with ease. There are an estimated one hundred million land mines distributed in roughly sixty countries around the globe (Grimmett, 1994).

The combination of market forces, civil conflict, and positive inducements to move has stimulated the global movement of people. Thus, people are on the move as never before in history, migrating voluntarily or as refugees. For example, in global terms, over one hundred million people are refugees, living against their choice in countries they were not born in (United Nations High Commission on Refugees, 1995). Of course, people do not move as easily as either goods or finance capital. In my country, Canada, money can move in and out between Mexico, the United States, and our financial institutions with ease, but people have much more difficulty. Indeed, the open capital market has not produced an open labor market.

As D'Arcy de Oliveira and Tandon (1994, p. 5) point out, "the weaker, the more vulnerable, the powerless, those who do not produce or consume anything of value for the world market, those who can hardly be privatized or internationalized are becoming expendable." The same sweeping forces for global economic integration are deepening the age-old divisions of the rich and the poor. Our global village has an expanding slum area, and the affluent are increasingly afraid of the poor. The many faces of globalization create, not surprisingly, new forms of resistance, new calls for community revitalization, a renewed emphasis on self-sufficiency, withdrawals into searches for security through the reinforcement of cultural identities, and new forms of community economic development. And as this chapter will explore, new forms of regional and global networks of activists, nongovernmental agencies, and citizens are actively contesting the movement toward poverty, ecological imbalance, and exclusion.

Critics of Flat-Earth Economics

Speaking before the October meeting of the International Monetary Fund in 1998, the finance minister of Canada, in a turn away from previous unrestrained support for free global market systems, noted the following: "Even the truest believers in free markets have long since acknowledged the need for sound domestic banking regulations . . . and other such instruments to protect individuals from the excesses of an unfettered market at home. *Clearly there is need for similar instruments and tools in international markets*" ("Finance Minister Addresses World Bank," 1998, p. 31; emphasis added). More than the finance ministers of the world have come to the edge of the flat earth just now; the sustained instability in global markets has for the first time raised, even in the minds of the most diehard economic fundamentalists, fundamental concerns about the risks of unregulated capital flows. What has caused me to think that we are quite literally at the edge—at the point of transition— have been the sustained voices from so many different disciplines and fields of study, so many views from the edge. Let us consider some of these views.

What about leaders of government and business? Ingvar Carlsson, the former prime minister of Sweden, and Shridath Ramphal (1995), former Commonwealth secretary general, were the authors of the report on the Commission on Global Governance, which looked at the potential reform of the United Nations system. They noted that we were at a point in time as momentous as the rise of Islam at the time of the death of the prophet Mohammed or as the time of the European expansion into the Americas. They write, "The world needs a new vision that can galvanize people everywhere to achieve higher levels of co-operation in areas of common concern and shared destiny" (p. 6). George Soros, the philanthropist and currency speculator who rose to fame on the basis of a one-day profit of $1 billion in the global currency game by betting against the British pound, has said in his book *The Crisis of Global Capitalism* (1998, p. xxii) that "market fundamentalism is today a greater threat to open society than any form of totalitarian ideology." He continues by saying, "One of the great defects of the global capitalist system is that it has allowed the market mechanism and the profit motive to penetrate into fields of activities where they do not properly belong" (p. xxiii).

What about the sociologists and social activists? Ulrich Beck, a much-respected German sociologist, notes, "More and more we find ourselves in situations which the prevailing institutions and concepts of politics can neither grasp nor adequately respond to" (1997, p. 7). He continues with specific reference to Europe: "Anyone who takes a look at the shifts and erosion in the basic structures of European modernity must ask the question of how and where new structures, coordinating systems and orientations will come from" (p. 13). Asoka Bandarage, author of *Women, Population and Global Crisis* (1997), notes that from her perspective, "We are at a critical juncture in the history of human and planetary evolution. . . . The world is experiencing an intensification of violence" (pp. 1–2). Charlene Spretnak, an ecofeminist from the United States, tells us, "Our situation as a species is the following: the life-support systems of this almost impossibly beautiful planet are being violated and degraded, causing often irreparable damage, yet only a small proportion of humans have focused on this crisis" (1990, p. 3). From Vandana Shiva (1989, p. xiv): "Somewhere along the way, the unbridled pursuit of progress, guided by science and development, began to destroy life without any assessment of how fast and how much of the diversity of life on this planet is disappearing."

What about the historians and political scientists? In his seminal history of the twentieth century, Eric Hobsbawn, one of the most respected Western historians, notes that "for the first time in two centuries, the world of the 1990s entirely lacked any international system or structure" (1994, p. 559). He goes on to say, "In short the century ended in a global disorder whose nature was unclear, and without an obvious mechanism for either ending it or keeping it under control" (p. 562). He closes out his work with a plea to look beyond the edge toward something new; he argues, "The forces generated by the techno-scientific economy are now great enough to destroy the environment, that is to say, the material foundations of life. The structures of human societies themselves including even some of the social foundations of the capitalist economy are on the point of being destroyed by the erosion of what we have inherited from the past. Our world risks both explosion and implosion. It must change" (pp. 584–585). Jorge Nef, a global security political scientist, in a study published by the Canada-based International Development Research Centre, cautions us that "the seemingly secure societies of the 'North' are increasingly vulnerable to events in the less secure and hence underdeveloped regions of our globe, in a manner that conventional international relations theory and development have failed to account for" (1997, p. 13). Nef states, "In the midst of the current crisis, the established flow of information, ideas, science and world views is being shattered" (p. 94). Benjamin Barber, a U.S.-based political scientist, has outlined his view from the edge in a fascinating book called *Jihad vs. McWorld* (1995, p. 7): "Jihad forges communities of blood rooted in exclusion and hatred. . . . McWorld forges global markets rooted in consumption and profit, leaving to an untrustworthy, if not altogether factitious invisible hand, issues of public interest and common good that once might have been nurtured by democratic citizenries and their watchful governments." Barber continues, "Unless we can offer an alternative to the struggle between Jihad and McWorld, the epoch on whose threshold we stand is likely to be terminally post-democratic" (p. 7).

What about geographers and economists? In the introduction to their book *An Unruly World? Globalization, Governance, and Geography,* Andrew Herod, Gearóid Ó Tuathail, and Susan Roberts of the United States note, "One might be tempted to proclaim at century's end the emergence of an 'unruly epoch' of ungovernable, turbulent and disorderly global space" (1998, p. 1). Lester R. Brown, the respected director of the World Watch Institute, notes, "In effect we are behaving as though we have no children, as though there will not be a next generation" (1998, p. 19). Herman Daly and John B. Cobb Jr. (1989), in their powerful plea for an economics that reflects the environmental and human realities of our planet, note that "at a deep level of our being we find it hard to suppress the cry of anguish, the scream of horror . . . the wild words required to express wild realities. We human beings are being led to a *dead* end . . . all too literally. . . . The global system will change during the next forty years, because it will be physically forced to change. But if humanity waits until it is physically compelled to change, its options will be few indeed" (p. 62).

What about educators? Edmund O'Sullivan, a Canadian educational scholar, has noted, "In their present form they [forces of transnational globalization] represent the most destructive and malignant forces of modernism. They are hydra-headed dominator hierarchies gone wild" (1999, p. 2). The Hamburg Declaration of 1997, arising from the fifth UNESCO International Conference on Adult Education, acknowledges that serious doubts about the future exist: it includes in the first paragraph the poignant words "if humanity is to survive" (UNESCO, 1997, p. 1).

What Lies Beyond the Edge?

The recently published *Which World? Scenarios for the Twenty-First Century* (Hammond, 1998) reports on a research project that extrapolates current global trends in three different scenarios. This research suggests that roughly speaking, the contemporary context provides evidence for what Hammond calls Market World, Fortress World, and Transformed World. In Market World, we see the extension of the global free trade agenda. Market World is the same as the flat earth of my metaphor. It is, however, a vision that still contains nearly all prevailing economic and political power and influence. Fortress World arises in the scenario that sees a market-led failure to redress social disparities, from which follow spreading stagnation and fragmentation. Resources are shifted rapidly to security issues to contain growing violence and conflict. In Transformed World also drawn from existing trends and beginnings of new movement, we see a society with transformed values and cultural norms in which power is more widely shared and in which new social coalitions work, from the grass roots up, to shape what governments do. The market still exists, but it is balanced by other needs. In reality, the future, as is true of the present, will contain aspects of all three scenarios, but in what combination, in what proportion, and for whose benefit?

Ulrich Beck (1997) sees the future this way: "There is no lack of ideas for changing society. Today (just as in earlier revolutions) many contemporaries carry plans for changing the world around with them in their breast pocket or their heart" (p. 174). The capacity of people to shape the future was also expressed, according to Vandana Shiva (1998), by Gandhi's concept of Swadeshi, or economic self-reliance. This concept was based on the conviction that "people possess both materially and morally what they need to evolve and design their society and economy and free themselves of oppressive structures" (p. 6). The report on the Commission on Global Governance (Carlsson & Ramphal, 1995, p. 27) also demonstrates hope for a positive future by highlighting the "increasing capacity of people to shape their lives and to assert their rights. The empowerment of people is reflected in the vigour of civil society and democratic processes." The veteran political economist Samir Amin is even more hopeful when he notes that "a humanistic response to the challenge of globalization inaugurated by capitalist expansion may be idealistic, but it is not utopian: on the contrary, it is the only realistic project possible (1997, p. 10).

In *The Cult of Impotence: Selling the Myth of Powerlessness in the Global Economy,* Linda McQuaig (1998, p. 283), a Canadian journalist, offers an explanation of what people are up against in shaping their own futures: "We have become convinced that we are collectively powerless in the face of international financial markets. And with the widespread acceptance of this view the rich have proceeded to create a world in which the rights of capital have been given precedence over and protection against interference from the electorate." She argues convincingly in the case of Canada that we have been "sold" a myth of powerlessness because it serves the interests of the current ruling alliances, not because we in fact do not have any power as citizens. Gramsci's (1971) analysis can be used to explain this situation in showing that when it comes to maintaining the political status quo, coercion by the state is less effective than the consent that we give as citizens when we limit our horizons of possibility. At the first World Assembly of Adult Education, which was sponsored by the International Council for Adult Education, Julius Nyerere recognized this problem and said that the first goal of adult education is to convince people of the possibility of change. All other goals can come if we can believe that change is possible.

The UNESCO Vision: At Hamburg and Beyond

Many of the delegates to the Fifth International Conference on Adult Education (CONFINTEA V), including me, had been expressing for years our vision for a better world, our views of the world beyond the edge of the flat earth. And what kind of vision is it? It is of a world in which people are not powerless, in which agency and possibility flourish. Our vision was embedded in the conference's "Hamburg Declaration on Adult Learning," which stated that adult education "is a powerful concept for fostering ecologically sustainable development, for promoting democracy, justice, gender equity . . . and for building a world in which violent conflict is replaced by dialogue and a culture of peace based on justice" (UNESCO, 1997, p. 1). We further stated in our declaration that "at the heart of this transformation is a new role for the state. . . . The state remains the essential vehicle for ensuring rights for all" (p. 3). Ours is to be a society in which education includes "the right to question and analyze" (p. 4). We called for a culture of peace; the empowerment of women; environmental sustainability; rights of indigenous and nomadic peoples, persons with disabilities, and the aging; a transformed economy; and improvements to health. "Our ultimate goal should be the creation of a learning society committed to social justice and general well-being" (p. 4).

Whither Adult Education?

CONFINTEA V was, in my opinion, the most remarkable meeting in the history of the adult education movement. Never before had so many governmental, nongovernmental, and other types of adult educators and officials been brought together in one space. Never before had such diversity been assembled in support of lifelong learning. Never before had such creativity and play been woven into the fabric of a UNESCO conference. It brought together the finest aspects of the remarkable tradition of learning, social action, and policy considerations for which adult education is collectively known. No one who was fortunate enough to have been in the halls of the Hamburg convention center or in the streets dancing away the night in celebration of the event will ever forget what was accomplished. It felt grand. But was CONFINTEA V the forward cry of a movement taking new flight, or was it the last great poetic song of a generation that is passing away? I am not sure.

If for a moment we accept the arguments being put forward by the various persons whom I mentioned in the first part of this chapter—that the timing is ripe for a rising global effort to create a dramatically new path—we then need to look at what roles adult education and adult educators might play. From Canada the picture is mixed. Let me be specific. In the past several years, we have seen the federal government cut support to both the English-speaking and French-speaking national adult education bodies. The Canadian Association for Adult Education, which began in the heady days of the 1930s, is gone. The Quebec association is still afloat thanks to more generous politicians in Quebec and perhaps a deeper organizational framework, but it too is diminished. The women-focused National Adult Education Association hangs on like an autumn leaf, still able to show its colors but waiting for the first crisp breeze. In the province of Ontario, the adult education provision in the school boards has been all but eliminated. The national network of development education centers, which educated Canadians about those in less rich parts of the world, has been shut down. Dozens of large and small community-based popular education organizations that had focused on social change have disappeared.

In contrast, adult education that is linked to job creation, skills training, or economic readjustment is booming. There has never been more funding for instrumental adult education linked to corporate or other forms of economic life. But it is telling that the newly organizing Canadian Association for Lifelong Learning has few members who have called themselves adult educators before now. Our university adult education departments have, we believe, weathered the storm for the most part and are even starting to hire new faculty members. Our enrollments across Canada, with some regional exceptions in postgraduate adult education, are holding their own in most jurisdictions. Indeed, at the Ontario Institute for Studies in Education (OISE), where I work, our department has the highest number of applications for master's and doctoral programs of any other department in the faculty.

What the Hamburg Declaration called the "new social agents" of adult education are active and moving forward. A small but dedicated band of environmental adult educators have made substantial progress over the past five years, with great help from the CONFINTEA V process. Indigenous adult educators are beginning to get organized for the first time ever within many countries and at the global level. Large citizen's movements against the Multilateral Agreement on Investments have succeeded in putting the global marketers at bay at least temporarily. Extraordinary measures are being taken by global adult education networks concerned with protecting indigenous rights to knowledge against multinational pharmaceutical corporations intent on patenting every inch of global genetic stock.

Implications for University-Based Adult Education Practice

Globalization, with its emphasis on consolidating the financial support structures for multinational corporations, creates challenges for those of us in university adult education and training departments. Edmund O'Sullivan, a colleague of mine at OISE, has recently published a book titled *Transformative Learning: Educational Vision for the Twenty-First Century* (1999), which offers a very broad analysis of the historic period in which we are living. O'Sullivan notes that as educators we face three challenges at this time: to survive, to critique, and to create. As I discuss in the following paragraphs, these three challenges frame our educational practice.

To those of us in the field of adult education who frame our work primarily within the democratic or social movement traditions of adult learning, there is a particular challenge to survive, in both a practical and a theoretical sense. Globalization has given primacy to economic structures, and adult learning related to job creation or market adaptations has expanded dramatically in the past ten years. At the same time, the social demand for adult education has also expanded dramatically but is not being responded to as fully. The rise of new forms of homelessness, threats to our biosphere and to green spaces in our cities, refugee movements and new waves of migration, new challenges to health care, and continuing issues around housing and permanent structural unemployment all call out for adult education applications. Those of us in universities whose adult education practice relates to these forms of social learning are under great pressure to survive. At the same time, however, we need to defend the centrality of a broad democratic and ecological intellectual space for adult learning in the face of "market-only" visions.

We have an opportunity to critique the ways in which some expressions of adult education theory and practice reinforce market or exclusionary social and economic patterns. We have an opportunity to critique the narrowness of a market-only vision of global society. And, very important, we have an opportunity to critique the narrow European–North American bias of our adult education theory base. A few years ago, I did a quick review of the main references used in the papers submitted to both the U.S.-based Adult Education Research Conference and the Canadian Association for the Study of Adult Education, to see where the majority of the cited authors were from. With the exception of Paulo Freire, some 95 to 100 percent of the authors cited were either Americans or Europeans (mostly British) (Hall, 1993), and among those, nearly all were white males—the point being that if we were to look at globalization from a cultural perspective we would want to democratize the theoretical base of adult education and begin to construct an intellectual base that would draw on the work of intellectuals from those parts of the world where the majority of the world's population lives.

Finally, we have many opportunities to create: to create new theory from engagement with community or social movement activities; to create in our courses new practices in teaching that allow students to come to their own awareness of challenges they face in practice; to create new structures in our universities that help bridge the gap between university and social movements; to create opportunities for "community scholars"—community-based thinkers who spend time in our universities sharing their insights with us and our students.

An Adult Education Department
Facing Life Beyond the Edge

What can we do as teachers, administrators, and learners organized within university adult education programs? How is our work influenced by the realities of global constraints and global possibilities?

I have approached this reflection by looking at the following questions: How do I approach my own teaching and learning? Who are we as faculty members? How do we structure our adult education program? What are our research and community outreach functions? What are our alliances within the university and within the local, national, and global civil societies?

What and How I Teach

This book calls on us to reflect on our practice. Teaching is one of my main activities. I teach four courses in which I try to respond to a new vision, a "globalization from below" perspective: (1) an introductory course to the field of adult education, (2) Political Economy of Adult Education in Global Perspectives, (3) Participatory Research, and (4) Poetry, Social Movements and Adult Learning.

In the introductory course, my practice is to present the field of adult education as an area of contestation, to share with students materials that lay out the ways various powerful currents in society influence our field of study. I share materials that support a more socially or ecologically engaged vision of adult education. In addition, I have tried to broaden the sources that I use in my teaching to go beyond the mostly North American and European texts. My vision of adult education is of a global movement that draws on visions and explanations from a variety of global, racial, and sectoral voices. As adult education teachers, we still have considerable power in determining the curriculum of our courses and the choices of readings to present to our students. The course in participatory research draws on the theoretical and practical base of projects in Tanzania, Asia, and Latin America.

The course on poetry, social movements, and adult learning is a very special one for me. It grew out of my witnessing over the years in many countries the ways in which poetry is often used in social movement settings—in newsletters, at political rallies, or just as something one friend passes along to another. Some twelve or so years ago I also began sharing my own poetry with others and found it to be a powerful personal practice. The course allows all of us (I myself act as a participant) to examine the relationships among poetry or poesis, learning, and the various social movement contexts that engage the students. The course is held in a literary cafe near the university and concludes with an open public reading. By poetic means, we interrogate social movements and learning. To explore issues of race and exclusion, we draw on poets who have written on these issues. To express our own complex responses to oppressive power dynamics in our lives, we write our own materials. To share our thoughts with others, we share our work with the public beyond the academic walls. Of the several courses that I teach, this one never fails to create a powerful and transformative atmosphere.

The Changing Face of Our Department

Globalization has changed the city of Toronto. Some thirty years ago, 6 percent of the population was of non-European origins. By the year 2002, over 50 percent of Toronto will be of non-European origins. Our department of adult education has taken this as a challenge in terms of changing the face of our faculty. As retirements have occurred, we have taken up the challenge of replacing faculty with persons who more closely reflect our community. In the past few years, our department has hired or recruited six new faculty members, two men and four women. The men are of New Zealand and Latin American origins; the women are from the Middle East, from the Cree First Nation in Canada, of South Asian origins, and of Chinese origins. We see the diversity in our department as part of what makes for overall academic excellence.

The Structure of Our Department

One of the structural innovations we have created in the department is a joint university-community participatory research and education center, the Transformative Learning Centre (TLC). It is a unique interdisciplinary OISE–University of Toronto center for the study and practice of transformative learning in adult and community education contexts. The TLC was created in September 1993 by the coming together of several OISE faculty members, some students, and interested community partners. The faculty who came together were basically senior scholar-activists who were looking, from a variety of diverse perspectives, at ways of combining interdisciplinary practices, new knowledge, and alternative strategies for local and global change. It became clear that we all shared an interest in transforming contemporary educational and social paradigms. We were also united by our interest in the role of learning in local and global change and by our preference for university and community partnerships in research and field development. With the merger of OISE and the former Faculty of Education at the University of Toronto in the mid-1990s, the TLC today represents much broader interests and has specific implications for community-based research and action as well as for instruction in both graduate and preservice programs.

The TLC has served as an administrative home for several projects that link our department to larger communities in both Toronto and around the world, including the United Nations Peace University Common Curriculum project, the Social Movement Learning project, the International Research Network of Kurdish Women, the Learning for Environmental Action Programme of the International Council for Adult Education, and the Dame Nita Barrow Distinguished Visitorship. Each of these projects forges links between the local and the global, between the academy and social movements, and between formal and informal learning opportunities.

Alliances and Partnerships

The challenges of globalization require alternative or oppositional forces to work together to move programs and projects forward—and sometimes simply to survive. In the case of our adult education and community development program, we have assiduously sought internal alliances within our faculty through links to other programs or departments that share a common perspective. Specifically, we operate through a set of explicit and tacit agreements with like-minded faculty and administrators. We have particularly close links to the Department of Sociology and Equity Studies in Education and some teaching groups within the Department of Curriculum, Teaching and Learning.

On the broader University of Toronto front, we have similarly intentionally developed alliances and partnerships with a variety of departments and disciplines, including public health, urban studies, industrial relations, geography, continuing studies, the Institute for Environmental Studies, the Institute for Women's Studies, the Transition Year Programme, the Faculty of Medicine, the student union, the Faculty of Social Work, and the college for mature students (Woodsworth College). We share a common concern in the transformation of the university into a structure that supports university-community linkages and a vision of lifelong learning.

The department further maintains strong partnerships in a number of national and international networks, such as the Canadian Association for the Study of Adult Education, the Canadian Network for Democratic Learning, the North American Alliance for Popular and Adult Education, the International Council for Adult Education, the International Congress for University-Based Adult Education, CIVICUS (a global civil society networking body), the Earth Council, United Nations Peace University, and numerous other such global networking organizations. These networks provide our students and us with access to information and ways of linking up that are necessary in the global age.

Conclusion

Universities play complex roles in our societies. They provide the background and training for new generations of researchers, scholars, and administrators who collectively occupy the higher-paid and most responsible positions in our community, state, and private sector institutions. Universities are the places where class differences are imprinted successively on new generations of women and men. Universities offer the few a chance to understand the world in order to think for and take action on behalf of the many. They are the places where the "professionals" are formed and where society nurtures the creative spark for maintaining a world where the privileged may have both a better conscience and a firmer grip on the majority.

Universities are also part of the larger struggles of our times. They are sites of struggles over whose histories are taught and studied and who can have access to university study. They offer a genuine opportunity for some women and men to overcome class, racial, ability, gender, or other stereotypes and take up positions as active citizens in their own communities. Departments of adult education that offer graduate study in the field of adult and life-long learning are no less sites of struggle. Adult education, which for many of us began in the great emancipatory movements of the early twentieth century, faces its biggest challenge in the economic globalization movement of the twenty-first century. For those of us engaged in teaching and research in the university world, the larger struggle over economic globalization will play out in the choices we make. What books do we put on our reading list? What kinds of papers do we encourage in our classes? For whom do we find time for that extra bit of support? Whom do we try to hire as colleagues?

Globalization in and of itself is not a bad thing. Long before the financial institutions created the supposed global market utopia we now see, ordinary working people spoke of the need for working together across international borders. The theme of "globalization of whom and for whom?" has seized the world stage as well as the world discourse. Adult educators, because of their unique positions working with women and men who are not among the global marketers, are in a unique position to address one of our most profound challenges in the twenty-first century. We should not be silent. We need not consent. Let us teach ourselves and create opportunities for others to learn about a world where peace, fairness, clean water and air, and good health for all tower, as our beacon, over the right to profit.

References

Amin, S. (1997). *Capitalism in the age of globalization.* London: Zed Books.

Bandarage, A. (1997). *Women, population, and global crisis.* London: Zed Books.

Barber, B. R. (1995). *Jihad vs. McWorld.* New York: Ballantine.

Beck, U. (1997). *The reinfection of politics: Rethinking modernity in the global social order.* Cambridge, England: Polity Press.

Brown, L. R. (1998). *The state of the world.* New York: Norton.

Carlsson, I., & Ramphal, S. (1995). *Our global neighborhood.* Oxford, England: Oxford University Press.

Daly, H. E., & Cobb, J. (1989). *For the common good: Redirecting the economy toward community, the environment and a sustainable future.* Needham Heights, MA: Allyn & Bacon.

de Oliveira, M. D., & Tandon, R. (1994). An emerging global civil society. In M. D. de Oliveira & R. Tandon (Eds.), *Citizens: Strengthening global civil society* (pp. 1–17). Washington, DC: CIVICUS.

"Finance Minister Addresses World Bank." (1998, September 29). *Globe and Mail*, p. 31.

Gramsci, A. (1971). *Selections from the prison notebooks*. (Q. Hoare & G. N. Smith, Eds. and Trans.). London: Lawrence and Wishart.

Grimmett, R. (1994). *Conventional arms transfers to the third world*. Washington, DC: Library of Congress.

Hall, B. L. (1993). Recentering adult education research: Whose world is first? *Studies in Continuing Education, 15*(2), 149–161.

Hammond, A. (1998). *Which world? Scenarios for the twenty-first century*. Washington, DC: Island Press.

Herod, A., Ó Tuathail, G., & Roberts, S. M. (1998). *An unruly world: Globalization, governance, and geography*. London: Routledge.

Hobsbawn, E. (1994). *Age of extremes: The short twentieth century, 1914–1991*. London: Abacas.

McQuaig, L. (1998). *The cult of impotence: Selling the myth of powerlessness in the global economy*. New York: Viking Penguin.

Nef, J. (1997). *Human security and mutual vulnerability*. Ottawa: International Development Research Centre.

O'Sullivan, E. (1999). *Transformative learning: Educational vision for the twenty-first century*. Toronto: University of Toronto Press.

Shiva, V. (1989). *Staying alive*. London: Zed Books.

Shiva, V. (1998, April 6). Swadeshi. *Weekend Observer of New Delhi*, p. 6.

Soros, G. (1998). *The crisis of global capitalism*. New York: Public Affairs.

Spretnak, C. (1990). Ecofeminism: Our roots and flowering. In I. Diamond & G. F. Orenstein (Eds.), *Re-weaving the world: The emergence of ecofeminism* (pp. 3–14). San Francisco: Sierra Club Books.

UNESCO. (1997). *The Hamburg Declaration: The agenda for the future*. Hamburg, Germany: Author.

United Nations Development Programme. (1999). *Human development report 1999*. New York: Oxford University Press.

United Nations High Commission on Refugees. (1995). *Annual report*. Geneva, Switzerland: Author.

Chapter Seven

The Power of Race and Gender

Black Women's Struggle and Survival in Higher Education

Juanita Johnson-Bailey

In 1978, Lena, a forty-eight-year-old Black woman who directs a public housing project, applied to graduate school at the public university where she had received her undergraduate degree. For several months she did not hear from the graduate coordinator. Finally, she made an appointment to see him. He informed her that her application had not left his desk because he did not feel that she was "graduate school material."

Lena recounted slowly and with stumbling speech: "The rejection held me back for years and years. I was afraid to try. It was just traumatic. So from 1978 to 1996 I waited. I wanted to be in graduate school. I said that there had to be a place for me. My job had gotten to the place where the challenges weren't there anymore. I had maxed out on the job with my previous education and work experience. I was determined to go to graduate school. I thought I was capable . . . I had to find out."

Eighteen years would pass before Lena found the courage to reapply to graduate school. This time she applied to a different college in the same university. She has now graduated with her master's degree. Her thesis project on forming grassroots community programs received national recognition.

When I think of the circumstances of Black reentry women's experiences in higher education, I am reminded of a Negro spiritual from my childhood, "How I Got Over": "I want to sing hallelujah. I want to shout the trouble is over. My soul looks back in wonder at how I got over." The song speaks of prevailing in the face of difficult obstacles and of looking back in amazement at one's survival.

The educational narratives of Black women like Lena who have returned to college as adults are stories of marginalization and struggle that serve as vivid examples of how power operates in higher education (Johnson-Bailey, 1994, 1998, 2000). This chapter examines events from the college sojourns of Black reentry women and offers critiques of the power relations in the academy. Parts of the stories of these women—Lena, Johnnie, Jean, and Faye—are laced throughout the chapter and are followed by an analysis that exposes the often concealed issues of power lodged in the formal and hidden curricula that drive our educational settings. In addition, by offering a historical and contemporary portrait of Black women in college, this chapter provides a context for understanding the pattern of disenfranchisement that frames the lives of reentry Black women. Finally, the chapter discusses the ways in which adult education, in praxis, can participate in creating a more democratic setting for Black reentry women.

Historical and Contemporary Perspectives

From primary school through higher education, the lives of Black women are touched either overtly or covertly by racism and sexism. The history of Black women's education documents their path as one of constant struggle, confrontation, resistance, negotiation, and marginality (hooks, 1984). Black women have much in common with Black men and with White women, as all were historically locked out of most arenas of higher education by custom or law. However, the routes taken by Black and White women diverged. White women were afforded higher education opportunities in the mid-1800s as private colleges were established for their specific schooling needs. Later, as state institutions became coeducational, White college women also found a place of acceptance. Black women were still excluded from most colleges, both private and state owned, because of their race. This condition changed somewhat with the emergence of Black colleges at the end of the nineteenth century.

The educational experience of Blacks is notably different from the experiences of other groups (Collins, 1990; Cuthbert, 1942/1987; Fleming, 1984; hooks, 1989; Ihle, 1986; Moses, 1989; Noble, 1956; Player, 1987; Washington, 1988). The lack of educational opportunity during slavery and the subsequent inequality of education after slavery made education even more important to Blacks as a race (DuBois, 1903/1953). Blacks immediately recognized the importance of educating their daughters as well as their sons (Solomon, 1985). However, because of gender discrimination, the Historically Black Colleges and Universities that were founded to educate Blacks conformed to custom and did not offer Black women the same place of acceptance that they offered Black men (Bell-Scott, 1984; Guy-Sheftall, 1982). Often Black women found a place only by studying in the caretaking professions of nursing and teaching.

As a result of the landmark desegregation case *Brown v. Topeka Board of Education,* most American colleges began to desegregate in the 1960s (Kluger, 1976; Weinberg, 1977; Wolters, 1975). In addition, the new women's movement of the 1970s called attention to entrenched gender biases and forced open the doors of many colleges to greater numbers of women. Now, forty-five years after the 1954 Supreme Court's *Brown* decision and more than thirty years after the beginning of the new women's movement, society's power structures remain unchanged and are replicated in higher education, a bastion of hegemonic culture.

Despite the myth that Black women possess an advantage because they hold membership in two groups (Blacks and women), Black women still find themselves without the accouterments that male or White privilege provide (Beal, 1970; King, 1988; McIntosh, 1995; Washington, 1988). The hierarchical system that exists in the Western world affords credence to Whiteness and maleness, and Black women possess neither attribute. The daily experience of Black women's lives is a synergistic composite of racism and sexism. Black women's positions are reflected in society by their place at the bottom of the economic totem pole, slightly above children, as the poorest individuals in society (Williams, 1988; Zinn, 1989). Even though White women have benefited the most from the women's movement and the civil rights movement (Hacker, 1995; Reskin & Roos, 1990) and Black men have gained more from the civil rights movement than have Black women (Hacker, 1995), it is still a popular belief among some members of both movements to justify inattention to Black women's issues by purporting that Black women are strong matriarchs capable of sustaining themselves (Washington, 1988). In contrast to such rhetoric, the lives of Black women reveal the power disparity between Blacks and Whites and between women and men.

Two landmark studies by Cuthbert (1942/1987), *Education and Marginality: A Study of the Negro Woman College Graduate,* and Noble (1956), *The Negro Woman's College Education,* present comprehensive pictures of the early history of Black women in higher education. According to Cuthbert, college women experienced isolation on their various campuses, were aware of their status as the "Other," and were faced with racism and sexism. Cuthbert characterized the circumstances of Black college women after the turn of the century succinctly: "They are lonely in a world in which they are striving to become acquainted" (p. 117). The literature abounds with accounts of this kind of experience, regardless of the academic setting or background of the adult Black woman student. For example, in a study by Ward (1997), *Black Female Graduate Students in the Academy: Re-Moving the Masks,* a participant explained that she understood the graduate school setting was not fair but that she would endeavor to negotiate the system because her ultimate goal was graduation. In two separate excerpts this same participant related stories of sabotage and inherent unfairness that she silently endured.

According to Ogbu (1978, 1992) and Everhart (1983), many minority students see education as an exclusive game that will never allow them an equal opportunity, and so they reject or resist education as an option. Those who choose to engage in education do so with the understanding that it is not fair. These students follow two simple rules. First, they resist believing in the equity of the system, and second, they resist giving up their home cultures in order to fully participate in this new academic world. Disenfranchised students often counter the system by trying to find alternative ways to coexist alongside the maneuverings of the hidden curriculum. Routinely, Black women graduate students establish research agendas that center on race and gender issues as a way of having an impact on a formal curriculum that excludes information on Black women and as a means of resistance (Margolis & Romero, 1998; Ward, 1997).

Currently, Black women describe a "chilly climate" in higher education and report that they are verbally abused, ignored, and silenced (Hall & Sandler, 1982). The educational lives of the women described by Cuthbert (1942/1987) are quite similar to the educational lives described by contemporary Black women. Racism and sexism, which structure American society, affect the educational experiences of Black women in many ways. Black women are thought to be intellectually and morally inferior because they are Black. As women, they are taken to task for their gender's alleged intellectual inadequacy and proclivity for subservience. Yet they are trapped, for they are given neither the benefit of being placed on a pedestal as the fairer and more virtuous gender nor the protection said to be guaranteed to the weaker sex. Among members of the Black race they are subordinated by their gender, and in society at large they are subjugated because of their race (Joseph & Lewis, 1981). The duality of their position as the conduit of two types of oppression carries into the classroom, as education reproduces societal inequities (Moses, 1989; Washington, 1988). These issues are brought into the classroom by the socialization process that occurs in the family and other social institutions.

Fleming (1984) considers the contemporary position of Black women and reports that Black women suffer from discrimination in all college settings, even those that are same-sex or same-race. She offers that most Black women attend predominantly White colleges and notes of this group that "there is always the clear sense that Black women are suffering from emotional pain, social isolation, or aroused fears about their competence. The pain may have to do with the lack of support in White colleges; but it may also have to do with the difficulty of overcoming inhibitions surrounding assertiveness" (p. 146).

In direct acknowledgment of these problems, the Project on the Status and Education of Women (Moses, 1989) offered the following observations: (1) Black women become less outspoken and socially confident when they are educated with men (both Black and White); (2) Black women lose some social assertiveness skills in Black colleges but not in White colleges; (3) Black women experience more emotional distress at predominantly White colleges; and (4) Black women internalize concerns of being less qualified and skilled than men. These difficulties are compounded by issues the Project on the Status and Education of Women (Hall & Sandler, 1982) found to be true for all women, namely that women are seldom mentored by professors, often overlooked and ignored by professors, interrupted by male students, and treated as less proficient. The findings by the project parallel the findings of the Fleming study (1984) conducted several years earlier.

The focus of the remainder of this chapter is women who have been out of school for at least five years and are over twenty-five years old. These Black reentry women have found that the identical societal forces that shaped their lives outside the academy are present inside its walls (Johnson-Bailey, 1994, 1998; Johnson-Bailey & Cervero, 1996). The primary systems of power that shape and patrol their various communities are the same ones that regulate the Western world: race, gender, class, physical ability, and sexual orientation (Banks, 1994; Hacker, 1995). Several studies describe how Black reentry women react to the power dynamics that operate in the academy. In one study (Johnson-Bailey, 1994), Black reentry women characterized their experiences by completing the phrase "School was like . . ." using the following words: a roller-coaster ride, an unarmed battle, an upset stomach, making a way out of no way, a radical mastectomy, and skipping barefoot through broken glass. These characterizations convey a wealth of information about the women's individual difficulties and collective experiences.

Camouflaged Power in the Academic Setting

In analysis it is apparent that the ways in which school administrators, professors, and students act in school settings are indicative of how power operates in our society. Overall, Black women students are not seen as capable scholars because of the stereotypical ways in which women and Blacks are regarded as intellectually inferior. This translates into subtle actions that occasionally lock Black women out of higher education.

A review of the studies conducted on nontraditional Black women students (Broach, 1984; Bunce, 1996; Johnson-Bailey, 1994; Lewter, 1995; Margolis & Romero, 1998; Miller, 1997; Tate, 1996; Ward, 1997; Withorn, 1986) reveal classic incidents that are rooted in the workings of power across the higher education landscape (community colleges, state institutions, research universities), regardless of the degree program (adult basic education, undergraduate, graduate, professional). The forces are particularly evident in two sites: the formal curriculum and the informal curriculum of the educational systems. In the formal curriculum, comprising the intentional components of schooling, such as the program design, textbooks, and activities, the issues of power are explicit (Apple & Beyer, 1988; McCutcheon, 1988). The hidden curriculum asks a very important question: Are disenfranchised groups important? Part of the answer lies in whether or not their participation is sought through the design of the program and whether or not their contributions are acknowledged in the texts. The answer routinely is, Disenfranchised groups are not important.

Black college women are aware of the policy-driven curriculum. Indeed, they see the built-in bias of the formal curriculum as inevitable. There appears to be resignation in their acceptance that the formal curriculum reflects the larger society outside academia. Aspects of the stated curriculum, textbooks, and institutional policies are unmistakable in their consistent message to minorities: (1) minorities are not included in the core subject areas; (2) minorities, if represented, are peripheral to the subject matter; and (3) minorities are not considered in nor do they benefit from institutional rules and policies.

However, the operation of the formal or overt curriculum reveals only a surface look at how power operates in higher education. It is the functioning of the hidden curriculum: the interactions between student and professor, the social relations between Black reentry women and their classmates, and the classroom policies that reveal tangible examples of how power works in higher education. The hidden curriculum is more intricate and more influential than the formal curriculum as regards the experiences of students and the intent of the academy.

Overwhelmingly, research on adult Black women in college relates accounts that focus primarily on how the hidden curriculum affects the women's academic tenure. The women explore their relationships with teachers and other students when they discuss student networks, research opportunities, mentoring relationships, study groups, class presentations, and grading practices. What is also salient in the literature is that the women used strategies cultivated in their everyday lives outside of academia to handle the hostility encountered in higher education: silence, negotiation, and resistance.

In an ethnographic study by Luttrell (1989), fifteen Black women from the rural South recounted their early learning experiences. They framed their educational lives as a struggle for access and ability, understanding that their access to an education was unequal and unfair when compared to White students and simultaneously questioning their ability to perform satisfactorily in school. Moreover, because they were not recognized for their achievements or given adequate teacher attention, they grappled with the problem of being invisible in the classroom. This issue of invisibility parallels findings by Grant (1992), who concluded that young Black girls are at the bottom of the classroom hierarchy in terms of time, attention, and encouragement.

Luttrell's analysis (1989) also reveals that the poverty of these women separated them from the middle-class teacher and from middle-class students. Working-class women received the subtle messages given by class distinctions that they were "lesser than" or somehow deficient. In addition, the Black women were encouraged through assignments and examples in their schooling to assume caretaking roles that were traditional to their race and gender. The matters of caretaking and feelings of inadequacy are again consistent with Grant's observations (1992). Luttrell concludes that the politics of gender, race, and class and the student's ability to negotiate these issues with teachers, as representatives of the larger society, affect the student's learning process.

The studies on Black adult women (Broach, 1984; Bunce, 1996; Johnson-Bailey, 1994; Lewter, 1995; Miller, 1997; Tate, 1996; Ward, 1997) show that women were aware of the power dynamics present in higher education. The oppositional stance of their lives outside the academy made them particularly astute at assessing their surroundings. Adult Black college women face a hostile environment in higher education, and higher education for them is a site of defiance and struggle.

An example of how an informal exercise of power operates is seen in the story of Lena that introduced this chapter. One person who thought her an incapable student greatly affected her academic career, actively dissuading Lena in her initial pursuit of school. She waited eighteen years before she reapplied to graduate school. Recounting the story twenty-two years later, she is incredulous that she was stymied by one negative and forceful act. Although the graduate coordinator who believed her inferior was discouraging, it was Lena's abandonment of her goal that allowed his actions to stand unchallenged. She assumed the place accorded her by society, one of deferential silence. She tacitly agreed with his assessment by leaving it unchallenged. Certainly, Lena's asking the coordinator to justify his decision or to reconsider his decision would not necessarily have resulted in Lena being admitted to graduate school; however, it is important to note that, according to Lena, it never entered her mind to dispute him or his assessment of her.

In a story similar to Lena's, another Black woman student, Faye, was warned during the welcoming reception by an official of her new program. The administrator told her that she should try hard to succeed, because most of the Blacks who entered could not seem to finish. Intuitively, Faye knew that his intentions were biased against her: "I walked out of the reception area and never looked back. I knew that the deck was stacked against me there. I found a more receptive program at another institution where the keeper of the gate did not have a ready-made stereotype in his mind about me—somewhere where they didn't expect me to fail."

Although the actions of the college official do not appear overtly racist, Faye felt that she recognized his tactics as prohibitive and reminiscent of previous discriminatory situations. She was confident enough of her feelings to attend another graduate program. Faye had positive experiences in her new graduate program and later reported that an associate of hers who stayed in the other program described it as "unfair to Blacks."

Both of these stories relate how representatives of two different colleges reacted to Black women students who were attempting to enroll in their institutions. Even though neither administrator appeared to have sufficient evidence to make a value judgment about the women, both discouraged them. Their actions appear to show a readiness on the part of both men to believe that the two Black women students were not capable. In analysis, the coordinator's unwillingness to process Lena's application and the second official's expressed belief that completing graduate school would be an almost impossible task for Faye seem irrational. Because they had not collected any of the routine data on which to base an assessment—letters of recommendation, test scores, or writing samples— their appraisal was based on personal reactions gleaned in brief encounters. Such actions reflect the stereotypical assessments that are made in society about certain groups. These socially constructed images of Blacks as lazy, intellectually inferior, emotional, and immature are created to make disparate treatment appear deserved. Diligently keeping such images alive in the everyday psyche through the media and by consistently manipulating them in everyday circumstances maintains and justifies the power hierarchies these socially constructed images serve.

Another way in which the politics of the hidden curriculum affect Black women students is by denying them access to opportunities that shape their academic careers. For example, Black women students are often locked out of study groups, research and publication opportunities, and assistantships and other funding opportunities. Although these prospects are said to be available to all students and are not controlled by any formal structures that exclude Black reentry women or any other minorities, the hidden curriculum and its representatives—professors and their designated students—arbitrate these opportunities by informally controlling information and by choosing through encouragement and sponsorship who will benefit and who will remain locked out. A solution to the exclusion has been to form alternative systems or to infiltrate existing structures. Black women students often form their own support and study groups and seek to manage information. Margolis and Romero (1998) stated that the women they interviewed went to great lengths to survive what they characterized as a "repressive social order."

Although Lena was finally admitted to a graduate program, she did not find acceptance. The issue of remaining in school and doing battle with the establishment presented itself as an early moment of truth in Lena's school career. She remembered being told that if she wished to be successful in graduate school, she should find an editor, because even though her grammar was understandably inferior, it was not acceptable. She was told by a White woman professor, "You talk White, but you write Black." Through trial and error and through a student network, Lena found out how to adapt her writing to this professor's style. She expressed that no matter how hard she tried, this professor consistently graded her harshly. She felt that this attitude was transmitted to the other students and served to establish an unfriendly classroom setting.

Another Black woman student, Johnnie, also found higher education unaccepting. Johnnie grew up in the proximity of the university she chose to attend. She was hesitant to apply to this university because of the stories she had heard regarding the inherent unfairness toward Black students. She had originally attended an out-of-town college because of these stories. After dropping out of school several times, she finally decided to come to the major research university in her hometown. "I decided it was convenient. It was on the bus line. I didn't have a car. . . . Scores were not the problem. I had been in the gifted program since fourth grade. My GREs were high. . . . So I did my master's and specialist degrees back-to-back in math. But it was a very biased place, exceptionally biased. So I decided to try a different department. If I could find an OK environment, I'd do my doctorate."

She found just such a program, where there seemed to be a "welcome sign." She thrived and graduated with her doctorate. However, she reported that her day-to-day experiences with the teachers, though pleasant, were not close or friendly. She felt that the professors made surface attempts to be fair but that the students were overt in their animosity. In her opinion, this palpable student attitude was tolerated and therefore silently approved of by the faculty. She registered strong suspicions about her fellow students: "There always seemed to be a question about why I was here—about my competency. When I first got here I thought I was graduate school material. I'd been in gifted programs since grade school. I thought I could handle it. I thought I was a smart little whippersnapper. But over the course of the first few quarters I thought that I wasn't smart. I kept trying to justify, rationalize why I got Bs and what was happening to me."

Johnnie felt lonely and considered quitting the program: "In some classes, early on, when I was the only Black student, I had trouble. People wouldn't eat with me at break, or they wouldn't want to sit by me, or when we'd pair up in groups nobody really wanted to be my partner. It was sort of like being the odd man out. Lately, I've been having more classes with African American women, so my interactions have been different. The other Black women are a support. They even call me after class. They tell me how wonderful I'm doing with my research."

The Means of Surviving in Higher Education

Although the literature illustrates that society constructs barriers to hinder Black women's educational pursuits, Black women have continued to survive and excel in academia. They have outnumbered Black men in higher education since the 1940s. But what have been the costs paid by this long line of educated Black women? Black women students reported that they were discouraged and stifled in the higher education environment in specific ways: (1) they were ignored when they raised their hands; (2) they were interrupted when speaking; (3) their comments were disregarded; (4) they voluntarily remained silent out of fear, habit, or necessity; (5) they were misadvised by professors; and (6) they were intentionally excluded from the student network. Each of these listed ways shows how the hidden curriculum operates. In the following incident (Johnson-Bailey, 1994, p. 191), Jean displays a typical representation of silence that occurred when a class of older students attempted to discuss the civil rights movement:

> There comes a time when we must deal with Civil Rights and prejudices and Black/White relationships and all of this. . . . I was the only Black in class. Antiquated and Black in class. Which meant that I have had the opportunity to not only read the changes but I've lived the changes. There were times in the class when even the professor felt uncomfortable. . . . Well, to be honest, after a while I felt that it was better for everybody concerned inasmuch as I was the only one. There were lots of times that questions were asked that even I did not respond to at all because I did not want to respond honestly or from my true feelings. A lot of times, I just

suppressed my own answers or my reactions. And oftentimes I would limit my remarks and statements—keeping in mind that it's not all it's cracked up to be.

This incident shows how the power dynamics in the classroom, which are regulated by the teacher, have effectively silenced Jean. She reasoned that she was making the professor and her classmates uncomfortable by giving her opinions about her experiences. Her solution was not only to refrain from talking but also to stop responding truthfully. According to Collins (1990), self-imposed silence should not be interpreted as a form of submission but rather as an active form of resistance that is part of a larger world-view used as a survival technique by Black adult women. Stated differently, Jean decided that the risk in speaking was too great. For her own protection, she decided to hold dear her individual truth and not to share it with the class.

For Black women who consider themselves as dwelling on the margins of their new higher education environment and in society in general, the politics of the academy are most apparent in personal interactions in small-group activities, study groups, and research pairs. Black reentry and graduate school students tell many stories concerning how they suffered in unethical situations and how they found a way or a reason to work through those situations.

Strategies for Inclusion

Adult Black women, as reentry students and as traditional undergraduate and graduate students, exist as the most significant minority group in higher education (Bennett, 1992; Carter, Pearson, & Shavlik, 1987–1988; Evangelauf, 1992; Johnson-Bailey, 1994). According to research, their experiences in academia do compare less favorably to those of other groups. They are particularly harmed by the operation of the hidden curriculum, which marginalizes them and discourages their full participation. Expressions of frustration and dejection are standard in their everyday experiences.

Adult education, as a field that claims to hold democratization as a core value, must examine the hidden curriculum that thwarts efforts to be inclusive and democratic. The power dynamics that are the manifestations of the politics of the academy convey a powerful message that is unheard or unacknowledged by most enfranchised students but seems obvious to minority students. The message is multifaceted: (1) you do not belong, and you are not wanted; (2) if admitted, you will be treated unfairly, and different standards and different rules will be used; (3) you must find your own means of survival; and (4) your degree, if achieved, will be considered inferior or unearned.

How can we address the politics that shape the experiences of adult Black women and other minorities who participate in higher education? The sections that follow describe a three-part strategy.

Examine the Hidden Curriculum

To examine the hidden curriculum is tantamount to opening the doors of our minds and the portals of the academy. Doing so involves abandoning a falsely claimed neutral position that only belies favoritism toward certain types of knowledge and groups. We must understand that students are cast in roles assigned by the positions they occupy in life. If a student has consistently experienced privilege in her life, then privilege will be accorded and expected in the classroom. Such a stance of power will advantage her in the classroom environment, encouraging her to participate and negotiate her needs. The student will expect to be respected, listened to, and treated fairly. In direct contrast, a student who has been underprivileged in our society will expect the direct opposite. In our hierarchical U.S. society, those who are overprivileged and those who are underprivileged are likely to be prescribed by their life positions. Are they of White, Hispanic, Asian, African, or Native American ancestry? Are their families of origin middle class, working class, or working poor? Are they able bodied? Do they fit in or stand out?

Adult education as a field needs to acknowledge that professors and students alike favor Eurocentric texts and forms of knowledge as well as White students. Although this was possibly unintentional in the past, to continue such preference to the exclusion of other knowledge and to the detriment of other groups of students would be malicious. We must admit that while affirmative action policy has existed in the academy, its presence was not allowed to effect real change. In addition, a recommitment to recruiting and retaining minority students is necessary to the mission of the field. Silence is not a possibility. It is necessary to assess the damage done by the power dynamics implicit in education through the formal and informal curricula, to acknowledge our part in their continuation, and to understand the ways in which we have benefited from those dynamics.

Create a New Educational Structure

As students and practitioners, we must negotiate for a new educational structure that does not reproduce the existing system. Such action requires a commitment to make clear where we stand, as practitioners, administrators, students, and program directors. This commitment requires active involvement in all aspects of our academic settings. Instructors must be aware of students' networks and must analyze how their actions as teachers influence those interactions. This negotiation must not remain passive, but should be an active method for changing the political vista. The power inherent in our positions as learners and educators gives us varied platforms from which to effect change. Whatever our positions, we can find ways to work within them to make a difference. Either as practitioners or students, we can attempt to find ways to be more inclusive. We can reach beyond the established barriers, whether physical, psychological, or social, by realizing why and by whom they were established.

Resist Acceptance or Exclusion

Finally, it is essential not only to resist the comfort of acceptance into that existing inner circle of power but also to resist our exclusion from it. A bidirectional resistant force can be effective in restructuring our educational setting. Being enfranchised makes resistance difficult. It commands rigorous introspection. How do you know if you are part of the problem? If things are comfortable, then your position may be an encumbrance for others. How do you resist from within? Actively resisting from this position can involve substantial risks that could result in expulsion from the inner circle, loss of status, and a turbulent praxis. Resisting from outside entails less risk because the only risk is the distant possibility of acceptance, or possibly of being labeled a troublemaker, a position already in proximity to one's preexisting marginality.

There are many benefits to be derived from refusing to be silent, from negotiating for change and equity, and from resisting conformity or resisting marginalization. In endeavoring to enact these strategies, the field of adult education can make a stride toward the social justice expounded in our literature. In addition, such actions would establish an inclusive setting that would benefit groups historically excluded and would in turn have a domino effect on changing the spirit of the formal and informal curriculums. Admitting new participants benefits all students by invigorating the educational setting—changing classroom discussion, broadening research agendas, and enhancing the knowledge base. These actions of speaking out, negotiation, and resistance are a necessary foray into new territory if we are to effect a welcoming climate for all students.

References
Apple, M. W., & Beyer, L. (1988). Social evaluation and curriculum. In L. Beyer & M. W. Apple (Eds.), *The curriculum: Problems, politics, and possibilities* (pp. 334–350). Albany: State University of New York Press.

Banks, J. A. (1994). *An introduction to multicultural education.* Needham Heights, MA: Allyn & Bacon.

Beal, F. M. (1970). Double jeopardy: To be Black and female. In R. Morgan (Ed.), *Sisterhood is powerful: An anthology of writings from the women's liberation movement* (pp. 340–353). New York: Vintage Books.

Bell-Scott, P. (1984). Black women's education: Our legacy. *Sage, 1*(1), 8–11.

Bennett, C. E. (1992). *The Black population in the United States: March 1991.* Washington, DC: U.S. Government Printing Office.

Broach, T. J. (1984). Concerns of Black women and White women returning to school (Doctoral dissertation, University of Florida, 1984). *Dissertation Abstracts International, 46,* 03A:0611.

Bunce, S. H. (1996). "It's always something": African-American women's college reentry experience (Doctoral dissertation, University of Southern California, 1996). *Dissertation Abstracts International, 58,* 01A:0302.

Carter, D., Pearson, C., & Shavlik, D. (1987–1988). Double jeopardy: Women of color in higher education. *Educational Record, 68*(4) & *69*(1), 98–103.

Collins, P. H. (1990). *Black feminist thought: Knowledge, consciousness, and the politics of empowerment.* New York: Routledge.

Cuthbert, M. V. (1987). *Education and marginality: A study of the Negro woman college graduate.* New York: Garland Press. (Original work published 1942)

DuBois, W.E.B. (1953). *The souls of Black folk.* Greenwich, CT: Fawcett. (Original work published 1903)

Evangelauf, J. (1992). Separate studies list top disciplines, big producers of minority graduates: Earned degrees. *Chronicle of Higher Education, 38*(36), A36–A37.

Everhart, R. B. (1983). *Reading, writing and resistance.* New York: Routledge.

Fleming, J. (1984). *Blacks in college: A comparative study of student success in Black and in White institutions.* San Francisco: Jossey-Bass.

Giddings, P. (1984). *When and where I enter: The impact of Black women on race and sex in America.* New York: Bantam Books.

Grant, L. (1992). Race and the schooling of young girls. In J. Wrigley (Ed.), *Education and gender equality* (pp. 91–113). Washington, DC: Falmer Press.

Guy-Sheftall, B. (1982). Black women and higher education: Spelman and Bennett Colleges revisited. *Journal of Negro Education, 51*(3), 278–287.

Hacker, A. (1995). *Two nations: Black and White, separate, hostile, unequal* (Rev. ed.). New York: Scribner.

Hall, R. M., & Sandler, B. R. (1982). *The classroom climate: A chilly one for women?* Washington, DC: Project on the Status and Education of Women, Association of American Colleges. (ERIC Document Reproduction Service No. ED 215 628)

hooks, b. (1984). *Feminist theory from margin to center.* Boston: South End Press.

hooks, b. (1989). *Talking back: Thinking feminist, thinking Black.* Boston: South End Press.

Ihle, E. L. (1986). *Black women's academic education in the South: History of Black women's education in the South, 1865-present.* (Report No. UD-025-516). Harrisonburg, VA: James Madison University. (ERIC Document Reproduction Service No. ED 281 959)

Johnson-Bailey, J. (1994). *Making a way out of no way: An analysis of the educational narratives of reentry Black women with emphasis on issues of race, gender, class and color.* Unpublished doctoral dissertation, University of Georgia, Athens.

Johnson-Bailey, J. (1998). Black reentry women in the academy: Making a way out of no way. *Initiatives, 58*(4), 37–48.

Johnson-Bailey, J. (2000). *Sistahs in college: Making a way out of no way.* Malabar, FL: Krieger.

Johnson-Bailey, J., & Cervero, R. M. (1996). An analysis of the educational narratives of reentry Black women. *Adult Education Quarterly, 46*(3), 142–157.

Joseph, G. I., & Lewis, J. (1981). *Common differences: Conflicts in Black and White perspectives.* Boston: South End Press.

King, D. (1988). Multiple jeopardy, multiple consciousness: The context of a Black feminist ideology. *Signs, 14*(1), 42–72.

Kluger, R. (1976). *Simple justice: The history of Brown v. Board of Education and Black America's struggle for equality.* New York: Knopf.

Lewter, A. J. (1995). Diamonds in the rough: A case study of college transfer African American reentry females at Halifax Community College. (Doctoral dissertation, North Carolina State University, 1995). *Dissertation Abstracts International, 56,* 04A:1212.

Luttrell, W. (1989). Working-class women's ways of knowing: Effects of gender, race, and class. *Sociology of Education, 62*(1), 33–46.

Margolis, E., & Romero, M. (1998). "The department is very male, very White, very old, and very conservative": The functioning of the hidden curriculum in graduate sociology departments. *Harvard Educational Review, 68*(1), 1–32.

McCutcheon, G. (1988). Curriculum and the work of teachers. In L. Beyer and M. W. Apple (Eds.), *The curriculum: Problems, politics, and possibilities* (pp. 191–203). Albany: State University of New York Press.

McIntosh, P. (1995). White privilege and male privilege: A personal accounting of coming to see correspondences through work in women's studies. In M. Anderson & P. Collins (Eds.), *Race, class, and gender: An anthology* (pp. 76–87). Belmont, CA: Wadsworth.

Miller, E. L. (1997). Fears expressed by female reentry students at an urban community college: A qualitative study. (Doctoral dissertation, Teachers College, Columbia University, 1997). *Dissertation Abstracts International, 58,* 09A:3393.

Moses, Y. T. (1989). *Black women in academe: Issues and strategies* (Report No. HE-022-909). Washington, DC: Project on the Status and Education of Women, Association of American Colleges. (ERIC Document Reproduction Service No. ED 311 817)

Noble, J. L. (1956). *The Negro woman's college education.* New York: Bureau of Publications, Teacher's College.

Ogbu, J. (1978). *Minority education and caste: The American system in cross cultural perspectives.* New York: Academic Press.

Ogbu, J. (1992). Understanding cultural diversity and learning. *Educational Researcher, 21*(8), 5–14.

Player, W. B. (1987). *Improving college education for women at Bennett College: A report of a type A project.* New York: Garland Press.

Reskin, B., & Roos, P. (1990). *Job queues, gender queues.* Philadelphia: Temple University Press.

Solomon, B. M. (1985). *In the company of educated women: A history of women and higher education in America.* New Haven, CT: Yale University Press.

Tate, L. H. (1996). The life structure development of African American women career officers. (Doctoral dissertation, University of Texas at Austin, 1996). *Dissertation Abstracts International, 57,* 06B:4061.

Ward, W. G. (1997). *Black female graduate students in the academy: Re-moving the masks* (Report No. HE-030-314). Chicago: American Educational Research Association. (ERIC Document Reproduction Service No. ED 410 779)

Washington, V. (1988). *The power of Black women: Progress, predicaments and possibilities* (Report No. HE-022-826). Albany, NY: Association of Black Women in Higher Education. (ERIC Document Reproduction Service No. ED 323 821)

Weinberg, M. (1977). *A chance to learn: The history of race and education in the United States.* Cambridge, England: Cambridge University Press.

Williams, P. J. (1988). On being the object of poverty. *Signs, 14*(1), 5–25.

Withorn, A. (1986). Dual citizenship: An interview with women of color in graduate school. *Women's Studies Quarterly, 25*(1&2), 132–138.

Wolters, R. (1975). *The new Negro on campus: Black college rebellions of the 1920s.* Princeton, NJ: Princeton University Press.

Zinn, M. B. (1989). Family, race, and poverty in the eighties. *Signs, 14*(4), 856–874.

Chapter Eight

The Politics of Positionality
Teaching for Social Change in Higher Education
Elizabeth J. Tisdell

It was the afternoon session of the last day of a master's level higher education class dealing with diversity issues in education. We were getting ready for the last small group's presentation based on their experience of working through a book of their own choosing dealing with diversity issues—in this case bell hooks's *Teaching to Transgress: Education as the Practice of Freedom* (1994). There were sixteen students in this class: five men and eleven women; four were students of color, the remainder white. One student was hearing impaired, so all classes were signed; another student openly acknowledged being bisexual. The remainder of the class was more or less representative of the white, dominant culture. I, a white woman and permanent full-time faculty member, was team teaching the class with an African American woman adjunct faculty member. In general, the class had been challenging and productive, although as is typical in these classes, there had been some conflict. It was fairly limited, however, and was related mostly to some frustration with a white male student's constant defense of the status quo (less as the semester went on due to relatively gentle confrontation by another white male).

This particular activity on *Teaching to Transgress* was facilitated by three very articulate students—Mary, an African American woman with considerable experience as a full-time adult educator in a postsecondary setting; Sam, a white hearing-impaired man who taught in a community college; and Nora, a white woman, a part-time foreign language teacher who also worked in the holistic health movement. They began their presentation by each taking a turn in setting the context. They discussed some of the conflict among them—largely between Mary and Nora, and based somewhat on race and class differences—in both working through the book and planning the presentation, and described how they worked through it. They explained that bell hooks (1994) talks about engaged pedagogy and that we were not going to *talk* about engaged pedagogy; rather, we were going to *do* it. Our task was to pass a "talking stick" around the room and comment on what this class meant in changing our consciousness. Participants had the option of speaking or passing.

The three facilitators first modeled the process. Mary spoke briefly about her experience in the class as an African American woman and about ways the class affected her teaching in a post-secondary setting. Sam spoke about being hearing impaired and dealing with staying engaged in engaged pedagogy when sometimes speakers talk much more quickly than signers can sign. Nora cried as she spoke movingly about dealing with issues of privilege and oppression and about what she learned about dealing with conflict from her work both in the small and large group. And so we passed the stick around the circle.

In going around the circle the first round, all the students of color spoke. Many of the white students passed, but some also spoke. Those that did cried as they talked about their experience or the development of their understanding of how systems of privilege and oppression work. I passed (thinking that I didn't want to do anything to affect the process). My teaching partner spoke. The stick was passed to Susan, a white high school teacher, who was both very well liked and highly respected by her peers. She tearfully explained what the class had brought up for her. Her father had been murdered a few years before by two African American men who had broken into the house during the night. Susan was there when it happened. She heard the door break down. She heard her father run downstairs. She heard the shots. She heard the running away. She heard the quiet. She went downstairs, finding her father's body in a pool of blood. She explained her response to this death: that the murderers were the victims of a racist society, a racist educational system. Although she didn't condone or accept their murderous behavior, this response was why she was doing her antiracist work as a teacher. She cried—the painful reality of the whole experience of her father's death was present with her, and now present within the circle of this group. There was silence in the room. You could hear a pin drop. Many were wiping their eyes. The stick passed, and finally arrived back at Mary after once around the circle. Mary paused, and then gently, slowly, in a voice both deliberate and filled with empathy, turned to Susan and said she was sorry that someone "who looks like me has caused you so much pain." Although these are not her exact words, Mary went on to say something like this:

> I just want to point something out here. I have been through many classes and in-services dealing with diversity issues. I am often one of the few people of color in the room. Often I feel like my pain is supposed to be on display, and that white folks often have the privilege of sitting in silence, and sometimes watch me bleed. Today, in going around this circle, I want to point out that all the people of color and differently abled people have spoken, and all the white folks that spoke cried. And I am struck with how willing those of you who spoke are to share your pain with me. And when you share you pain with me, I am much more willing to share mine with you.

She turned to Susan, who by this time had stopped crying, and thanked her for her courage and willingness to share her pain. The stick went around the circle one more time. Some people spoke, making some closing remarks (myself included). The three student facilitators closed the exercise. We took a break. Then we attempted to put closure on the course, knowing that many of us were forever changed by this experience.

This vignette describes a critical incident that happened in one of my classes a couple of years ago. Although some of the details have been changed out of respect to the participants and to the class, this incident really took place, and the salient points remain intact. To say this was a powerful moment in the class would be an understatement. In fact, this may have been the single most powerful moment I have ever experienced in a classroom. Many participants also indicated as much in their final paper, in which they had to apply the theory and intellectual material of the course to an analysis of their experiences dealing with diversity and equity issues in and outside of the class. Further, upon graduation many students cited this event as a defining moment in their educational history.

I cannot know for sure exactly what made the event so powerful to other people in the room. I suspect it's that it brought together rationality and affect, theory and practice, passion and possibility, pain and transformation. That's part of what made it so powerful for me, too. But it also made me rethink how aspects of power and privilege work in classrooms, particularly in those designed to "teach against the grain," to challenge society's power relations that typically privilege those who are white, moneyed, male, heterosexual, and able bodied. It made me think more about how the positionality of instructors and students affects the way classroom dynamics unfold, and about the effect of positionality on how participants construct knowledge in higher education settings in classes where the course content is about challenging power relations. By positionality, I am referring to how aspects of one's identity such as race, gender, class, sexual orientation, or ableness significantly affect how one is "positioned" relative to the dominant culture. Indeed, higher education has been about constructing and disseminating knowledge, but it has historically been focused almost exclusively on rational forms of knowledge that are created, for the most part, by and for white males. Yet one cannot teach classes for social justice that focus on dealing with power relations based on gender, race, and class without at times getting into conflict, controversy, and strong (and sometimes painful) emotions in the classroom.

How are instructors to deal with these issues in the academy that typically privilege constructions of knowledge based on rationality and ways of interrelating more typical of and comfortable for members of the white dominant culture? What is the responsibility of higher education to society in general, particularly in regard to creating a more equitable and just society, and how does this responsibility interrelate with the politics of positionality in power relations in the classroom, and in the knowledge construction process? It is these issues—power relations in classes focusing on diversity issues and the role of the positionality of instructors and students in the construction of knowledge in such classes—that are central to this chapter. Using an analysis of the opening critical incident as a grounding place, I will consider the possibilities and limitations of the higher education classroom as a site of resistance and social justice education. I begin by focusing on power relations in classrooms and in the higher education system. Then I will consider how this focus on power relations in the classroom relates to the politics of positionality in the knowledge production and dissemination process. Finally, I will consider some strategies that adult educators might use in dealing with these issues.

Sites of Resistance to Power and Privilege in Higher Education Classrooms

To be sure, higher education has a responsibility to society, not only to fulfill the traditional role of creating and disseminating knowledge but also to contribute to creating a more equitable and just society. In recognizing this role, most institutions of higher education offer classes in various places in the university—in each department and through programs such as ethnic studies or women's studies—that deal with diversity issues of various types. Such classes are often seen as sites of resistance to the dominant culture. Power relations are indeed challenged in these and other higher education classes. Yet despite best attempts to do otherwise, these power relations are sometimes also reproduced.

We can see evidence of both resistance and reproduction even in the snapshot of the class provided by the critical incident. This critical incident can best be understood by considering some of the dimensions of power at play in this particular site of resistance. To begin, this was a *powerful* experience—indeed, one of the most powerful in my experience as a teacher. What made it so powerful? I think Marilyn French's discussion of power (1986) may be helpful to our analysis here. She makes a distinction between "power over," or power as dominance, and "power with," or power that comes from within. Usually when neo-Marxist, resistance postmodernist, and feminist writers talk about power relations, they are referring to the power that dominant groups often exert over oppressed groups, on both a conscious and an unconscious level. In this respect they are talking about "power over." Although such writers rarely discuss power from within, they do refer to the ability of individuals and groups to have a sense of agency—the ability to act on their own and others' behalf to change the world. Much education for social justice, including the class I have described here, is trying to activate a sense of agency among participants. From my perspective, both types of power were very much present in this critical incident.

Structured Power Relations as "Power Over"

Clearly, the mechanisms of "power over" are structured into the very fabric of society in general and are manifested in structural power relations based on gender, race, class, sexuality, and ableness in nearly all institutions in society. Higher education is no exception. Indeed, the effects of structured power relations are present before students ever get to the door of the classroom—in who is given access to academic preparation and is mentored even to seek out, apply, and get admitted to higher education. The result is that typically the further one goes up the educational ladder, the fewer people of color are represented both in the student body and in faculty and administrative positions in higher education; often there are fewer women as well. Thus, when one considers the positionality alone of the participants in the critical incident described, it is not insignificant that only one-fourth of the students are people of color.

It is also not merely coincidental that I, the white instructor, was the permanent full-time faculty member, whereas my African American teaching partner was the adjunct instructor. What is not obvious in the vignette is that at the time I was team-teaching this particular class, there were no full-time permanent faculty of color in the education department made up of twelve faculty members. I had made a request a couple of years earlier that such classes be team taught. There was a need for a greater range of cultural representation and for ways of foregrounding forms of cultural knowledge that are not embodied in my positionality and life experience as a white woman. Further, because of the controversial and emotionally laden nature of the course content, these classes are difficult to teach alone. I was given permission either to create a teaching internship for an experienced graduate student or (as was the case in the foregoing scenario) to team teach the class with an adjunct faculty member. But a primary power relation was present in the team teaching. I, the white woman with a doctoral degree, was the full-time permanent faculty member and the adviser to many of the students in the class. My positionality—as a white woman and as a permanent faculty member—resulted in the fact that I had more power in the classroom than my master's level African American teaching partner. I was seen (both by the institution and probably by the students, as I was the adviser to many of them) as having primary responsibility for the course. This perception was manifested in the fact that questions about assignments and the organization of the course from both the students and the administration (such as the department chair or the registrar's office) tended to be directed to me. My point is that some of these power relations are structured into the university itself. My higher status *position* as a permanent faculty member, which intersects with my *positionality* as a white woman, gives me power that others without these position markers do not have. In the five times that I have team taught the course (with three different people), including the class in the incident described here, my teaching partners and I have made every effort to structure the class to alter some of society's power relations. We have tried to make our teaching time and responsibility more equal, by alternating in taking a lead role and through the focus of the course content. Further, we structure activities so that students have a turn in being in teaching roles as well. But in spite of our best attempts, no matter what we did in these classrooms, we could not completely get outside some of the power relations structured into the university itself. In discussing the limitations placed on how emancipatory a higher education classroom can be, Jennifer Gore (1993) refers to some of these institutional factors, along with the required faculty evaluation of students, as "institutionalized pedagogy as regulation."

There were also power relations present in the foregoing incident beyond those structured into higher education. One of the most striking was in who was silent and who chose to speak during the incident. I have generally thought of speaking as being a sign of power, and over the years I have observed that those who benefit more by virtue of their positionality are more likely to dominate the classroom speaking space and in general have more power in the classroom. I had not thought of silence necessarily as a way of maintaining power and privilege in a classroom. Further, I had not initially noticed that it was the most marginalized (namely the people of color and the person with a disability) and the white folks most willing to be vulnerable who spoke in the first round of the circle. Mary's very important insight in this regard was transformative for me at that moment. Indeed, silence can have multiple meanings; it can be an unwillingness to be open or vulnerable, which can be a way of maintaining power and control. On a conscious level, I thought my own initial silence was about not wanting to disrupt the process. But my African American teaching partner spoke. Perhaps on a less conscious level, I too, along with the other white folks who said nothing, did not want to be vulnerable. In what way does our positionality shape our willingness to be vulnerable in classes focusing on systems of privilege and oppression? In thinking about this issue, one white woman student asked in her final paper (due a week later), "Is [the silence of some of the white folks] due to *not having to* [speak] *or not really wanting to?* Do we (I include myself) not want to let others know us because we don't have to? Is that part of our privilege?" Like this student, I am still pondering this question. As I have discussed at length elsewhere, the positionality of teachers and students always affects how classroom dynamics unfold (Tisdell, 1995, 1998). But in my mind, what determines the success of classes like this is the extent to which teachers and students honestly deal with *how* the positionality of participants is operative in teaching and learning.

Resisting Structured Power Relations: Agency as Power from Within

Classes such as the one I have described are intended to be sites of resistance in higher education. They are about activating a sense of agency—an ability to act and make change happen. They are about getting in touch with the second type of power—power from within—which was operative in this class. Social change, or the transformation of power relations between dominant and oppressed groups, requires action. Thus part of the point of these classes is what black feminist writer Audre Lorde (1984) refers to as "the transformation of silence into language and action" (p. 40).

Our class was successful to some degree in activating this power from within to transform silence into action. This success was due partly to the way the class is structured. The course content is about power issues based on the politics of positionality—race, gender, class, sexuality, and ableness. Thus, unlike most classes in the academy, the work of people of color, women, and members of other marginalized groups is foregrounded in the curriculum. In addition, participants in this class write about what it means to be a member of a particular group—for example, what it means to be white, or Latino, or female. This is often the first time that members of privileged groups think about what it means to be heterosexual or white or able bodied, whereas most people of color, or people who are lesbian or gay, have thought a lot about what it means to be members of a marginalized group. As McIntosh (1988), Delpit (1995), and Sleeter (1996) have observed, privilege is often most invisible to those who have it. But this class is only a beginning, and as we have discussed in this chapter, privilege still asserts itself to some degree in these classes.

As incidents arise in the class, we also try to critique how some power relations are present in the classroom. We see how Mary did this in the foregoing incident: by pointing out how silence can sometimes be a way of hanging on to privilege, whereas giving voice can result in shared vulnerability. At that moment, Mary was pointing out how our process was shaped by positionality and by the willingness of the white folks who moved out of their privileged position to share some of their own vulnerability. Her calling attention to and critiquing how privilege works served to challenge power relations. Her doing so increased our consciousness about how privilege works so that we had more power to act to challenge systems of power and privilege.

As we have seen, due to the nature of the course content, these classes are often controversial and emotionally laden. In trying to figure out how to deal with this in the many times we have taught it, my teaching partners and I have learned to create activities that are likely to access people's emotions early in the course. Examples include the use of films, and the writing and sharing of each participant's cultural story around awareness of positionality itself. We have found that such activities allow for the discharge of emotion, which, ironically, actually gives participants more intellectual energy to deal with the theoretical material in the course. Further, requiring people to be in teaching roles not only helps foreground and makes apparent how participants are constructing knowledge but also provides participants a forum for the creative expression of their own ideas as well as their affect and passion. It facilitates their ownership of the course and alters some of the teacher-student power relations.

The general structure of the class created the possibility of the foregoing incident taking place. But if the participants hadn't activated their own power from within, the incident never would have occurred. So what activated this sense of power from within that resulted in this powerful experience? I cannot know for sure what made it so powerful for others in the room. It may have been the very honest comments of so many, or Susan's sharing of the tragic death of her father. Perhaps it was the poignant exchange between Mary and Susan, the very articulate way each spoke to their experience, and the obvious emotion that was attached to both of their comments. Perhaps it was the interaction of participants' emotion and passion related to their past experience, as well as the intellectual and affective experiences we had had together in this class, that gave us new insight into how power relations are played out in society. But I think what was most powerful was that this open exchange of vulnerability among many participants *offered hope.* Susan herself did not go down the road of racial hatred in the aftermath of her father's murder. She had been doing antiracist work in her own teaching long before she arrived in our class. Our knowing this offered hope and offered a sign that deep pain, loss, and grief could result in positive action. Mary also responded to Susan's pain with empathy, insight, and her own vulnerability. Her bringing this before the group offered hope. In addition, Nora, Sam, and Mary's beginning insights and their willingness to share with the group some of their internal conflicts with each other and how they were resolved offered hope. In their own vulnerability, all the students in the group, particularly those who spoke in the first round, offered hope.

It is not strictly the sharing of participants' vulnerability that offered hope, however, because hope is not based on affect alone. There was also a critical analysis that took place during the event itself. The clearest analysis was in Mary's remarks to the entire group. But there was some analysis both in my own and in my teaching partner's closing remarks. Further, the students needed to analyze power relations in the class itself as a portion of their final paper. Many talked specifically about this particular incident, and one student in particular noted that she had wondered prior to this event what bell hooks's engaged pedagogy might really look like in a class. She suggested that engaged pedagogy united affect and intellect, emotion and critical analysis, and she pointed out that when this happens, "It works!" And indeed, engaged pedagogy had "worked" in this particular situation. Further, this uniting of emotion, passion, and critical analysis in this particular event was facilitated by three students, not by either of the teaching partners. Although the three student facilitators did not know exactly what was going to happen, it was their own taking of action integrated with their passion, affect, and intellectual analysis in facilitating the experience that was also powerful. Integrating emotion, intellect, and action perhaps is an example of what can happen, as Ira Shor (1996) suggests, when students have power. Such integration leads to new ways of constructing knowledge.

Higher Education's Responsibility to Society: The Construction of Knowledge

Higher education's responsibility to society has traditionally been to construct, generate, and disseminate knowledge. More accurately, higher education has served as the guardian and gatekeeper of what counts as "official" knowledge. This is why people attend universities: to get degrees that are a sign that they are the possessors of this official knowledge. But as Elizabeth Minnich (1990, p. 151) notes, "behind any particular body of accepted knowledge are the definitions, the boundaries, established by those who have held power." Certain people have had the power to determine what has counted as "valid" knowledge—largely those who are white, Western, and, for the most part, male. And as was mentioned earlier in this chapter, the forms of knowledge that those in power in the academy have determined are valid are almost exclusively based in rationality. What does this privileging of certain forms of knowledge have to do with the critical incident? And more broadly, what does this privileging mean when one is teaching classes focusing on the politics of positionality and power relations based on race, gender, and class—courses that are inherently controversial, and at times emotional, in institutions that reify rationality? This privileging will be made clearer following a discussion of the politics of knowledge production.

Those who are teaching for social change are generally trying to alter the power relations of the dominant culture by calling attention to the politics of positionality in all institutions of society, including higher education. Doing so means calling attention—through the analysis of curriculum and pedagogy of higher education institutions—to how positionality informs the politics of the knowledge production process. But it is also important to do something different: to create a more inclusive curriculum that is representative of people of color and other marginalized groups and to conduct classes in a way that takes into account the myriad ways people construct knowledge. In essence, calling attention to how positionality informs knowledge production both challenges the boundaries and definitions of knowledge and expands the parameters of what has counted as knowledge, and creates what Hill (1996) refers to as fugitive knowledge—knowledge that resists the dominant culture.

To teach against the grain like this can sometimes be seen as dangerous. In speaking to this point, Elizabeth Minnich (1990) notes that to challenge the boundaries and definitions of what has counted as knowledge "is to mark oneself as mad, heretical, dangerous. The assumptions and the form of a position mark it as admissible or inadmissible to the discourses of knowledge. So too does the kind of person (a person whose 'kind' has been pre-established by the culture) affect whether what is said or written is listened to as knowledge or not" (pp. 151–152). In essence, Minnich is calling attention to what is involved in the politics of knowledge production. She points out that often those who have attempted to expand what counts as knowledge, particularly if they are women and people of color, have not only been met with resistance from those who have more power in the system but also are often marked as dangerous. Further, often the "kinds" of people (women, people of color, working-class people) trying to expand the knowledge base as well as the definitions of knowledge have not traditionally been viewed as producers of knowledge. Minnich argues that positionality—that is, *who* people are who are doing the speaking or writing—affects "whether what is said or written is listened to as knowledge or not" (p. 152). This explains why white men teaching classes like the ones described in this chapter or writing about these issues are more likely to be taken seriously. In fact they often come off as heroes for doing this work if they have high enough status in their institution (for example, as tenured professors). People of color (and white women to some degree) may be seen as "pushing their own agenda" and are more often considered suspect; they are thus discounted in the knowledge production process.

Minnich (1990) also observes that the "form of a position" marks it as admissible or inadmissible to the discourses of knowledge. This is an extremely significant point when one considers the forms of knowledge that have been reified in the academy: primarily rational forms of knowledge expressed in a way that is more or less devoid of passion or emotion. This pronounced rationality suggests that if a student or a professor explains a point with too much passion, anger, and emotion, he or she may be discounted as being "irrational" or "too emotional" or "not academic enough." In terms of positionality, people who tend to express and privilege such rational forms of knowledge also tend to be white or male. (By contrast, feminist writers have shown the significance of affective forms of knowledge for women learners [Belenky, Clinchy, Goldberger, & Tarule, 1986]). This overreliance on rationality reifies a way of knowing that is also more associated with white culture. Many of us who are white have been socialized to be a bit distant from our emotions and passions, which easily carries over to how we behave in the classroom. Other cultural groups are not necessarily socialized in this way. How this plays out pedagogically in classrooms is that some people of different cultural backgrounds will speak with a good bit of passion (sometimes read as hostility) or speak with more modulation in their voice intonation and affect in their ordinary day-to-day interactions than is typical of much of Anglo culture. These differences of expression are examples of how positionality shapes the knowledge construction process. Those students and professors who do not conform to the proper "form" in expressing knowledge risk being discounted by others in the higher education system.

This discounting did not occur in the critical incident; people were not discounted overall even though they did not entirely conform to the reign of rationality in the academy. But I think there are particular reasons why this was so. First, as mentioned earlier, critical analysis, which is typical of the rationality of higher education, was still very much present in the course, along with the affective and experiential dimension. Students needed to critically analyze curricula and pedagogy in light of the reading in their written assignments and in their class discussions. Second, there were some very strong allies in the class among those positioned relatively close to the dominant culture. Steve, the white male who tended to defend the status quo, did so throughout the semester until he was gently confronted by Jerry, another white male. By virtue of his positionality, Jerry had much more power to get through to Steve than anyone else. In essence, the fact that Jerry valued examining these resistance forms of knowledge appeared to make it more admissible to Steve. But there were other allies besides Jerry. As the white teacher, I had also been a strong ally to people of color; my teaching partner was a strong ally on disability and gay and lesbian issues. Susan also had been an extremely strong ally throughout the semester, which is part of what made her sharing the story of the murder of her father so powerful; Susan had already shown herself to be extremely capable in terms of participating in the discourses of rationality. Although Mary and Sam, as members of marginalized groups (along with three other students), were least representative of the dominant culture, throughout the quarter they had also shown themselves to be extremely capable in participating in the discourses of rationality. As the main players in this very powerful and emotional critical incident, Mary, Susan, and Sam had all shown strong ability in critical analysis (based on rationality). I believe it is both because these individuals had strong allies and because they were all proficient in the discourse of critical analysis that this expression of emotion and passion not only was tolerated but also was key in facilitating an extremely powerful way of constructing knowledge in this particular situation. Indeed this was a way of doing something different.

There is no question that higher education's responsibility to society is the construction and dissemination of knowledge. But the critical incident begs the question of what higher education's

role should be in constructing transformative and culturally relevant knowledge. If one is teaching for social change, clearly one is
in essence teaching for social transformation. Is this within the
domain of higher education? I would say yes, although teaching
for social change is not its exclusive domain. But if higher education is serious about teaching for cultural relevance, then we must
begin creating new models of teaching and learning. As Mary Hanley observes:

> The academy has always been about the Eurocentric aspects of the
> dominant society. To not introduce other ways of knowing and
> other ways of thinking is to do a disservice to people whom we are
> trying to educate, because they will have to deal with other people
> from other cultures. It's also intellectually dishonest and an affront
> to other people from other cultures that are knocking at the door
> of the academy and saying, look, this is a distortion of reality, this
> Anglo-centric distortion of reality, this is not how reality is. This old
> reality is based on White supremacy; it's based on a certain class
> position. If we are going to be intellectually honest we've got to
> look at other ways of knowing, because they are as intrinsic or as
> necessary to the dominant culture as is Anglo-centric ways of know-
> ing. If we're going to claim to be intellectuals, and boast that the
> academy is intellectually challenging, then we're going to have to
> address the true complexity of our culture—now *that's* an academic
> challenge! [Tisdell, Hanley, & Taylor, 2000, p. 138]

Difficult Dilemmas: Creating a Community of Practice

In light of the politics of positionality inherent in the knowledge
production process, and in light of the power dynamics in classes
that are intended to be sites of resistance, those who are teaching
for social change or social transformation are indeed faced with
some difficult dilemmas. Some of these teachers obviously focus on
how to create resistance forms of knowledge in an academy that has
historically privileged white ways of knowing based in rationality,
and on how to deal with controversy and strong emotions that arise
in such classes. If institutions of higher education are serious about
teaching for social justice and developing and disseminating culturally relevant knowledge, they need to be concerned about moving beyond the acceptable (rational) forms of knowledge; not all

forms of cultural knowledge can be captured by rationality. Furthermore, transforming our understanding and creating new knowledge that can facilitate the challenge of power relations between dominant and oppressed groups require more than just critical analysis; they require the transformation of the heart. Higher education has some responsibility to do this. I do believe there is a place for this within higher education: the uniting of heart knowledge with rational forms of knowledge so as to lead to transformative learning.

In discussing his theory of transformative learning, Jack Mezirow (1995) argues that critical reflection is a necessary condition for transformational learning to happen. Many have criticized Mezirow's theory as being overly focused on rationality, and Mezirow in his later work has acknowledged in a limited way the importance of affect. Clearly, critical reflection is necessary for transformational learning; it was crucial in the critical incident described in this chapter. But I do not think it is possible to have a transformational experience by merely "critically reflecting" on experience. Further, an overreliance on rationality can *prevent* a transformational learning experience from happening. I do not think that we participants in the critical incident would have had a transformational experience only by critically reflecting or rationally thinking about our experience. The affective component—the sharing of our vulnerability—along with the critical analysis was what made the experience transformational. I would argue, contrary to Mezirow, that affective involvement and expression is also a *necessary condition* for transformational learning to happen.

If higher education is interested in allowing transformative education to occur, it seems to me that we must develop opportunities for it to happen. bell hooks (1994) suggests that part of what we must do is create a community in which we can practice engaged pedagogy by bringing our whole selves into the learning environment and examining how we engage with our educational practice. Doing so involves our affect, passion, bodies, spirituality, and critical minds. These parts of us are markers of our positionality and cannot be splintered off. Acknowledging this and working with it by creating a teaching community is what engaged pedagogy is about. It is what the three student facilitators in the critical incident were trying to do. I believe they were successful; many reported this to be a transformational educational experience.

There is also the question of what the teacher's role should be in doing transformative social justice education; after all, three students, not my teaching partner or I, facilitated the foregoing exercise. Even though I can say this was the single most significant experience I have had in a classroom as a teacher or a student, I know that as a teacher, I probably would not even now facilitate such an experience. As an instructor, I do have institutional power over students. Students might have felt that I was requiring them to be emotionally more vulnerable than they had bargained for in higher education. As it happened, students facilitated this emotional vulnerability for each other. And of course, each student was free to share what he or she chose. With the students facilitating the exercise, there was no arm twisting. But if I had facilitated the exercise, students might have felt pressured to "please the teacher" by being more vulnerable than they might have wanted. I believe students should have the power to make that choice. So as I said, as a teacher I would be leery of facilitating or appearing to require students to be vulnerable to that degree, although clearly I value such experiences in classrooms. But my teaching partner and I made choices too: we chose to structure the course in such a way that it did incorporate affective and more passionate forms of cultural knowledge. We were trying to create a teaching community in this group of experienced educators. Our efforts probably set the stage for the three student facilitators to try this particular exercise based on their understanding of engaged pedagogy. But even though we set the stage for this possibility, the power of their own choosing helped to make this experience of engaged pedagogy really work.

Higher education does indeed have a responsibility to participate in creating a more just society. There are no cookbook solutions for how best to do it. But there are a few things that adult educators can pay attention to in trying to teach for social change:

- Integrate affective and experiential knowledge with theoretical concepts.
- Pay attention to the politics of positionality inherent in knowledge production and among participants in the class.

- Acknowledge the power disparity between teachers and students.
- If possible, team teach with someone who is positioned differently relative to the dominant culture.
- Require students to be in teaching roles.
- Consider how curricular choices implicitly or explicitly contribute to challenging structured power relations.
- Be conscious of the ways in which unconscious behavior contributes to challenging or reproducing unequal power relations.
- Build a community based on openness, affect, and intellectual rigor to create a democratic classroom.

Clearly there are no easy solutions, and there are limitations to what can be done in a higher education. But higher education has a responsibility to do its part in teaching for social change. Creating a community of practice can be powerful if students have power to practice their own understanding of engaged pedagogy and to examine the politics of positionality. We can hope that doing so leads to social transformation.

References

Belenky, M. F., Clinchy, B. M., Goldberger, N. R., & Tarule, J. M. (1986). *Women's ways of knowing: The development of self, voice, and mind.* New York: Basic Books.

Delpit, L. (1995). *Other people's children: Cultural conflict in the classroom.* New York: New Press.

French, M. (1986). *Beyond power.* New York: Ballantine Books.

Gore, J. (1993). *The struggle for pedagogies.* New York: Routledge.

Hill, R. (1996). Learning to transgress: A sociohistorical conspectus of the American gay lifeworld as a site of struggle and resistance. *Studies in the Education of Adults, 28*(2), 253–279.

hooks, b. (1994). *Teaching to transgress: Education as the practice of freedom.* New York: Routledge.

Lorde, A. (1984). *Sister outsider.* Freedom, CA: Crossing Press.

McIntosh, P. (1988, July/August). White privilege: Unpacking the invisible knapsack. *Peace and Freedom,* pp. 10–12.

Mezirow, J. (1995). Transformation theory of adult learning. In M. Welton (Ed.), *In defense of the lifeworld: Critical perspectives on adult learning* (pp. 39–70). Albany: State University of New York Press.

Minnich, E. K. (1990). *Transforming knowledge*. Philadelphia: Temple University Press.

Shor, I. (1996). *When students have power.* Chicago: University of Chicago Press.

Sleeter, C. (1996). *Multicultural education as social action.* Albany: State University of New York Press.

Tisdell, E. J. (1995). *Creating inclusive adult learning environments: Insights from multicultural education and feminist pedagogy* (Information Series No. 361). Columbus, OH: ERIC Clearinghouse on Adult, Career, and Vocational Education.

Tisdell, E. J. (1998). Poststructural feminist pedagogies: The possibilities and limitations of a feminist emancipatory adult learning theory and practice. *Adult Education Quarterly, 48*(3), 139–156.

Tisdell, E. J., Hanley, M., & Taylor, E. (2000). Adult education for critical consciousness: How positionality shapes teaching and learning for social transformation. In A. L. Wilson & E. R. Hayes (Eds.), *Handbook of Adult and Continuing Education: New Edition* (pp. 132–146). San Francisco: Jossey-Bass.

Chapter Nine

Transforming Boundaries of Power in the Classroom

Learning from La Mestiza

Mechthild Hart

"I am not just a White person," a student exclaimed in one of my classes during a discussion on race relations. "My parents are Irish, and that puts them at war with the English, whom you would also call White." The class had been reading about issues related to poverty and to poor mothers dependent on public aid. Our discussion had focused on the racist public image of the Black teenage mother who presumably represents the typical welfare mother. Based on the readings and on the way I structured class discussion, our premise had been that "the racial hierarchy is fairly stable, with Whites always at the top and Blacks at the bottom" (Reddy, 1999, p. 6). We had not yet talked about the fact that other groups were "moving between these two poles at different points in history" (p. 6); that some, such as the East European immigrants or the Irish, could become "Whiter" once they had sufficiently assimilated into the dominant culture; or that Whites did not constitute one homogenous group.

We also had not yet approached the issue of people moving back and forth between different kinds of identities throughout their entire lives because they claim, or are ascribed to, multiple group affiliations. Some of these identities are visibly marked, especially by skin color and phenotype but also by clothes or clothing style. These markers have tremendous evocative power as they are inserted in a social, political, and economic power matrix. It was brought home to me in one of my classes that I myself easily fall into the trap of categorizing people according to these evocative markers. The majority of students were Black, and at first glance I identified them as African American. As it turned out, the students represented several African nationalities, and one woman, Frances, was Puerto Rican. She told the class that she constantly had to explain to African American students that she was not African American, that is, "one of us," and to White students that she was not African American, that is, "one of them." In addition, because she did not live in her own country, only by her switching from English to Spanish did Puerto Ricans themselves recognize her as one of their own. However, Frances actively contributed to discussions that centered on male sexism; her generally strongly proclaimed loyalty to all Puerto Ricans, female or male, did not prevent her being quite critical of rather divisive tendencies within her own Puerto Rican community.

In this chapter, I describe the steps I have taken in expanding my understanding of *la mestiza,* a concept that signifies cultural, political, and epistemological border crossings. Frances's story could give me only a glimpse of the struggle and reality of *la mestiza,* who is "the product of the transfer of the cultural and spiritual values of one group to another" (Anzaldúa, 1990, p. 377). As *la mestiza* moves between different cultures, she may experience multiple, often conflicting messages about who she is or how she should act. It was not surprising that Frances was either silent or speaking rather angrily. Having her in class taught me two important lessons. First, I had to work on gaining an understanding of what it means to a person's sense of self when she constantly has to juggle between several identities that are tied to social and political power relations. Second, I had to be able to provide space for acknowledging these multiple identities, thereby making it possible to hear and learn from voices that speak different languages, that emanate from different cultural and political positionalities and from different locations on the topography of power.

The topography of the social world inhabited by all of us is a topography of power. I cannot assume the alleged vantage point of the neutral, unattached facilitator of learning similar to that of the enlightened scientist who uses the latest digital information technology of geomatics. For example, in geomatics, technology is used for "acquiring, analyzing, and manipulating earth images," and maps remain "symbols and instruments of power" (Poole, 1995, p. 1). However, geomatics does not address the question, How can we live off this land and keep it well? Instead, this question is asked by indigenous people who are "using maps to re-name and reclaim their lands." In their hands, the power of map making becomes "a creative and restorative power," the power of "re-mapping," "power-mapping," "counter-mapping," and "defending the land with maps" (p. 1).

As an educator I have to find where others and I are located in the topography of power. Only then can I enlarge the map of my world by remapping and countermapping this topography and by finding and nourishing common ground among people I encounter in my educational practices. I have to recognize and acknowledge my particular, specific location in this topography if I want to engage in transformative educational practice that follows a "process of pivoting the center . . . , for the assumed center (Europe and the United States) will no longer hold," and where people have multiple identities, and are therefore placed in a "discontinuous location" (Mohanty, 1991, pp. 2, 3). Friedman (1998) points to "the complex interplay of differences" within each of the cultures in which a person temporarily dwells, producing "contradictory and relational subject positions" (p. 100). People with multiple identities have lives that are full of pain, conflict, and contradiction. They also harbor the potential for developing a mestiza consciousness, a consciousness of the borderlands that turns ambivalence into something else, into the possibility of uniting all that is separate (Anzaldúa, 1990).

As I discuss in this chapter, the notion of a mestiza consciousness is especially important for educational work that engages in a process of remapping or countermapping as it grapples with the injustice and violence of a topography of power. The mestiza consciousness is a consciousness that is "simultaneously singular and plural, located in a theorization of being 'on the border'" (Mohanty, 1991, p. 37). It can provide a blueprint for transforming the topography of power into a source of creative energy that transcends divisions and fragmentation. Whether and how it is possible to engage in various steps toward developing such a consciousness of the borderlands in educational contexts is a question I address in this chapter.

World-Traveling

All learners—students and educators—live in or represent fundamentally different places on the map. Some people move about more than others, not as tourists but as border dwellers who do not adhere to expected social patterns but instead resist "social homogeneity, domination through unification, and hierarchical ordering of split social groups" (Lugones, 1994, p. 475). In recent years, theorizing about cultural hybridity or mixing has "emerged explosively," variously being called "syncretism, hybridity, creolization, mongrelization, *mestizaje, métissage,* and *tahjien*" (Friedman, 1998, p. 82). Friedman describes in detail the different kinds of cultural mixing that the various branches of hybridity theory, or "hybridity-talk," have to offer, especially with respect to the kinds of power relations these theories romanticize, criticize, or try to transcend. She also traces the history of the term *hybridity,* which originally had a strictly biological meaning referring to "the cross-breeding of plant or animal species" (p. 83). As biology does not exist in a social vacuum, its "common synonyms—*mongrel, half-breed, cross-breed, mixed blood*—have been largely derogatory, implying a degeneration from purebred or thoroughbred" (p. 83).

Educational theorists have also addressed the issue of métissage, borderlands, border crossings, creolization, cultural hybridization, syncretization, or diaspora space (Brah, 1996; Edwards & Usher, 1998; Giroux, 1992; McLaren, 1997; Willis, 1997). All these writings address the issue of globalization, but from quite different perspectives; these differences signal different approaches to the problem of power hierarchies. One perspective regards globalization as representative of the "contemporary condition" (Edwards & Usher, 1998, p. 161). This condition is characterized by "networks of transnational identifications" and "a process of multi-locality across geographical, cultural and psychic barriers" (Brah, 1996, p. 196). Another perspective highlights the dangers inherent in this kind of "difference-talk" (Friedman, 1998, p. 91), a version of hybridity-talk that constructs a border identity "without paying sufficient attention to the asymmetry of power relations that occur in

the process of cultural mixing" (McLaren, 1997, p. 8). The difference-talk of multiculturalism reinforces the widespread fragmentation of people all over the globe. Therefore, staying within the
parameters of this "difference-as-pluralism model" means having
no conception of the fact that it is women in the Third World who
"bear the disproportionate burden of difference" (Alexander &
Mohanty, 1997, p. xviii). In people's daily and nightly realities, difference does not refer to "a benign cultural form." Instead, it has
"a deeper and exploitative" meaning (Bannerji, 1995, p. 71). To
be different means to deviate from the norm and thus to be different *and* inferior.

Most likely, if not certainly, it will be educators who claim at
least partial membership in the dominant group for whom border
crossing becomes an emotionally manageable exercise. Border
crossing is fundamentally different for people who are the survivors
of imperialism and colonialism and who are now subject to various
forms of neocolonialism (Alexander & Mohanty, 1997). As one of
McLaren's students remarked with respect to the Chicana/
Chicano experience: "We didn't cross the border, the border
crossed us" (1997, p. 8). To look at my experience and validate the
particularities of my subjectivity and my direct agency are acts that
are inseparable from a cognitive approach that looks at the ways
this subjectivity is mediated. A "reliable understanding of the
world" (Bannerji, 1995, p. 65) needs to be gained, however, in
order to examine how subjectivity is mediated by this world. Such
an understanding is likewise mediated and formed by my unique
experience of it. I am therefore looking at a map of the world as
given to me from the outside, but I am also drawing and redrawing it as my understanding of this world—of the forces that shape
it or rule—is growing.

The White Other

Locating myself in the topography of power means becoming
aware of core aspects of White privilege, which includes an "invisible package of unearned assets . . . an invisible weightless
knapsack of special provisions, assurance, tools, maps, guides, code-
books, passports, visas, clothes, compass, emergency gear, and
blank checks" (McIntosh, 1995, p. 77). Whiteness is a racialized
category, and White people have to dismantle "the colossal unseen

dimensions" of a social system of White privilege, as well as uncover the "denials that veil the facts of white privilege" (p. 77).

Frankenberg's study (1993) of White women's views on race and racism shows how difficult it is for White people to be able or willing to leave behind the paradigms of either color-blindness or racial essentialism (which looks at race differences as being biologically founded). These responses to Whiteness indicate two related but nevertheless different political and educational challenges. One is to see Whiteness within a "relational framework" where "identities shift with a changing context, dependent always upon the point of reference" (Friedman, 1995, p. 17). Seeing Whiteness in relation to Blackness would dismantle the normative fixity of Whiteness, and Whiteness could be seen to be as socially constructed as Blackness. This is, however, only one aspect of the process of escaping color-blindness.

A second challenge is that, although seeing identities in a relational framework does address one's misperception of or ignorance about people's true reality, recognizing the relational aspects of Blackness and Whiteness may leave untouched one's misperception of one's own (undeserved) merits that are based on skin privilege. This kind of misperception not only distorts others but the self as well, or one's sense of self. Reddy (1999) puts it quite succinctly: Whiteness is "the unspoken norm and center of everything," and chief among White privileges, "indeed, the one that represents the sum of all the others is never having to think about race unless [one] chooses to do so" (p. 5). In Patricia Williams's (1995) words, "the very definition of white middle-classness is the complete lack of ethnic markers," thus making Blacks in the United States "the 'unassimilable ethnics'" (p. 64).

White people's notion that race is not an issue for them is a prime example of assuming an allegedly neutral "view from nowhere" (Harding, 1991, p. 273). A "race cognizant" (Frankenberg, 1993) paradigm would reject this color-blind view from nowhere and would instead look at racial difference from an explicitly antiracist perspective. Such a perspective would, however, entail more than becoming conscious of one's own color-blindness. It would also require people to acknowledge, and therefore move beyond, the social denigration of sources of knowledge that are tied to an identity they "were taught to despise." This knowledge originates from people's "own socially devalued lives instead of from 'nowhere' or from somebody else's life" (Harding, 1991, p. 273).

In order to be able to learn from others, and in order to assist in the common task of building bridges across boundaries, I therefore need to acknowledge and understand, analyze and reflect on the boundaries created by my own White culture. As a German American, I speak two "once-colonial tongues" (Busia, 1993, p. 208). At the same time, I am using that part of my own heritage that is rooted in political struggles of resistance and change. It is this heritage that has assisted me in learning about and from people who have been "othered" by my own culture and who have been dominated, exploited, and violated by White, or Aryan, patriarchal-industrial supremacy. I am trying to get a handle on my Whiteness and the privileges it accords in a racist culture. But I am also learning to see my privileges as sources of deficit, of blindness and ignorance with respect to the knowledge created and preserved by those the White culture has othered and whom it continues to violate and destroy. I had to learn to move beyond feelings of guilt because I am German or White, learn to understand the deep-seated rage of people who have been persecuted or killed because of their difference, and move on to my own fury about what my country and my race have done.

Seeing race as part of a relational framework means to see where Whiteness and Otherness are placed within the social hierarchy. By using the term *Otherness* I am, however, already moving within the White master narrative. As Jean Graveline (1998), a Métis woman who sees herself as "located in the intersection of Aboriginal and Western cultures" (p. 7), pointed out during a conversation, she does not like to be referred to as the Other, irrespective of the critical intent behind the use of the term. Thus, although it requires a lot from people who are members of the dominant group to recognize how Whiteness defines Blackness as inferior Otherness, doing so is also a further step away from the "othering-talk." Where Whiteness rather than Blackness is defined as Otherness, power relations are turned upside down. It is difficult to look at myself as the White Other, but it is also very effective in dismantling the pairing of Whiteness with that of normalcy, or of locating Whiteness at the center and Otherness at the margin. However, because the White Other is a member of the group that holds power over all the non-Others, taking this step is more than simply turning the tables.

As a teacher I have to be fully aware of the tremendous process of learning that is required, especially for members of the dominant groups. Students may sometimes not be willing to recognize the implications of changing their views of themselves and of the world around them. Shankar (1996), for instance, writes how White ("especially male") students "either feel guilty and become silenced, or become defensive and/or (mildly) aggressive when the discussion centers around slavery or colonization" (p. 198). To acknowledge one's socially guaranteed privilege means to acknowledge how one's collective identity is part and parcel of historical and current forms of injustice. This is often the hardest learning route to take.

Voice and Silence

Valuing the knowledge lodged in experiences that are fundamentally different from one's own means being able to be silent and to truly listen to others' life stories. The themes of voice and silence have been debated rather frequently within the field of critical/feminist pedagogy, where both voice and silence have been addressed in often conflicting ways. For instance, silence has been described as a form of muteness, a loss of voice (Belenky, Clinchy, Goldberger, & Tarule, 1986). Silence has also been described as a powerful strategy. As Hurtado (1996b) writes, "the knowledge obtained by remaining silent is like a reconnaissance flight into enemy territory that allows for individual and group survival" (p. 382).

Hurtado describes the "outspokenness" of women of color as "the complement of the strategy of silence," and notes how many "feminists of Color have written extensively about how they are more outspoken, or ferociously outspoken, than many White feminists" (1996b, p. 382). In a similar vein, hooks (1990) writes, "This emphasis on women's silence may be an accurate remembering of what has taken place in the households of women from WASP backgrounds in the United States, but in black communities (and diverse ethnic communities), women have not been silent. Their voices can be heard. Certainly for black women, our struggle has not been to emerge from silence into speech but to change the nature and direction of our speech, to make a speech that compels listeners, one that is heard" (pp. 207–208).

Whether Black students or students who are not members of the dominant group are silent or outspoken clearly depends on the institutional framework of the learning situation, on the topic of the class, and on the racial-ethnic, or "ethnoracial" (Reddy, 1999), mix of the learning group. In my regular college classes, Black students are always a minority. This may contribute to their strategic silence. For instance, in one of my courses on "mother-work," two Black women told the class about their own encounters with the welfare system only after a White woman had mentioned that she was on welfare herself. Until then the Black students had been silent, and during the rest of the quarter they stayed on guard in terms of how much they would reveal to the class about their experiences. Clearly, although their colearners had opened some discursive and emotional space, the class had just begun to understand how the experiences of women on welfare and their own views of themselves and the world around them remained embedded in the overall structure of inequality. It will therefore take more than creating some space for thus far silenced voices to be heard if we are to undo the pain this silencing continues to inflict, or to simply let go of the well-trained ability to "bridle the anger and outspokenness—in a sense to tame it" (Hurtado, 1996b, p. 379). Creating space for silenced voices to be heard would be much too risky without a clear sense that everyone in class could be trusted and that everyone fully understood the overall social power structure that makes the taming of one's outspokenness a matter of survival.

By coteaching a class called Child, Family, and Community Relations in one of Chicago's city colleges, I could see that the racial-ethnic makeup of the learning group can make all the difference in terms of who speaks and who is silent. The majority of the students were African American, African, and Latina/Latino. There was only one White female and one White male student in class. Silence was therefore not strategically placed at the center of political survival as in my other college classes. On the contrary, it was especially the women of color who were indeed ferociously outspoken. It was a joy, but also a pedagogical challenge, to have students voice strong opinions about parts of their individual and social reality, opinions that were fueled by anger and fury but also by a strong sense of humor.

Learning from *La Mestiza*

In a chapter called "Straight Teacher/Queer Classroom: Teaching as an Ally," Winkler (1996) addresses the complexities of political allegiance from the perspective of someone who belongs to the dominant group but whose sense of political allegiance to nondominant groups is nourished by a profound dedication to social justice. She therefore asks, "How do we understand our own embodiment of privilege and oppression, both historical and current? How do we teach as allies to oppressed groups of which we are not a part? What does it mean to teach as an ally?" (p. 49).

In Winkler's definition, teaching as an ally means to "approach authority and the creation of classroom community as a condition for the production of knowledge and transformation of consciousness" (1996, p. 48). To enter an educational situation after a sufficient amount of intellectual and emotional preparation does not mean to be able to pick apart and sort out the many different issues that are all bundled up in the notion of political allegiance. However, it is possible to understand key ingredients of a process that critically and creatively examines the relationship of one's identity (or identities) and one's political standpoint. Clearly, none of the various dimensions of my multiple identities are fixed (although some of them are more stable and continuous than others); rather, they rest on an achieved political standpoint that is inseparable from an achieved identity. Miles (1996) describes these achievements as "an oppositional/transformative identity and politics" in which my achieved political standpoint and my achieved identity are "consciously, reciprocally, and continuously shaping one another" (p. 78).

In an earlier writing, which is influenced by Sandra Harding's theories (Hart, 1998), I summarize the main aspects of such an achieved standpoint. Here I want to focus on the notion of an achieved identity as it is intimately linked to the notion of a mestiza consciousness. I believe it is the mestiza consciousness that most poignantly captures the complexity of "interlocked, intermeshed oppressions" (Lugones, 1994, p. 459) and also the difficult and creative process of resisting them. Creating resistance poses tremendous challenges to explicitly educational endeavors.

Anzaldúa (1990) describes the many ways the mestiza has to move between an understanding of the complexity of her own multilayered history, which is inseparable from colonialism and imperialism, and an understanding of how different cultures clash in her own many selves. In Anzaldúa's words (1990, p. 379), "That focal point or fulcrum, that juncture where the mestiza stands, is where phenomena tend to collide. This assembly is not one where severed or separated pieces merely come together. Nor is it a balancing of opposing powers. In attempting to work out a synthesis, the self has added a third element which is greater than the sum of its severed parts. That third element is a new consciousness—a mestiza consciousness—and though it is a source of intense pain, its energy comes from continual creative motion that keeps breaking down the unitary aspects of each new paradigm." To gain such a new consciousness is clearly a tremendous struggle, an ongoing process of effort and accomplishment, particularly for people who, like Anzaldúa, are ascribed to or affiliated with quite disparate social groups. Her "Indian mother" and her "Spanish father," for instance, belong to social groups that are differently inserted into the overall matrix of power relations dominated by the Anglo. How can a teacher who is at least a partial member of the dominant group draw on the notion of *la mestiza* and a mestiza consciousness?

Taking Inventory

There is a first step that I require myself to take and that I also guide my students to take in educational situations: to locate myself on the power map and take inventory. I try to locate myself on the power map by looking at the many different strands of my multiple identities. Although I am of German origin, I have been an immigrant or have lived in exile for almost three decades. Although I am middle class, my consciousness is somewhat split or ambivalent in terms of class. I was born and raised in utter poverty, and I learned to respect and appreciate the hard and unpaid subsistence labor my mother and her children had to perform on a daily basis. Although my skin color makes me a member of the dominant group, I am a woman, with all the disadvantages and experiences of discrimination that being a woman entails. In addition, my being a lesbian seriously jeopardizes my claim to membership in the dominant group.

Clearly, my own inventory taking is built on an ongoing process of analyzing the multiple meanings of various identities by placing them into a larger political-ethical framework. In concrete educational situations, moving back and forth between the personal and the impersonal (or general) is a major pedagogical challenge. As a teacher, I have to assist in creating conditions under which people can begin to look at the fragments of their identity and see that certain fragments are only split, or "pure," because they are coerced into "the logic of this and that" (Lugones, 1994, p. 476). This is the logic of control, of "social homogeneity, domination through unification, and hierarchical ordering of split social groups" (p. 475). Thus the process of inventory taking only starts with, and ultimately has to move beyond, ordering the fragments of one's identity along the lines of the general social fragmentation into split, homogeneous groups that can be "had" or controlled. As Lugones writes, this fragmentation is replayed in a "fragmentation in the person," a person who is "affiliated to separate groups"; and because "the parts of individuals are separate, the groups are separate, in an insidious dialectic" (p. 475).

From an educational perspective, the situation becomes more complex as more identities are "counted." At the same time, people identifying with and representing nondominant groups still see very clearly the political importance of a less fluid collective identity. Friedman (1995), for instance, emphasizes that the fluidity of identities does not simply translate into a pluralism that denies the existence of relations of dominance, although "power and powerlessness, privilege and oppression, move fluidly through the axes of race, ethnicity, gender, class, and national origin" (p. 19). In a similar manner, Busia (1993) speaks of "the indeterminate aspects of 'identity' [that] cannot contain . . . the issues at stake for those of us—migrants, exiles and other kinds of homeless—troubled by the anxiety of trying to name ourselves in different tongues and voices, and place ourselves in or out of the manifold places from which we speak" (p. 204).

Likewise, in direct reference to the "archetypally postmodern" critique of feminist standpoint theories, Collins (1997) writes that "fluidity does not mean that groups themselves disappear, to be replaced by an accumulation of decontextualized, unique women whose complexity erases politics. . . . Group-based realities . . . grounded in an equally central notion of oppression, . . . race, gender, social class, ethnicity, age and sexuality are not descriptive categories of identity applied to individuals. Instead, these elements of social structure emerge as fundamental devices that foster inequality resulting in groups" (pp. 376–377). In *Teaching to Transgress*, bell hooks (1994) also writes about the importance of a collective political identity, and how it is rooted in the experience of oppression. She states that "identity politics emerges out of the struggles of oppressed or exploited groups to have a standpoint on which to critique dominant structures, a position that gives purpose and meaning to struggle" (pp. 88–89).

In addition, all cultures and religions have their own oppressive traditions, and as a lesbian feminist, Anzaldúa is "cultureless," has "no homeland," has "no race," because her own people "disclaim her." She therefore challenges "the collective cultural/religious male-derived beliefs of Indo-Hispanics and Anglos" (1990, p. 380). There is, of course, the issue of sexism, which requires women of color not to question "our loyalty and silence to those who may oppress us because they have also been our companeras/companeros in struggle" (Hurtado, 1996a, p. xi). Lugones (1994) makes a similar point by portraying "a complex version of identity politics and a complex conception of groups" (p. 475). Groups often relegate "needs, interests, ways . . . to the margins in the politics of intragroup contestation" (p. 474). For instance, the title of an introductory book to Black women's studies is a telling example of the way categorizations hierarchically order, fragment, or erase social groups and, correspondingly, aspects of one's sense of self. The title reads *All the Women Are White, All the Blacks Are Men, But Some of Us Are Brave* (Hull, Scott, & Smith, 1982). As Lugones (1994, p. 474) writes, "White women are transparent as women; black men are transparent as black. Black women are erased and fighting against erasure. Black women are fighting for their understanding of social relations, their personal possibilities, their particular sense of history, their mode of reasoning and values and expressive styles being understood as neither reducible to anything else nor as outside the meaning of being black and being women. Blacks and women are thus conceived as plural, multiplicitous, without fragmentation." Thus, "Unless one understands groups as explicitly rejecting the logic of fragmentation and embracing a nonfragmented multiplicity that requires an understanding of oppression as interlocked, group representation does most group members little good" (p. 475).

Lugones (1994, p. 460) uses the term *impure, curdled multiple state* to describe a mestiza consciousness (*mestizaje*) that rejects "fragmentation into pure parts. In this play of assertion and rejection, the mestiza is unclassifiable, unmanageable." Lugones derives the metaphor of curdling from the process of making mayonnaise, which "is an oil-in-water emulsion": "As an emulsion, it is unstable. When an emulsion curdles, the ingredients become separate from each other. But that is not altogether an accurate description: rather, they coalesce toward oil or toward water, most of the water becomes separate from most of the oil—it is instead, a matter of different degrees of coalescence. The same with mayonnaise; when it separates, you are left with yolky oil and oily yolk" (p. 458).

The mestiza is a complex, nonfragmented, heterogeneous person with an equally heterogeneous history of group affiliations. This history includes "the formation of voices in contestation that reveal the enmeshing of race, gender, culture, class, and other differences that affect and constitute the identity of the group's members" (Lugones, 1994, p. 475). Therefore, inventory taking also includes taking inventory of one's history of group loyalties and of where one suffered exclusion, discrimination, or violation from the groups with which one affiliated. This is a difficult, if not impossible, task to accomplish in a regular class setting, depending on a number of circumstances. Some can be shaped or influenced from the outside, whereas others may simply be unalterable givens. For instance, in my city college class, where Black people and Latinas/Latinos were in the majority, the themes of racism and ethnocentrism were a constant undercurrent in all discussions. However, although discussions around issues of racism were rather lively, they were not as emotionally charged and as directly confrontational as the ones that addressed forms of inequality between the sexes. I assume that because Black women were clearly the largest group in the class, they were empowered to voice their quite outspoken criticism of all sexist behavior, including that of Black men. In other words, when women of color were the majority in the class, they never questioned race-based loyalties, although they would challenge power relations, such as sexism, that threatened or undermined a strong sense of group solidarity.

Seeing Myself in the Other and the Other in Myself

In the context of a chapter called "Reinventing Ourselves as Other," Harding (1991) discusses the relationship between standpoint theory and knowledge and experience. In terms of the epistemological premise of an interaction that can be called pedagogically and politically successful, such an interaction must go beyond the formality of politely expressing opinions (or simply shouting at each other). Instead, for me to create a politically successful interaction means to be able to identify with the Other, and to see where the Other is part of myself, my sense of self, and therefore my life. As previously discussed, the Other has, or can have, multiple, fluid, and shifting meanings. The Other is the person different from myself, be it in terms of cultural background, sexual difference, age, class, able-bodiedness, and so on. Depending on the concrete context, some of these differences may be foregrounded while others remain in the background of attention. However, as a White person I must be vigilant about not falling into the trap of what Adrienne Rich (1979) called "white solipsism," where the Other is seen from the White perspective, the only perspective acknowledged and therefore available to White people. Nondominant groups face another challenge, as there is also the danger of denying the power of assimilation, of saying "I'm just like them," that is, White people. In both cases the power hierarchy is solidified rather than challenged.

Although it is tremendously difficult, it is also possible to try to stand in the Other's shoes, to attempt to see the world from someone else's perspective. Sondra Jackson, one of my colleagues, takes up a story reported in the news media that involved members from various ethnic or racial groups. After she asks students to name their particular identity, she asks them to assume the role of the Other in the story. The students have to first research the story in some detail and then tell it to the class from the perspective of the person or persons with which they were asked to identify. This experience invariably leads to the shattering of various stereotypical assumptions about the Other. On the most basic political level, it fosters a strong identification with politically motivated efforts to address and do away with some of the concrete, material consequences of such assumptions. On a deeper level, it also helps create a common ground, because students learn to empathize with the emotions and motivations of the Other. It clearly requires the soul and the heart to take a major leap so as to come closer to the emotional and spiritual reality of a human being who cannot be reduced, or is no longer reducible, to categorical group membership. As Lugones (1990) explains, students (and teacher alike) move out of the orbit of control, or "split-separation," but engage in a process of "curdle-separation," this time by looking at or moving into the interior of an experience of the Other. The Other is no longer othered by the logic of control, but she, or at least some aspects of her, are also seen and felt in one's own self, and thereby become parts of one's curdled self.

Clearly, in a system that is dependent on and keeps perpetuating an entire matrix of power relations, engaging in a process of curdle-separation can give only a glimpse of the complex and ambiguous reality of the Other. At the same time, I strongly believe that once this step is taken, others are bound to follow. When I listened to a blond and blue-eyed student's story about her angry response to her coworkers' racist remarks about Black people, and seeing tears of fury in her eyes, I realized that she had made that vital first step. Her heart had been transformed, and there was no way back. However, the education of one's heart and soul also requires moving beyond immediate emotional responses. Transformation requires being or becoming aware of the general powers of injustice and finding the thread common to all humanity. This transformation can take many different forms. In my classes, for instance, I can see that Black students appreciate the assigned readings. Some of these readings validate their experiences by placing them in a larger social and political framework. Other readings show that people who belong to quite different social groups can also be placed into this larger framework. This allows all students to discern areas of commonality and displays how various forms of oppression intermesh.

Once these steps have been taken, cultural differences can be looked at as another area of investigation, vital for learning *about* the Other. What makes her different? What are the core values nurtured by her particular culture? This moves the mestiza consciousness onto the plane of understanding and valuing cultural differences as treasures, some of which can be or should be carried into one's own culture. The "should" is directly linked to a critical perspective on one's own hierarchically organized society, its potentially or actually destructive forces, and the cultural norms associated with it. Other cultures may have preserved ways of living that affirm rather than extract from life. Some of these ways may have been preserved in various narrative forms or in pieces of art. As an educator, I have the responsibility of making these cultural tropes available to students, thereby assisting them in moving ahead in the complex, multifaceted learning process of understanding or developing a mestiza consciousness.

Conclusions

La mestiza conjures up notions of diversity, multiculturalism, and globalization, but it also has a radical political agenda. Cartographies of struggle testify to the attempt to reconnect divisions and fragmentation into a self-created whole. As an educator trying to foster such connectedness by redrawing our social relations, I cannot forget to achieve clarity about my own particular location on the map of power and identity. My own location determines the possibilities of and limitations on what I can or should learn, unlearn, or relearn. If I do not take the trouble to figure out what I need to learn about myself and about the world surrounding me, I cannot learn from others and cannot assist in remapping the world. People who are not members of the dominant social or political group and who *became* people of color (those consciously achieving a sense of their identity) are confronted with the challenge of becoming aware of the "psychic residues of different colonialism" and of engaging in a process of countermapping. This means they have to grapple with "the nuances of the interconnections of struggles for decolonization" (Alexander & Mohanty, 1997, p. xiv).

To remap or countermap means to acknowledge, learn about, and attempt to understand the many different struggles of many different groups of people to survive, to resist or battle against the onslaught of injustice and destruction, and to gain or regain some power over their lives in a way that acknowledges the dignity of life in all its forms. For me to do these things, I have to be able to be silent, to listen and observe, to open myself up for critique, and to make myself vulnerable. In other words, I have to engage in a process of developing my own version of a mestiza consciousness. But my original position of privilege granted to me by a hierarchical social system will give a very specific content to this openness and vulnerability and to the kind of pain and anguish that always accompanies true learning. Learning about the habit of taking such privileges for granted, and unlearning that habit, will also open the doors to the joys of learning about Others and to discovering parts of Others in my own self.

It is the pain and joy of unlearning, relearning, and learning that I carry into my everyday educational practice as an ally teacher and an ally learner. I learn from women of color who "struggle to develop a voice that is representative of the complexity of all the groups they belong to because, unlike many middle-class White feminists, they do not wish to reject their communities of origin" (Hurtado, 1996b, p. 382). Consequently, "voice" has to be translated into "multiple voices (or multiple *lenguas* [tongues])" (p. 385). Only then can I participate in the larger political struggle of developing a mestiza consciousness, which gives the term *global* a truly radical meaning by linking it to the "psychic and pedagogical aspects of decolonization" (Alexander & Mohanty, 1997, p. xxviii). For Himani Bannerji, a Bengali woman living in Canada, a global consciousness is a consciousness that spans different worlds connected by the fragments of her own subjectivity. As Bannerji writes, "For me, this process of discovering the many names of my oppression in all its complexity brought sanity. My world became larger and populated" (1995, p. 10).

References

Alexander, M. J., & Mohanty, C. T. (Eds.). (1997). *Feminist genealogies, colonial legacies, democratic futures.* New York: Routledge.

Anzaldúa, G. (1990). La consciencia de la mestiza: Towards a new consciousness. In G. Anzaldúa (Ed.), *Making face, making soul. Haciendo caras: Creative and critical perspectives by women of color* (pp. 377–389). San Francisco: Aunt Lute Books.

Bannerji, H. (1995). *Thinking through: Essays on feminism, Marxism, and anti-racism.* Toronto: Women's Press.

Belenky, M. F., Clinchy, B. M., Goldberger, N. R., & Tarule, J. M. (1986). *Women's ways of knowing: The development of self, voice, and mind.* New York: Basic Books.

Brah, A. (1996). *Cartographies of diaspora: Contesting identities.* New York: Routledge.

Busia, A.P.A. (1993). Performance, transcription and the languages of the self: Interrogating identity as a "post-colonial" poet. In S. M. James & A.P.A. Busia (Eds.), *Theorizing Black feminisms: The visionary pragmatism of Black women* (pp. 203–213). London: Routledge.

Collins, P. H. (1997). Comment on Hekman's "Truth and method: Feminist standpoint theory revisited": Where's the power? *Signs, 22*(2), 375–381.

Edwards, R., & Usher, R. (1998). "Moving" experiences: Globalisation, pedagogy and experiential learning. *Studies in Continuing Education, 20*(2), 159–174.

Frankenberg, R. (1993). *White women, race matters: The social construction of whiteness.* Minneapolis: University of Minnesota Press.

Friedman, S. S. (1995). Beyond White and other: Relationality and narratives of race in feminist discourse. *Signs, 21*(1), 1–49.

Friedman, S. S. (1998). *Mappings: Feminism and the cultural geographies of encounter.* Princeton, NJ: Princeton University Press.

Giroux, H. (1992). *Border crossings: Cultural workers and the politics of education.* London: Routledge.

Graveline, F. J. (1998). *Circle works: Transforming Eurocentric consciousness.* Halifax, NS: Fernwood.

Harding, S. (1991). *Whose science? Whose knowledge? Thinking from women's lives.* Ithaca: Cornell University Press.

Hart, M. (1998). The experience of living and learning in different worlds. *Studies in Continuing Education, 20*(2), 187–200.

hooks, b. (1990). Talking back. In G. Anzaldúa (Ed.), *Making face, making soul. Haciendo caras: Creative and critical perspectives by women of color* (pp. 207–211). San Francisco: Aunt Lute Books.

hooks, b. (1994). *Teaching to transgress: Education as the practice of freedom.* New York: Routledge.

Hull, G. T., Scott, P. B., & Smith, B. (Eds.). (1982). *All the women are White, all the Blacks are men, but some of us are brave: Black women's studies.* Westbury, NY: Feminist Press.

Hurtado, A. (1996a). *The color of privilege: Three blasphemies on race and feminism.* Ann Arbor: University of Michigan Press.

Hurtado, A. (1996b). Strategic suspensions: Feminists of color theorize the production of knowledge. In N. R. Goldberger, J. M. Tarule, B. M. Clinchy, & M. F. Belenky (Eds.), *Knowledge, difference, and power: Essays inspired by women's ways of knowing* (pp. 372–392). New York: Basic Books.

Lugones, M. (1990). Playfulness, "world"-traveling, and loving perception. In G. Anzaldúa (Ed.), *Making face, making soul. Haciendo caras: Creative and critical perspectives by women of color* (pp. 390–402). San Francisco: Aunt Lute Books.

Lugones, M. (1994). Purity, impurity, and separation. *Signs, 9*(2), 458–479.

McIntosh, P. (1995). White and male privilege: A personal account of coming to see correspondences through work in women's studies. In M. L. Anderson & P. H. Collins (Eds.), *Race, class, and gender* (pp. 76–87). Belmont, CA: Wadsworth.

McLaren, P. (1997). Decentering Whiteness: In search of a revolutionary multiculturalism. *Multicultural Education, 5*(1), 4–11.

Miles, A. (1996). *Integrative feminisms: Building global visions, 1960s–1990s.* New York: Routledge.

Mohanty, C. T. (1991). Cartographies of struggle: Third world women and the politics of feminism. In C. T. Mohanty, A. Russo, & L. Torres (Eds.), *Third world women and the politics of feminism* (pp. 1–47). Bloomington: Indiana University Press.

Poole, P. (1995). Geomatics: Who needs it? *Cultural Survival Quarterly, 1*(4), 1.

Reddy, M. T. (1999). White, Whiter, Whitest. *Women's Review of Books, 16*(6), 5–6.

Rich, A. (1979). *On lies, secrets, and silence.* New York: Norton.

Shankar, L. D. (1996). Pro/(con)fessing otherness: Trans(cending) national identities in the English classroom. In K. J. Mayberry (Ed.), *Teaching what you're not: Identity politics in higher education* (pp. 195–214). New York: New York University Press.

Williams, P. J. (1995). *The rooster's egg: On the persistence of prejudice.* Cambridge, MA: Harvard University Press.

Willis, D. B. (1997). An outsider's view inside: Twenty-first century directions for multicultural education. *Multicultural Education, 5*(2), 4–10.

Winkler, B. S. (1996). Straight teacher/queer classroom: Teaching as an ally. In K. J. Mayberry (Ed.), *Teaching what you're not: Identity politics in higher education* (pp. 47–69). New York: New York University Press.

Technologies
of Practice
in Adult Education

Adult educators too often view practice technologies as apolitical processes. In contrast to this stance, the chapters in Part Three assume that educators' technologies of practice produce and reproduce relations of power in society.

In Chapter Ten, Nod Miller highlights the gap between the rhetoric about the potential of new media technologies to transform adult education and the messy realities of a project designed to enhance access to higher education for black women from an economically deprived area in a large English city. Her analysis deals with power dynamics in this program at both the institutional level and the classroom and interpersonal level.

In Chapter Eleven, Stephen D. Brookfield takes on a much older teaching technology, the discussion group, showing how forces in the wider society always intrude into the classroom. He shows how discussion groups are contested areas defined by the contradictory struggles for material superiority and ideological legitimacy that exist in the world outside.

The remaining chapters in Part Three focus on political issues embedded in the planning of educational programs. In Chapter Twelve, Arthur L. Wilson takes the seemingly commonplace decision of selecting a site for a continuing education program and shows the many ways a geographic location is crucial for the distribution of power and knowledge in adult education. In Chapter

Thirteen, Kimberly B. Sessions and Ronald M. Cervero show how the political dynamics of an urban gay community are played out in the process of planning programs for HIV-negative gay men in a community agency. They discuss the struggles between the interests of solidarity in an urban gay community and of offering programs that are most likely to be effective in keeping HIV-negative men from becoming infected.

Chapter Ten

The Politics of Access and Communication
Using Distance Learning Technologies
Nod Miller

In this chapter I highlight issues of power in relation to the use of new information and communication technologies (ICTs) in adult education through an examination of my experience over the course of a project, referred to here as Minerva. This project was designed to enhance access to technology-related higher education by way of a part-distance course delivered through multimedia and networked computers. The names of the individuals mentioned in the narrative have been changed.

Utopian and Dystopian Visions of New Technologies in Education

Analyses of the use of new technologies in education and predictions about such use tend to be constructed within one of two sharply contrasting discourses. Some see new technologies as having the power to transform education, providing learners with greater choice, flexibility, and control in relation to what, where, and when they study (Negroponte, 1995). Recent policy documents on education (in the United Kingdom, at least) have tended to espouse this utopian vision. Others, however, argue that the increased use of new technologies for course delivery will serve to increase the gap between information-rich and -poor and to dehumanize education, putting learners at risk of being more easily controlled and manipulated. For example, Apple (1992) inclines toward this view. In this chapter, I attempt to steer a course between utopian and dystopian extremes. I highlight the gap between the rhetoric about the potential of new technologies to transform education and the messier realities of lived experience. I outline some of the issues that I believe adult educators need to take into account in order to make effective use of new technologies in the course of their professional practice.

I address power dynamics at both structural and interpersonal levels in the course of my discussion. At the structural level, the issues concern the ways in which the construction and use of new technologies relate to patterns and processes of social stratification. Access to new technologies (seen here as hardware, software, skills, and knowledge) is not distributed equally across all social groups: use of ICTs has been skewed toward white, middle-class men and boys; Kirkup (1999) provides a recent examination of this pattern. Minerva, the project dealt with here, attempted to address this aspect of inequality by loaning computers to students from groups underrepresented in the population of those literate in the use of ICTs, as well as by providing them with network connectivity and by developing their knowledge and skills. However, the project demonstrated that overcoming the combination of financial, technical, pedagogic, and cultural challenges posed in this context is by no means an easy task. Furthermore, I shall argue that access to the technologies is not the only issue; consideration of how interpersonal power dynamics are mediated through new technologies is also essential. Analysis of the critical incident that serves as the focus of my discussion shows how the micropolitics of communication via new technologies requires that adult education take into account many other issues, including class, gender, and ethnicity.

The Policy Context of Minerva

The Minerva project needs to be understood against the background of current government policy in the United Kingdom. Shortly after the election of a new Labor government in 1997, several policy documents were published that indicated the likely direction of educational change at the beginning of the twenty-first century. Those documents particularly relevant to adult and higher education included the Dearing Report on the future of higher education (Department for Education and Employment, 1997b); the Fryer Report, *Learning in the Twenty-First Century* (Department for Education and Employment, 1997a); and *The Learning Age: A Renaissance for a New Britain,* a consultation paper on lifelong learning (Department for Education and Employment, 1998). These papers stress the importance of widening participation in higher education and encouraging partnerships between universities and other providers of learning opportunities, and they enshrine the belief that increased use of new technologies for teaching and learning can make an important contribution to these goals.

One of the themes that runs through the Dearing Report is the potential for the innovative use of ICTs to improve the quality and flexibility of higher education and its management. The authors of the report believe that such usage gives scope for a reduction in costs, although they acknowledge that "in the short term, implementation requires investment in terms of time, thought and resources" (Department for Education and Employment, 1997b, section 65). They recommended that all higher education institutions in the United Kingdom have overarching communication and information strategies in place by 2000. The suggestion is that the main challenges for the future are to harness the United Kingdom's existing information technology infrastructure and to ensure good management of educational and technological systems and the production of high-quality materials in order to meet the needs of students and other clients. They state, "students will soon need their own portable computers as a means of access to information and learning via a network" and that "students will need access to high quality networked desktop computers that permit the use of the latest multimedia materials and other applications" (Department for Education and Employment, 1997b, section 68).

The authors of the Fryer Report predict that universities and colleges are likely to see enormous growth in part-time study, distance learning, and technology-based programs in the next few years. They see universities as having particularly important parts to play in developing expertise in these areas and applaud the principle of universities and other educational providers and learners working in close partnership with one another to provide flexible, technology-based systems of learning. Fryer and his colleagues are clearly excited by what they refer to as the digital revolution, which they see as offering the opportunity for active learning via multimedia technologies; they state, "New digital technologies will create learning opportunities which are not dependent on being available at a particular time or place. Learning at home and outside conventional educational establishments will become more widespread with implications for institutions, teachers and content creators (like broadcasters) as well as individual learners. Tailoring resources to individual needs will eventually become possible" (Department for Education and Employment, 1997a, section 15.5). They recommend that the government adopt policies to secure access to new technologies, such as Internet connectivity, for everyone, including those for whom financial barriers would otherwise be insuperable. In addition, they stress the importance of government, funders, and providers in establishing arrangements that encourage individuals to acquire relevant skills and knowledge (Department for Education and Employment, 1997a, section 15.10).

It is not difficult to distill out some of the assumptions in these papers regarding the relationship of technology to education. Despite the importance assigned to technology, the term is seldom if ever defined or seen as problematic. Its usage seems most often to connote hardware, and there is relatively little mention of technological skills or knowledge other than occasional mentions of the need for students to acquire keyboard skills. This narrow definition of technology contrasts with the view widely expounded by sociologists of technology: that technology should be seen as comprising physical objects, the knowledge required to use them, and the knowledge required to create them (MacKenzie & Wajcman, 1985). The use of new technologies generally seems to be seen as a key feature of a "learning society" where all may be learners, where all may study where and what they want, and where a system of mass higher education offers choice, flexibility, quality, and coherence. Digital technologies are seen as having the power to transform distance learning, enabling geography, space, and time to be manipulated and managed in ways that benefit learners and cut costs.

An earlier paper to which I contributed (Miller, Leung, & Kennedy, 1997) examined the polarity in the academic literature on technology and learning between utopian and dystopian discourses: between those who view the use of new technologies in education optimistically and those who are convinced that increasing use of technology will increase social divisions and inequalities. The government policy papers examined here have generally been constructed in the utopian discourse. The Minerva project attempted to negotiate the boundaries between extremes of technophilia and technophobia and of evangelical enthusiasm and Luddite despair.

Minerva: The Critical Incident

The Minerva project, which forms the focus for my analysis in this chapter, was designed to enhance access to technology courses in higher education for mature black women from an economically deprived area of a large English city. The educational program undertaken by these women made use of new ICTs that both delivered part of the program and themselves formed the content of the curriculum. The project responded to current policy imperatives to open up educational opportunities to groups traditionally underrepresented in the university sector. It also sought to test some of the assumptions embedded in policy documents about ICTs and their power to transform education. The pedagogic approach in the program was based on principles of experiential learning; students were encouraged to reflect on their experiences of using technologies such as computers and the Internet in the course of their studies and on the place of technologies in their everyday lives. The name of the project was chosen to link it with a goddess of classical mythology who was the patron of technology and women's crafts. My role in Minerva was that of project director.

The project was funded through an award from a large multinational telecommunications company and involved a partnership between a university department and a women's training center situated in a working-class urban area. The grant from the company enabled the purchase of computers, which were installed in the students' homes for the duration of the program, and the employment of two tutor-researchers who contributed to the production of distance learning materials, the delivery of the distance elements of the course, and the implementation of research designed to identify the strengths and weaknesses of new technologies for teaching and learning. The yearlong course was designed as a foundation or "year zero" course leading to three-year, full-time undergraduate programs. Students were admitted to the year zero program on the basis of an interview and were not required to have formal educational qualifications in order to enroll. Successful completion of the year zero program enabled the students to enter the undergraduate program automatically. The delivery of the year zero program was shared between the university department and the community-based women's training center.

The critical incident that crystallized much of my thinking about the subject matter of this chapter arose toward the end of the course delivery phase. As project director, I was asked by the distance learning tutor (Teresa) to intervene in a conflict that had arisen between her and one of the students (Jacqui). According to the tutor, the student had failed to submit one of the e-mail assignments. The student asserted that the assignment had indeed been dispatched by the deadline, but the tutor had no record of its being received. It emerged later that the work had been sent to an incorrect e-mail address. Before this became apparent, the student had sent another e-mail to the distance learning tutor accusing her of lying and expressing a lack of confidence in the way in which the course was organized and assessment procedures conducted.

The distance learning tutor was angry and hurt at the tone of the communication from the student and anxious about the possible repercussions of this incident in terms of her relations with other students in the course. Once it had been established that the student had made a mistake when typing the tutor's e-mail address, so that it was impossible for the assignment to have reached her, Teresa felt that she was owed an apology. She wanted me to use my authority to "sort things out." I telephoned the student and explained that I had been alerted to a problem in relation to the course, that I needed to understand what had happened, and that I wanted to resolve matters in a way that was satisfactory from everyone's point of view. Jacqui said she was pleased to have the opportunity to discuss aspects of the course. She quickly shifted the focus of the conversation away from the particular incident to expressing her unhappiness with the feedback she had received about earlier assignments, some dissatisfaction with aspects of course organization (which she claimed were shared with other students), and her belief that she had suffered discrimination in some of her dealings with university tutors. At the end of a lengthy conversation, Jacqui said she was prepared to apologize to Teresa for the last e-mail she had sent but only if I "ordered her to do it," and further stated that she "wouldn't really mean it."

In the course of several weeks following the incident, I became involved in a number of telephone conversations, e-mail exchanges, and face-to-face discussions with Teresa and Jacqui. At several points I became concerned that this small but significant incident was in danger of souring relations within the course team and that it might lead to the student leaving the course. I was anxious that neither of these consequences ensued. I was prompted to review my own behavior and my assumptions about power relations in educational settings and to consider the limits of my own power to effect a satisfactory outcome to the incident. I felt that it might help matters to get the parties concerned into a face-to-face meeting, but Jacqui was resistant to this idea, arguing that the best solution was for her to maintain her distance from Teresa and to complete the course with minimum contact with this particular tutor. I was reluctant to make recourse to disciplinary procedures, which I felt would be likely to polarize the individuals concerned and amplify the incident out of all reasonable proportion. At the end of the project, all tutors and students met in the context of a conference to review the project experience. During the course of the day, Jacqui made an intervention that I interpreted as an indirect apology to Teresa: she acknowledged the dedication and hard work of the teaching staff and the difficulties involved in electronic communication. Teresa was pacified, and I judged that honor had been satisfied sufficiently to let the matter rest, despite a lingering uneasiness about the heat of the emotions stirred up and the issues raised by the incident. I wanted to do as much as I could to learn something from the experience and to use the learning to inform future action—hence this chapter.

Critical Perspectives on Technology

The policy documents to which I made reference earlier do not engage in any critical analysis of the technologies that are seen as contributing to the advancement of education. Although the Fryer

Report makes brief mention of the need for government policies to ensure that access to ICTs is available to all, there is little evidence that policymakers appreciate that the purchase and use of hardware and software are beyond the financial reach of some people in the population. During the course of the Minerva project, members of the project team were regularly reminded of the economic realities of Minerva students, who worried a good deal about paying their telephone bills and about the costs of office chairs and tables to accommodate the computers that were being loaned to them. Despite my own upbringing in a working-class community with some features in common with the neighborhoods in which the Minerva students were located, I had to confess to some surprise on discovering that most of the students lived in houses without telephone connections; the grant from the telecommunications company that funded the project contributed to the costs of line installation and students' telephone bills. It became clear that without this financial support, most Minerva students would have been unable to participate in the program. The university and the commercial sponsor subsidized the students to an extent that could not be replicated on a large scale. Yet without funding for computers, connectivity, technical support, and child care, people in the social classes represented by the Minerva target group will remain excluded from technology courses.

A further issue arising from the policy documents relates to their view of the technologies as neutral and unproblematic: tools to be used for good (in this case) or possibly for evil, but in themselves free from values or culture. If there is a theoretical view of technology to be detected, it is that of technological determinism, whereby social change is seen as being caused by technological development. However, there is now a substantial social scientific literature (Edge, 1995; MacKenzie & Wajcman, 1985; Williams, 1990) that counters the view of technology as neutral and contests the one-way causal link implied in technological determinism. Robins and Webster (1987) argue that the notion of the neutrality of technology runs counter to the principles of social scientific inquiry and investigation:

> The presumption that technology is neutral, and thereby that it is
> in crucial ways asocial, is anathema to everything the social sciences

and humanities stand for. It unavoidably makes them secondary, as disciplines, to science and technology because it relegates their role to study of the effects of technological innovations which are presumed to be the major motor of change. Technology is seen as a deus ex machina, a phenomenon that has been developed outside of the social world yet which arrives in society with such consequence that society, more or less rapidly adjusting and always responding to technology, can be defined by that technology: The Railway Age, The Nuclear Society, The Cybernetic Society. [p. 157]

Exponents of the "social shaping" perspective see technologies as shaped by the interests of particular social groups, the effects of which are seen in the technologies' design, production, and use. Wyatt (1998) illustrates this social constructivist position with examples ranging from the construction of the Paris Metro during the late nineteenth century, in which the width of the tunnels was deliberately restricted in order to discourage takeover bids from the private railway companies, to the introduction by the Nazi authorities in Germany during the 1930s of radios with restricted reception capacity so as to prevent users from receiving BBC broadcasts from London. The restricted-reception radios led the BBC to develop alternative transmission technologies.

A number of feminist writers employ a social constructivist perspective to interrogate assumptions about gender that they see as built into the design and use of ICTs. Some argue that technological competence ("mastery") in relation to computers is tied up with notions of masculinity so that women are discouraged from developing skills in using ICTs (Cole, Conlon, Jackson, & Welsh, 1994; Faulkner & Arnold, 1985). Other writers contest the view of computers as essentially male. Spender (1996) applauds the possibilities opened up for women by digital technologies and celebrates the experience of "nattering on the Net," and Plant (1998) challenges the view of women as victims of technological change and argues that generations of women from Ada Lovelace onward have enjoyed intimate relations with the machinery of the digital age. A useful summary of the debates about gender and technology is provided by Grint and Gill (1995).

The literature on the social relations of technology has given little attention to important issues having to do with the relationship between technology and ethnicity and to the cultural values built into ICTs. Because a central aim of the Minerva project was to enhance access to technology courses for black women, questions concerning ethnic discrimination and difference were at the heart of the project. I found that my experience of the project highlighted the ways in which cultural tensions are embedded in certain aspects of the educational deployment of ICTs. I now return to a consideration of processes bound up in the incident I have described in order to reflect on how various dimensions of power relations surfaced in the project.

"Race" in the Minerva Project

One important factor in the incident described earlier was that the conflict had arisen between a black student and a white tutor (and I should say that I too am white). Although Jacqui did not directly accuse anyone of racism, there were certainly subtextual suggestions in her complaints of discriminatory attitudes and practices embedded in institutional procedures. Thus the incident raised a set of troubling issues related to the politics of "race" in higher education. The quotation marks around *race* signal the difficulties and sensitivities, acknowledged in much contemporary literature on ethnic identities and conflict, involved in framing the relationships between people from different ethnic groups in language that captures complexity and dissensus. Although the concept of race features frequently in public discourse in Britain, and phrases like *race relations* and *racially motivated crime* are commonly encountered in speech and print, people of widely varying origins find such usages and the categories they imply to be inaccurate, oversimplified, or downright offensive.

Some extremely disturbing incidents in Britain in recent times have drawn attention to the persistence of racism in public institutions and private lives. A major news story during 1999 was about the handling of events surrounding the murder of Stephen Lawrence, a black teenager apparently killed by a group of white youths motivated solely by hatred of black people. The Macpherson Report, which followed a public inquiry into the Lawrence case, expressed grave concerns about the police handling of the murder investigation and pointed to "institutional racism" in the police service, which the report defined in the following way:

"'Institutional Racism' consists of the collective failure of an organization to provide an appropriate and professional service to people because of their color, culture or ethnic origin. It can be seen or detected in processes, attitudes and behavior which amount to discrimination through unwitting prejudice, ignorance, thoughtlessness, and racist stereotyping which disadvantage minority ethnic people" (Home Office, 1999, p. 321).

A full exploration of the implications of the Macpherson findings for public organizations is outside the scope of this chapter. Nevertheless, few people in the ethnically diverse urban area where I live and work and where the Minerva project is based can have remained untouched and untroubled by the issues raised. The university where the project was located promotes policies designed to widen participation in higher education by "nontraditional" students (generally a euphemism for black people, women, those of working-class origin, and those with disabilities) and has achieved considerable success in terms of the diversity of its student profile. But it remains the case that the large majority of academic staff is white. Because the project was aimed at countering inequalities of gender and ethnicity in access to and knowledge of new technologies, the project management group strove as far as possible to recruit a project team that was ethnically diverse as well as predominantly female. The team included one Afro-Caribbean member and two members of Asian origin, but the majority were white Europeans. The contrast between the ethnic origins of the students and the members of the staff group was a matter debated frequently in meetings of the project team. Some members of the team felt that, although individual colleagues were generally well intentioned and indeed often strongly committed to acting to counter racism, there were aspects of institutional structure and organization that nevertheless might be seen as constituting institutional racism as defined by Macpherson.

Problems also arose in relation to the behavior and attitudes of some employees of the commercial company that was contracted to provide technical support for students in their homes for the duration of the project. Early on in the project, I approached the company with a request that female technicians be used for house calls as far as possible, as some of the Minerva students were Muslims, whose beliefs rendered problematic any interaction in the home with men who were not relatives. My inquiry was met with some embarrassment, and eventually it emerged that the company did not employ female technicians. In meetings with the staff of the company, it became apparent that the Minerva students, being mature black women, were seen as problem clients and were not expected to display technological competence. A frequent complaint from students was that their accounts of problems with computer technology were not taken seriously by the male technicians. The students felt that it was assumed their problems stemmed from their own lack of knowledge or skill. A sales manager with whom I dealt confided that he was surprised at the smart appearance of the homes of some students, which I felt implied that he had assumed black people lived in slums.

The topic of the representation of differing ethnicities on the Internet formed part of the content of the Minerva course, and we took considerable care in attempting to ensure interrogation of the cultural assumptions embedded in course materials and processes. The discomfort some students experienced in their dealings with the technical support staff were aired and analyzed in the course of discussions of the cultural values built into technologies. Nevertheless, I was left uncomfortably aware that there were no easy liberal solutions to the structural issues of ethnic inequality.

Power Relations and E-Mail

In some ways, the incident on which I have focused is typical of what happens in many educational courses. However, although it is true that conflicts and misunderstandings between tutors and students may arise in the course of face-to-face programs of teaching and learning, there are features of this sequence of events that are particular to the context of computer-mediated communication. Many of those engaged in using electronic technologies may be unaware of the existence of "netiquette" guidelines; communication norms on the Internet are still evolving, and the technologies employed permit high degrees of speed and spontaneity so that communications can be sent in haste and regretted at leisure. Furthermore, e-mail is literally an "in-your-face" medium. Many colleagues remark on how they find angry or critical e-mails particularly intrusive and distressing. A letter or other form of written communication somehow carries less of a charge than an electronic message delivered to the close-up intimacy of a workstation.

It may be helpful to provide some more details of the use of e-mail in the Minerva project. One of the aims of the project was to explore the application of computer-mediated communication in teaching and learning, and we wanted to examine how e-mail compared and combined with other means of communication such as lectures and tutorials (conducted both face-to-face and by telephone). Some elements of the program were taught using exclusively face-to-face methods. Other elements included conventional tutorials and lectures but also included tasks that students were asked to carry out on the computers loaned to them. One of the elements (that for which Teresa carried responsibility) was taught entirely by distance, and we decided that in order to test the strengths and weaknesses of this approach, Teresa should restrict as far as possible her contact with students to e-mail and telephone communication. Teresa's course unit was designed to promote students' learning about technology in everyday life by encouraging them to reflect on their experiences with using technologies, including those employed in the course as modes of delivery. The students were asked to keep diaries logging their uses of and reactions to various kinds of hardware and software. These diaries were used as the basis for reflective accounts of their experiences and for other assignments designed to foster understanding of their changing conceptions of and relationships with technology. The submission of these assignments via e-mail at intervals throughout the program constituted the assessment strategy for Teresa's unit.

I acted as internal moderator for the assessed work on this unit, so I read all of the assignments submitted by students. At an early stage I was impressed by the lively style and clearly expressed insights that I found in many of the e-mail assignments. This contrasted strongly with much of the prose to be found in the formal essays that formed the basis of assessment for other parts of the students' program, which tended to reflect the students' lack of acquaintance with the linguistic codes of higher education. Most of the students had been away from formal education for some years, and many of them complained of difficulties in knowing how to plan and produce essays that met the university's requirements. However, most students seemed to take enthusiastically to the opportunities afforded by e-mail; several of them said they felt relaxed when producing their electronic assignments, in contrast to the anxiety they experienced when writing essays. They felt able to express themselves freely, unconstrained by the need to worry constantly about spelling, grammar, and "proper" English. One student likened composing an e-mail assignment to talking to a friend; another remarked that she felt able to "throw her thoughts onto the screen," and contrasted the positive feelings about e-mail assignments with the worries and frustrations she experienced in connection with other aspects of her studies.

The tensions that emerged between Teresa and Jacqui illustrate that there were drawbacks, in this project at least, to the freedom of expression and spontaneity that students were able to explore in the context of their e-mail communication. Early on in my dealings with this case, I became convinced that the conflict between them would not have found such intense expression if their communication had been conducted through the medium of letters of the snail-mail variety. Jacqui herself admitted that she would have hesitated to call someone a liar if she had needed to type and print a letter for which she would also have had to find an envelope and stamp. However, the e-mail medium permitted a note to be written and dispatched at the touch of a button, all in the heat of anger.

An additional factor that I came to see as significant in shaping the relationships that evolved between Teresa and the Minerva students was that for the duration of the project the students seldom or never encountered Teresa face-to-face, although many of them communicated with her on a weekly or even daily basis by e-mail or telephone (or both). As I have mentioned, this was a deliberate strategy adopted by the project team in order to enable the dynamics of distance, electronic, and (often) asynchronous communication to be explored. Although the maintenance of the spatial distance between Teresa and the students enabled us to amass a rich body of data, the strategy had its costs, particularly for Teresa, who became the target for many of the students' anxieties and resentments. It seemed to me that the students felt freer to express anger and dissatisfaction toward her than toward other tutors, partly because they did not have to manage such communication elements as eye contact in their dealings with her, and partly because, as the distance tutor, she remained a somewhat shadowy figure, more cyborg than flesh-and-blood creature. It seems that the maintenance of distance in a relationship enables a person to construct the Other in stereotypical terms, as a category rather than as a human subject.

One of our observations during the Minerva project concerned the pattern and timing of students' completion of e-mail tasks. Because all the students had child-care responsibilities and because many of them had paid employment outside the home during the day, much of their university work was carried out late at night or early in the morning. Our impressions of this pattern were confirmed by empirical data; because times are automatically recorded in electronic messages, e-mail enables monitoring of the times when work is dispatched, in a way that is impossible with conventional essays. This monitoring facility is one of the features of educational programs employing electronic communication that leads some writers to argue that such technologies serve to facilitate surveillance and policing of students by tutors (Boshier & Wilson, 1998). Messages composed during the hours of darkness may well appear inappropriate in the light of day, but if they have already been dispatched, the damage has already been done.

Rules of Interaction in Higher Education

A remark I have heard made by colleagues about the nontraditional learners represented by the Minerva students (that is, mature black women) is that "they don't know how to be students." Sometimes this kind of observation refers to the students' lack of skills concerning time management and essay writing, skills in which students who have entered higher education directly from school are generally expected to have been trained. But often what is being referred to in this context is a lack of deference to and regard for authority and academic status. Although British universities have adjusted to the greater diversity of students by making provision for training in study skills, much less attention has generally been given to implicit rules and assumptions about what is "proper" in relations between staff and students. At the same time there has been a move away from the use of formal titles in universities; during the twenty-five years I have spent in the higher education sector, the norms of classroom interaction have shifted from students and teachers addressing each other as Miss X or Dr. Y to an almost universal application of first names. Many middle-class students imbibe recognition of the significance of academic titles, honors, and rituals along with the elaborated codes of formal education during their early socialization, but these remain mysteries not revealed to most working-class people. It is therefore not surprising that when such people become university students, many find themselves transgressing the implicit rules and boundaries operating in higher education.

My experience of the successes and failures of the Minerva project provoked me to reflect a good deal on implicit and explicit rules in educational settings, as well as on my own and others' assumptions about the boundaries to be drawn around relationships between tutors and students, and indeed about the rights and responsibilities of academic colleagues in relation to one another. Early on in the unfolding of the critical incident, I became enmeshed in a series of dilemmas about my own behavior and responses. When Teresa first approached me with her concerns about Jacqui's "offensive" e-mail message, she clearly assumed I would accept her interpretation of events: we were academic colleagues, and I was "in charge" of the project. I was constructed as a powerful individual in Teresa's eyes, my personal power to shape effects and determine outcomes being enhanced by virtue of the fact that I was also the supervisor of Teresa's doctoral studies. I had strong loyalties toward Teresa and felt protective toward her as a colleague who was shouldering heavy responsibilities at an early stage of her academic career, responsibilities that I had thrust upon her by selecting her to work on the project. Nevertheless, I felt I had to balance my concern for her with my responsibilities toward Jacqui as a student involved in a program for which I was responsible. In view of the sensitivities surrounding the politics of ethnicity in the program, I was anxious to avoid any possibility of the situation being construed as one in which white tutors were uniting in the face of complaints from troublesome black students. When Teresa reacted angrily to what I thought was a measured comment during one of our meetings, I began to wonder if I had exacerbated the problems by failing to establish clear boundaries around aspects of our work relationship. I had been aware of the tensions that sometimes arise when hierarchical relationships of different kinds get tangled together. In Teresa's case, I was acting both as line manager and as Ph.D. supervisor. I had attempted to manage these relationships ethically, as I thought, by trying to foster a culture of negotiation and consultation in all aspects of the project. In my anxiety to avoid problems arising out of the asymmetry in the power relations, I had perhaps overstepped the boundary into a space where I was expected to operate as an uncritical ally in all matters. Thus my questioning of her judgment was interpreted by Theresa as a betrayal. In this, as in other aspects of this incident, there were clearly differences of perception about what constituted the rules of interaction.

In this examination of my experience of the Minerva project I have tried to show how questions regarding the use of new media technologies for teaching and learning and the micropolitics of electronic communication intersect with other aspects of power relations, such as the inequalities in relation to gender, ethnicity, and class and the implicit rules governing interaction between tutors and students in higher education. I conclude with brief reference to some possible implications for the practice of adult education.

Implications for Adult Educators

Computer-mediated learning of course information shares many of the potential pitfalls and challenges of traditional educational practice, but there are elements in this particular case that illustrate how the micropolitics of distance communication may be particularly difficult to manage. Power relations between learner and teacher may be less explicit in computer-mediated teaching than they are in face-to-face interaction, but that makes it all the more important for educators to be sensitive to these issues.

Adult educators need to engage in debates about new media technologies in order to be able to use them in the course of their work. But it is not sufficient for them simply to have the technical skills necessary to operate networked computer systems or to design multimedia products. They also need to recognize that technologies are neither neutral nor separate from the social structures within which they are designed and used. If technologies are recognized as being socially shaped, clearly there are assumptions built into their production and consumption that are class, gender, and culture specific. If adult educators are to contribute to the educational advancement of all social groups, they need to identify and render visible these assumptions, as well as interrogate their own practice and evaluate critically the claims of both technophiles and technophobes.

References

Apple, M. W. (1992). Is the new technology part of the solution or part of the problem in education? In J. Beynon & H. Mace (Eds.), *Technological history and the curriculum* (pp. 105–124). London: Falmer Press.

Boshier, R., & Wilson, M. (1998). Panopticon variations: Surveillance and discipline in Web courses. In J. C. Kimmel (Ed.), *Proceedings of the 39th Annual Adult Education Research Conference* (pp. 43–48). College Station: Texas A&M University.

Cole, A., Conlon, T., Jackson, S., & Welsh, D. (1994). Information technology and gender: Problems and proposals. *Gender and Education, 6*(1), 77–86.

Department for Education and Employment. (1997a). *Report of the national advisory group for continuing education and lifelong learning: Learning in the twenty-first century* (The Fryer Report). London: Stationery Office.

Department for Education and Employment. (1997b). *Report of the national committee of inquiry into higher education: Higher education in the learning society* (The Dearing Report). London: Stationery Office.

Department for Education and Employment. (1998). *The learning age: A renaissance for a new Britain*. London: Stationery Office.

Edge, D. (1995). The social shaping of technology. In N. Heap, R. Thomas, G. Einon, R. Mason, & H. Mackay (Eds.), *Information technology and society* (pp. 14–32). London: Sage/Open University.

Faulkner, W., & Arnold, E. (Eds.). (1985). *Smothered by invention*. London: Pluto Press.

Grint, K., & Gill, R. (Eds.). (1995). *The gender-technology relationship: Contemporary theory and research*. London: Taylor and Francis.

Home Office. (1999). *The Stephen Lawrence inquiry: Report of an inquiry by Sir William Macpherson of Cluny* (The Macpherson Report). London: Stationery Office.

Kirkup, G. (1999). A computer of one's own (with an Internet connection!). *Adults Learning, 10*(8), 23–25.

MacKenzie, D., & Wajcman, J. (Eds.). (1985). *The social shaping of technology: How the refrigerator got its hum*. Bristol, PA: Open University Press.

Miller, N., Leung, L., & Kennedy, H. (1997). Challenging boundaries in adult and higher education through technological innovation. In P. Armstrong, N. Miller, & M. Zukas (Eds.), *Crossing borders, breaking boundaries: Research in the education of adults. Proceedings of the 27th Annual SCUTREA Conference* (pp. 333–337). London: Standing Conference of University Teachers and Researchers in the Education of Adults (SCUTREA).

Negroponte, N. (1995). *Being digital.* London: Hodder & Stoughton.

Plant, S. (1998). *Zeros and ones: Digital women and the new technoculture.* London: Fourth Estate.

Robins, K., & Webster, F. (1987). Dangers of information technology and responsibilities of education. In R. Finnegan, G. Salaman, & K. Thompson (Eds.), *Information technology: Social issues. A reader* (pp. 145–162). London: Hodder & Stoughton/Open University.

Spender, D. (1996). *Nattering on the Net: Women, power and cyberspace.* Melbourne, Australia: Spinifex Press.

Williams, R. (1990). *Television: Technology and cultural form* (2nd ed.). London: Routledge.

Wyatt, S. (1998). *Technology's arrow: Developing information networks for public administration in Britain and the United States.* Maastricht, Netherlands: Universitaire Pers Maastricht.

Chapter Eleven

A Political Analysis of Discussion Groups

Can the Circle Be Unbroken?

Stephen D. Brookfield

Within the progressive-humanist orthodoxy that reigns in adult education, democratic discussion holds a central place in the pantheon of practices. Discussion is usually lauded for a mix of pedagogic and political reasons. Pedagogically, it is held to engage learners in participatory learning, which helps them come to a deeper understanding of the topics considered. Politically, discussion is supposed to provide an analog of democratic process, a space where all voices are heard and respected in equal measure. Mezirow (1991) and Collins (1991), among others, invoke Habermas's ideal speech situation—which to many is exemplified in the rational discourse of respectful open discussion—as the organizing concept for good adult educational practice.

Vignettes of Participating and Facilitating

My concern for understanding discussion as a political event, and analyzing the dynamics of discussion as a political process, springs from my own experiences of learning through discussion. As a learner, I rarely found participating in discussion to be the liberatory, democratizing experience it was proclaimed to be. Rather, I experienced discussion as a competitive ordeal, the occasion for a Darwinian survival of the loquaciously fittest. Participating in discussion became translated into a form of competitive intellectual besting in which triumph was claimed by those who said the most or made the most brilliantly articulate and insightful comment. We knew we were engaged in the same kind of name dropping that grips guests at an academic cocktail party as they struggle for recognition and status. Our participation was framed by the need to speak as often and intelligently as we could, thereby impressing the teacher with how smart we were. The idea that we might be involved in a group creation of knowledge never occurred to us. It was also very clear that those who did well in discussion were those who brought the appropriate cultural capital to the occasion—a wide-ranging vocabulary, a confident manner, an ease at speaking in public, and an expectation of being listened to and taken seriously. My practice of discussion has been framed by this experience of learning, in that I believe discussion reproduces patterns of inequity based on race, class, and gender found in the wider society unless adult educators intervene to create a space for those voices that would otherwise be excluded by default. In this chapter, I offer five personal vignettes of my experience as either a learner or a facilitator in a discussion group. I then discuss these vignettes from the perspective of three allied theoretical perspectives: Marxist structuralist analysis, resistance theory, and poststructuralism, each of which has something important to contribute to a political analysis of classroom discussion practices.

Experiential Deflowering

I am seventeen years old in the final year of grammar school in England. A group of my peers and I have been chosen to participate in a weeklong symposium at Oxford University, designed for high school students who show academic promise. I am flattered by being chosen to be part of this group and to have the chance to play at being a bona fide intellectual—an Oxford undergraduate, no less. The first morning of the symposium arrives, and we are told we will spend most of our time in seminar groups. Our opening event is a general address by a well-known Oxford professor of moral philosophy. I understand his greeting of welcome to the symposium but am baffled by pretty much everything else he says. A couple of phrases register—moral imperative, existential dilemma—largely because they are uttered in a tone of portentousness. I dutifully write them down.

After morning coffee we split into discussion groups. As I take my chair I am gripped by panic. I know I am stupid—a hard worker but someone with no intellectual flair. I knew it was an accident that I was selected to attend this symposium. What can I do to stave off the humiliation that awaits me? I decide to beat the game of intellectual one-upmanship that is coming by working the phrase *existential dilemma* into the conversation in the first sixty seconds of the discussion. This I manage somehow to do. The discussion leader asks me why I think something is an example of an existential dilemma. There is a long silence before I stumble out a pitiful explanation—a stream of consciousness string of the most impressive words I know—that actually is devoid of any meaning. Another silence follows. I know the group is embarrassed at my idiocy and the fact that they have to endure this dolt in their midst. Then and there I resolve to keep my mouth shut for the duration of the week—a resolution I follow to the letter.

Counterfeit Discussion

We jump now to about twenty years later. I am a professor of adult education (how did *that* happen?) and am attending an informal conference discussion group on emancipatory practice. The leader announces that he wants to work democratically by getting us to set the agenda for discussion. We each express our concerns, and the leader lists these on a flip chart—except that what gets listed on the chart resembles nothing so much as his already announced interests. Somehow the words that have come out of our mouths have been transmogrified into something completely different by the time they are listed on the flip chart. I realize that what is taking shape as the group's agenda for discussion bears an uncanny resemblance to what this person is known to be expert on and committed to. The consequent discussion, not surprisingly, ends with the leader giving his sense of what the group has agreed on. To me it bears at best only a passing resemblance to what we discussed but a very strong resemblance to the leader's declared ideology. This ideology is one I happen to share, but I am astounded that a group of adult educators who profess a commitment to democratic, liberatory praxis can be so easily hoodwinked or un-aware of groupthink.

The Automatic Presumption of Authority

I am running a discussion in graduate school. It is the second or third evening of the course. After an introductory minilecture, we are moving to consider some of the ideas I introduced. I begin by playing devil's advocate and critiquing some of the ideas I argued in the opening lecture. Students pick up on some of these criticisms and begin to argue them with each other. Every two or three minutes one gentleman—a white male—intervenes in a loud, confident voice to deliver a minilecture. This individual has a friendly, gregarious personality and enjoys a position of considerable authority in his own field. He is used to people listening to him and doing what he asks of them.

Each time he contributes, he speaks uninterruptedly for five minutes or so, packing his comments with allusions to the recommended texts for the class plus several other theoretical works not prescribed. It is a dazzling display that shows the rest of us just how seriously he has read the materials for the course and how much he knows. After the third time this happens, the class dynamic changes markedly, and conversation fizzles. My guess is that no one will venture into conversation for fear of being steamrollered or outperformed by this same person. It is not that he is vehemently disagreeing with anyone or putting them down. It is just that for him no others exist as partners in conversation. The rest of us are mute witnesses to his erudite monologues.

The Unwitting Diktat

A different semester, a different group of adults. This time I am running my graduate seminar with an increased awareness of how patterns of domination structured by participants' race, class, and gender can emerge in discussion groups unless a deliberate intervention is made to prevent this happening. I do not want anyone (in particular, males, whites, or middle-class students) to take up a disproportionate amount of air time, so I raise this issue early in the course. Students seem to agree with the need to equalize the chance to contribute to the discussion and suggest a number of ways this might happen: for example, by posting a charter for respectful discourse on the wall at the start of each class session, by appointing a different student each session to watch out for people who are trying to say something but not being noticed, or by doing a regular "circle of voices" exercise. I airily throw a suggestion into the mix to the effect that we could have a "three-person rule" whereby once you have said something, you do not speak again until at least three other people have spoken (unless you are explicitly asked to say something by another member of the group). There is no particular response to my three-person rule, so I drop the idea.

Six or seven weeks later, I am reading the end-of-evening evaluations for that week's class. Out of eighteen completed forms there are five mentions of how students are finding it increasingly difficult to speak in the group and how they think I, the teacher, am continuously stifling discussion. I am staggered. Here I had been priding myself on my awareness of the traps of antidemocratic discourse and my sophistication in democratic process. Yet it seemed that I had created exactly the consequence—students feeling inhibited from speaking by my apparently arbitrary exercise of teacher power—that I had been seeking to avoid. The next class session I ask the students why they wrote that they felt inhibited. It emerges that they had been slavishly following the three-person rule since the time I had airily mentioned it. What I believed had been a suggestion that had fallen flat on its face had been heard by them as a diktat, a teacher imperative. As a consequence, they had been strenuously monitoring their own speech and feeling frustrated at the constraint I had imposed on their pattern of participation.

Successfully Sabotaged by Silence

I am teaching a course on the principles of adult education to a mix of students from across the institution. I decide that the course should mirror my understanding of best practices in the field: it should be dialogic and responsive, with students as cocreators of knowledge. To this end, on the first night I meet the class without a syllabus. I explain that we will be on a journey together for the next sixteen weeks or so and that we will make the road by walking (Bell, Gaventa, & Peters, 1990). I expect a welcome release of tension to greet my statements as students realize that finally they are participating in a course where they will be treated like adults—as equal partners in discourse and knowledge creation.

The reception is decidedly mixed. Some seem to like the idea and begin to talk excitedly with me and among themselves about the different directions they want the course to take. Others look mostly puzzled, confused, and anxious. But about one-third of the class either glowers in anger or determinedly refuses to let anything disturb their look of sullen disinterest. I notice when we take our break that the members of this group go to coffee together and seem at ease with each other. Subsequently I find out that they are all from the same organization and have been dragooned into joining the course because someone thought it would be good for them.

As the weeks pass, this group refuses to make any contribution to class discussion about the directions for the course, the activities the other students are proposing, or the forms of assessment they are coming up with. I make the point publicly that anything can be negotiated and that people have almost total control over what we do and how they will be judged. I say that unless they make the effort to contribute to the conversation, decisions will be made for them by default as their peers move forward. Nada—no discernible response.

A schism develops between this minority and the rest of the class. The minority is now seen by the majority as uncooperative, hostile, and disrespectful to their peers. People start to cluster into two groups as the class divides, with all decisions being taken by the majority. But the influence of the minority persists even though they do not say anything and certainly never object to any proposal put forward by the majority. The majority group makes intermittent attempts to involve the minority through humor or appeals to the once-in-a-lifetime chance for them to shape what happens in their education. Nothing. The minority are immovable, truly impressive in their majestic negativity, a black hole sucking the energy from the room. The course ends in an uncomfortable atmosphere, with much of the majority's energy fluctuating between trying to cajole the minority of noncontributors into participation and blaming them for their taciturnity and uncooperativeness.

These five vignettes illustrate the undoubted truth that discussion can never be thought of as a unitary experience. Indeed, talking of the discussion method as if it were a single, integrated approach to facilitating learning that achieves broadly the same consequences each time it is used is hopelessly naive and simplistic. Discussion is a problematic form of practice that is culturally situated. Its meaning and significance vary according to (among other things) the race, class, and gender of its participants, the institutional and cultural location of the speech acts that compose discussion, and the ways in which the facilitator's behavior is interpreted. The purpose for which discussion is held—for example, to check whether students have properly understood concepts reviewed in readings and lectures, or to engage in ideology critique as a way of unmasking dominant cultural values—always represents a political stance, an ideological agenda. The criteria underlying the evaluation of what counts as "good" discussion spring from a particular sociopolitical milieu and represent the values of those who have managed to lever themselves into positions as professional gatekeepers. Not surprisingly, these values are often in accord with the prevailing values of laissez-faire capitalism. In fact, many teachers adopt a more or less conscious metaphor of the free market toward their practice, believing that the less interaction by the teacher, the better and more authentically student centered the discussion. But intellectual exchanges in discussion never occur on a level playing field. Those who bring the greatest cultural capital to discussion find that participating in this activity ensures that they accrue yet more capital. Even the language teachers use to describe the outcomes they desire for discussion—getting students to "own" a concept or "buy into" an idea—buttress capitalist ideology.

So adult discussion groups in colleges and universities are not limpid, tranquil eddies cut off from the river of social, cultural, and political life. They are contested arenas—whirlpools containing the contradictory crosscurrents of the struggles for material superiority and ideological legitimacy that exist in the world outside. Power is omnipresent in discussion. The flow of power can be named and redirected, and its seat can shift around the group, but it can never be denied or erased. Becoming aware of how the dynamics of power permeate and move among discussion group members helps us realize that forces present in the wider society always intrude into the classroom. Patterns of participation and deference based on race, class, and gender, unless deliberately named and challenged, invariably reproduce themselves as the natural order of things in the discussion.

Political Analyses of Discussion Groups

In considering the way in which discussion mores represent or challenge dominant cultural values, I draw particularly on three allied theoretical traditions, each of which has something important to contribute to a power analysis of classroom discussion. The first is the tradition of Marxist structuralist analysis, which focuses on the ways in which education serves as a sorting device that mirrors and preserves economic relations in the wider society. The second is that of resistance theory, which accepts the importance of structuralist analysis but holds that resistance and change are possible within educational institutions. The third is that of poststructuralism, represented chiefly by Michel Foucault's analysis of the way power relations are inscribed in the specific practices of everyday life (such as classroom conversation). This perspective examines the way in which classroom discourse serves to create and maintain regimes of truth, and the possibility of resistance being exercised at the very site at which dominant power is embedded in speech.

Structuralist Analysis

For many adult educators, a central purpose of discussion is to help students engage in ideology critique by becoming aware of, and challenging, dominant cultural values. This politically laden conception of discussion is strongly influenced by the perspective of Marxist structuralist analysis. This intellectual tradition investigates the process by which social structures (even those that are manifestly unjust) maintain themselves. People are born, they live and die, yet the system stays relatively unchanged—how can this be? Should not humans' ability to change their lives—their sense of agency—mean that each generation creates a new world? Why does this not happen? Macrosociological studies of schooling by Carnoy and Levin (1985) and Bowles and Gintis (1974) show how education functions as a sorting device for the economy, socializing students to accept their subsequent occupational roles as white-collar or blue-collar workers, service personnel or self-employed professionals, owners of capital or sellers of their labor power. Schools reproduce the hierarchical organization of factories and supply the different kinds of mental and physical labor that the capitalist system needs to function.

How does this sorting process manifest itself in discussion in adult higher education? Here the concept of cultural capital proposed by the French thinker Pierre Bourdieu (1986) is useful. Cultural capital refers to the style and patterns of speaking, dress, and posture, the command of language, and the knowledge of cultural matters that one brings to an educational situation. Class-based differences in the amount of cultural capital people possess explain why students from middle- and upper-class homes consistently do better as a group than working-class students. Adults from middle- and upper-class homes bring culturally approved ways of speaking, writing, and thinking into higher education discussions. To many teachers these students appear smarter, quicker, and more knowledgeable. Just as in a capitalist economy resources accrue to those who already possess capital, so it goes in discussion. Students who speak the right way, who use academic terminology correctly, and who make their arguments with confidence, quickly come to be regarded favorably as "good," academically able students.

In the vignettes described in this chapter, the concept of cultural capital framed my own sense of paranoia that accompanied my visit to the Oxford symposium. I knew I did not possess this capital. I did not sound right (a Liverpool accent overlain with Oxfordshire dialect), I did not carry my body in the right way (I slouched in a deferential pose), and I did not possess the knowledge proper to an educated person (what the hell is existentialism?). The vignette focusing on the automatic presumption of authority, in contrast, featured a student with strong cultural capital. Such a student—with his commanding presence and history of taking center stage in speech acts—was accruing ever greater amounts of cultural capital through the exercise of what to him were natural, automatic ways of behaving in discussion.

The mores governing what counts as cultural capital in higher educational discussion groups bestow privilege (among other things) on rationality, calmness of expression, evenness of tone, the absence of strong emotions, and the censoring of curse words. These mores reflect middle-class modes of communication, which themselves spring from Eurocentric conceptions of discourse, such as the Socratic dialogue and the jury system. That these mores reflect middle-class values does not automatically invalidate them. We should be wary of collapsing into a romantic but artificial and distorted dichotomy of pretentious, anal-compulsive, and exclusionary middle-class speech and robust, inherently honest, unpretentious working-class dialogue. But we should acknowledge that middle-class norms of discourse place working-class students at a disadvantage. hooks (1994) describes a "collective professorial investment in bourgeois decorum" (p. 188) that shapes notions of appropriate tone and speech forms in discussion. What hooks describes as bourgeois decorum is strongly middle class, a form of high-status discourse (Shor, 1996). As hooks observes, "students from upper and middle class backgrounds are disturbed if heated exchange takes place in the classroom. Many of them equate loud talk or interruptions with rude and threatening behavior. Yet those of us from working class backgrounds may feel that discussion is deeper and richer if it arouses intense responses" (p. 186).

The research of British sociologist Basil Bernstein (1990) extends our understanding of how social class manifests itself through speech patterns in discussion. Over the past three decades, Bernstein has shown us how formal, more elaborate codes of language are valued over more restricted codes both in education and in the wider society. The *elaborated code* is a broadly middle-class form of speech comprising a wide vocabulary, the giving of reasons and justifications, and frequent use of clauses, subclauses, and qualifiers. The *restricted code* is a broadly working-class form of speech comprising a smaller vocabulary; appealing to authority rather than giving reasons ("Why should I do this?" "Because I'm telling you to"); shorter, terser sentences; and frequent repetition of colloquialisms.

Teachers use these ways of talking as signals to distinguish and sort smart students from dumb students. Richness of language, precision of definition, frequent use of authors' names or of specialized terms, fluidity of sentence construction, and the use of subclauses are all taken as evidence of intelligence and scholarly diligence. Colloquialisms and the use of general descriptors such as "stuff" or "neat" evince a lack of seriousness. Curse words are banished as the last resort of the unimaginative. It was because I knew this difference by the time I was seventeen years old (even if I did not use Bernstein's formulation) that I was paralyzed with a fear of looking stupid in my flirtation with Oxford described in the first vignette.

Resistance Theory

The structuralist perspective comprises a sort of sociological Calvinism: if you are born into a certain social class and learn a certain set of values, behaviors, and speech patterns, then your future course in life is inexorably set. Reacting against this, radical educators like Henry Giroux (1983) criticize how "in the structuralist perspective human agents are registered simply as the effects of structural determinants that appear to work with the certainty of biological processes" (p. 136). Opposing this radical pessimism regarding the possibility of change, educators such as Giroux and Stanley Aronowitz have focused on the ways in which schools should be viewed as sites of contestation in which teachers and students often struggle against the imposition of dominant cultural values and subvert the attempt to organize schools as efficient units of production. Microethnographies of schooling, such as those conducted by Willis (1977) and McLaren (1994), document the forms of resistance displayed—from sabotage to outright challenge—and explore what Freire (1994) calls the pedagogy of hope. Building on Gramsci's idea of the organic intellectual—a cultural worker drawn from the people who works with them to help them penetrate dominant ideologies—Giroux (1988) proposes that teachers consider themselves intellectuals. This belief in the possibility that teachers and students can mount critical challenges to the dominant ideology has recently inspired attempts to blend postmodern perspectives with critical theory, resulting in what its advocates refer to as oppositional postmodernism, resistance postmodernism, or critical postmodernism (McLaren, 1995). As is argued at the end of this chapter, however, the subjectivist epistemology of postmodernism is in direct contradiction to the objectivist epistemology of structuralism and resistance theory.

This tradition of resistance, opposition, and activism is strong in adult education. A strain of modernist optimism informs the critical perspective and activist efforts of such longtime adult educational luminaries as Eduard Lindeman (1926), Myles Horton (1990) and Paulo Freire (1994). The focus of Horton's work at the Highlander folk school was the exchange and analysis of participants' experiences in the circle of discussion. Horton believed that if people could be helped to analyze their experiences collaboratively and critically, they would realize how much knowledge and skill they already possessed, and they would learn how they could use these to fight for democratic social change. Freire's pedagogy of hope (1994) and his conversations with American educators (Bell, Gaventa, & Peters, 1990; Shor & Freire, 1987) elaborated a dialogical approach to adult education in which naming the world encouraged people to act on and in it.

To Lindeman (who went so far as to link discussion to world peace), the existence of formal and informal adult discussion groups was the prime indicator of American political health. As long as a vigorous network of living room discussion groups was in existence, and the discussion habit was encouraged in education, the chances for demagoguery and authoritarianism were much reduced. In a 1951 essay titled "Democratic Discussion and the People's Voice" (in Brookfield, 1987), Lindeman echoed George Orwell in his observation that "if democracies can combat totalitarianism only by becoming totalitarian, then the battle is already decided: totalitarianism has won" (p. 181). A populace that acquired the habit of discussion would keep the democratic spirit alive by fostering a continuous critical questioning of the directives and justifications of political leaders. Anticipating postmodernism by more than two decades, Lindeman argued that a prime virtue of discussion was that it helped participants avoid thinking in terms of binary, polar opposites, and it acquainted them with a plurality of choices and alternatives. For him, "so long as there are more than two alternatives human relations may manifest the qualities of peace rather than war" (p. 183).

The vignette "Counterfeit Discussion" illustrates an explicit attempt to develop an oppositional discussion practice, even though that attempt was distorted and manipulated. In my own career, I have been involved as a participant in initiatives within the adult educational community, for example, the transformative research network, the international league for social commitment in adult education, and the critical theory interest group of the Commission of Professors of Adult Education. All these initiatives are premised on the possibility that adult education can be an oppositional form of practice through which participants learn to unmask oppression, penetrate dominant cultural values, and develop strategies and energy to work for collective social change. That such efforts can be easily perverted, and are much more ambiguous than they sometimes appear, is evident in "Counterfeit Discussion" and "Unwitting Diktat." That adults can subvert educational authority (even authority that names itself as liberatory) with quite as much determination, stubbornness, and success as the working-class "lads" in Willis's classic study (1977) is demonstrated in the vignette "Successfully Sabotaged by Silence." It is the problematic nature of apparently oppositional and emancipatory practices such as discussion that leads us to our final theoretical tradition, poststructuralism.

Poststructuralism, Foucault, and Regimes of Truth

The work of the French cultural critic Michel Foucault questioned and then extended structuralist analysis. Foucault (1980) argued that the structuralist analysis was based on understanding power as the exercise of sovereign authority. Structuralism viewed power as emanating from a central source, such as the monarch, the state, the president, the military, and the central committee of the Communist Party. Sometimes the dominant group masked its identity and intentions and used ideology to maintain its hegemony, but a skilled Frankfurt school theorist could usually ferret out these ideological distortions. Foucault, however, maintained that in modern society, sovereign power has been replaced by disciplinary power—that is, power that is inscribed and exercised in the specific day-to-day practices of people's lives. In an adult discussion group, for example, power is exercised in such practices as the raising of hands to signify one wants to speak, the way eye contact is made by the teacher to confer the message that now a particular student can speak, the nod of teacher approval to register that a particularly insightful comment has been made, the preferred seating arrangement (usually a circle), and the form of speech and terminology that is approved. Foucault observed that modern society is so complex that a permanent army of police and informers would be necessary to make sure people accepted prevailing power relations. Because this is logistically impossible, he argued that overt surveillance has been replaced by self-surveillance—that we monitor and censor our own thoughts and behaviors in discussion groups and elsewhere.

Educators such as Gore (1993) and Usher and Edwards (1994) have extended Foucault's analysis to the use of the adult discussion circle (so sacred and reified in adult education as to be an unchallengeable sign of practitioners' democratic purity and learner-centeredness). They point out that although the discussion circle "may create different discursive possibilities, it nonetheless simply reconfigures the regulation of students. They may not be so directly subject to the teacher/lecturer but they remain under the immediate scrutiny and surveillance of their peers. . . . Changing practices do not, then, do away with power but displace it and reconfigure it in different ways" (Usher & Edwards, 1994, p. 91). Gore (1993) eloquently argues that beneath the circle's democratic veneer there may exist a much more troubling and ambivalent reality. For learners who are confident, loquacious, and used to academic culture, the circle holds relatively few terrors. It is an experience that is congenial, authentic, and liberating. But for students who are shy; aware of their different skin color, physical appearance, or form of dress; unused to intellectual discourse; intimidated by disciplinary jargon and the culture of academe; or conscious of their accent or lack of vocabulary, the circle can be a painful and humiliating experience. These learners have been stripped of their right to privacy. They are denied the chance to check teachers out by watching them closely before deciding whether or not they can be trusted. Yet learners' trust of teachers is often a necessary precondition for learners to speak out. This trust only develops over time as teachers are seen to act consistently, honestly, and fairly. Yet the circle, with its implicit pressure to participate and perform, may preclude the time and opportunity for this trust to develop.

Gore (1993) argues that a Foucauldian analysis leads us to a point where we see that no educational practice is inherently liberating or inherently oppressive—it is all in how the practice is experienced contextually and differently by those involved. I would not take the argument quite that far, but this line of analysis does throw the easy certainty of the progressive adult educational orthodoxy into productive confusion. No longer can we pride ourselves on the transparently democratic, learner-centered nature of andragogical practices. Things become much trickier and more elusive as we are robbed of the heady joys of celebrating our apparent commitment to, and practice of, democratic purity. The fourth vignette, "Unwitting Diktat," provides an example of how an intervention made with the best of intentions to equalize participation and foster inclusion actually worked to exclude some students.

This is not to suggest that we throw the discussion circle out and go back to the dark days of teachers talking uninterruptedly at rows of desks. I continue to use the circle in my own practice. But critical reflection makes me aware of its oppressive potential and reminds me that I must continually research how students experience the discussion circle. I now explain to students as they take their seats that I know that being in the circle does not remove power relations from the group and that I realize that the circle is sometimes experienced as an oppressive mandating of participation. Being aware that the circle does not remove power relations from the group means that I sometimes make a no-speech policy: I tell students they have the right not to speak and that I will not interpret their silence as indicating apathy, hostility, or mental inertia.

A central concept in Foucault's analysis is the regime of truth—"the types of discourse which [society] accepts and makes function as true" (1980, p. 131). In the second vignette, "Counterfeit Discussion," it is clear that a regime of truth is in operation. The fact that this regime is one I happen to agree with—the regime of liberatory education's values and practices—does not obscure the fact that the knowledge comprised by this regime supports teacher power. Power and knowledge are intertwined as the group is led, apparently spontaneously, to support an ideological agenda that matches the group leader's agenda. In the limited universe of the leader's conference classroom, his authority is buttressed and maintained by the regime of truth he propagates. Again, I accept that it may be a counterhegemonic regime of truth, a space for ideological resistance, but it conforms nonetheless to Foucault's analysis of the way power and knowledge interweave. Whenever a teacher ends a discussion by saying, "Well, I think we're all agreed that . . . ," or whenever you feel as a participant that you know where the conversation is leading, the regime of truth is close to being exposed.

Depending on how you read Foucault, you can either collapse into nihilism concerning the possibility of ever unraveling the interwoven and shifting conjunctions of power and knowledge, or you can take heart from his belief that because power is locally dispersed and contextually variable, resistance is possible at the site at which power is exercised. Foucault (1980) wrote that "there are no relations of power without resistances; the latter are all the more real and effective because they are formed right at the point where relations of power are exercised" (p. 142). The absence of monolithic sovereign power sometimes makes resistance seem more possible to activists who can work on a local, rather than national, level. The fifth vignette, "Successfully Sabotaged by Silence," shows how students can resist a regime of truth (in this case my own imposition of a dialogic ethic) to strip the teacher of his authority. Shor (1996) also vividly documents how students can skillfully use silence to challenge the power of liberal and liberatory teachers.

What Do Power Analyses Mean for the Practice of Discussion?

I want now to respond to these power analyses by examining specific discussion practices and responsibilities, focusing particularly on the role of the teacher. As adult educators, we cannot avoid taking action. The adult discussion leader cannot be a laissez-faire facilitator, exercising a minimum of control. Taking this stance only serves to allow patterns of inequity present in the wider society to reproduce themselves automatically in the classroom. Instead, the teacher must intervene to introduce a variety of practices—such as the circle of voices, periods when only those who have not spoken are allowed to speak, the ground rule that we can only speak about others' ideas (not our own), and the circular response technique developed by Eduard Lindeman (in Brookfield, 1987, p. 187)—to ensure some sort of equity of participation.

Many adult educators would like to believe either that they have no special power over adult learners or that any power mistakenly attributed to them by students is an illusion that can quickly be dissolved by a refusal to dominate the group. But avoiding our responsibilities for managing power is not that easy. No matter how much we protest our desire to be at one with learners, there is often a predictable flow of attention focused on us. Although it is important to privilege learners' voices and to create multiple foci of attention in the classroom, it is disingenuous to pretend that as adult educators we are the same as our learners. Better to acknowledge publicly our position of power, to engage students in deconstructing that power, and to attempt to model a critical analysis of our own source of authority in front of them; doing so will sometimes involve us in becoming alert to, and publicly admitting, oppressive dimensions to practices that we had thought were neutral or even benevolent. The following are some steps I take to accomplish these ends. These steps and others are described more fully in Brookfield and Preskill (1999):

1. Ensuring early in any discussion-based course that the group wrestle with creating what Bridges (1988) calls a moral culture for discourse—more prosaically, ground rules for conversation. These rules can be developed in several ways. The leader can suggest them, but doing so can seem a somewhat arbitrary exercise of teacher power. A better option is for students to generate these rules by reviewing their past autobiographical experiences as discussion participants to identify features they want to emphasize and avoid, and then generating specific procedures that encapsulate these preferences. Usually these ground rules focus strongly on equalizing participation, guarding against hate speech, preserving students' right to silence, and reducing the power of the teacher's voice.

2. Making sure that the group's experience of discussion is constantly researched through a classroom assessment or action research approach, such as the critical incident questionnaire (CIQ) (Brookfield, 1995, pp. 114–139) or discussion audit. In the CIQ, students write a weekly anonymous commentary on their experience of discussion, which is compiled and reported back to the class. The security this instrument's anonymity affords emboldens students to make explicit the inequities of participation they observe, the imbalances in voice they notice, possible discrepancies between the group's espoused rules of conduct and its actual behavior, and any arbitrary abuses of power by the teacher or other group members. In the weekly reporting out of the previous week's CIQ data, the problematic nature of power relationships in the group becomes a matter for public discussion. The group learns to delve deeper and deeper into understanding how power is exercised and resisted at the specific site of a discussion-based course.

3. Exercising teacher power to change relations of power is important for increasing opportunities for participation. A question invariably arises concerning whether teachers should require all students to participate in discussion. Mandating speech seems like an exercise of teacher power that stands in direct contrast to the spirit of democratic conversation. However, hooks (1994) argues forcibly that there are occasions when it is justifiable to exercise power in this way. She requires students to read out paragraphs from their journals in class so that none feel invisible or silenced. To her this is a responsible exercise of teacher power. Always allowing students the option to pass in discussion circles means that those who are shy and introverted, or uncomfortable because they perceive themselves as members of a minority race, gender, or class, end up not contributing. The longer this pattern of nonparticipation persists, the harder it is to break. So what seems like an empathic, benign action by the leader—allowing students the right to silence—serves to reinforce existing differences in status and power. Those who are used to holding forth will move automatically to speak, while those whose voices are rarely heard will be silenced.

I know that I can never entirely escape the web of power relationships within which an adult discussion class exists. Structures of inequity existing outside the class frequently reproduce themselves within. I know, too, that a universal democratic purity of practice is an illusion and that if I measure my work by whether or not I achieve this purity, I am doomed to perpetual guilt. But I know too that discussion groups can be more or less democratic, that the problematic nature of discussion can be continually revealed, and that we can come to more informed and sophisticated under-standings of how we are implicated in the unwitting maintenance of regimes of truth.

References

Bell, B., Gaventa, J., & Peters, J. (Eds.). (1990). *We make the road by walk-ing: Conversations on educational and social change with Myles Horton and Paulo Freire.* Philadelphia: Temple University Press.

Bernstein, B. (1990). *The structuring of pedagogic discourse: Vol. 4. Class, codes and control.* New York: Routledge.

Bourdieu, P. (1986). Forms of capital. In J. G. Richardson (Ed.), *Hand-book of theory and research for the sociology of education.* New York: Green-wood Press.

Bowles, S., & Gintis, H. (1974). *Schooling in capitalist America.* New York: Basic Books.

Bridges, D. (1988). *Education, democracy, and discussion.* Lanham, MD: Uni-versity Press of America.

Brookfield, S. D. (1987). *Learning democracy: Eduard Lindeman on adult edu-cation and social change.* London: Croom Helm.

Brookfield, S. D. (1995). *Becoming a critically reflective teacher.* San Francisco: Jossey-Bass.

Brookfield, S. D., & Preskill, S. (1999). *Discussion as a way of teaching: Tools and techniques for democratic classrooms.* San Francisco: Jossey-Bass.

Carnoy, M., & Levin, H. (1985). *Schooling and work in the democratic state.* Stanford, CA: Stanford University Press.

Collins, M. (1991). *Adult education as vocation: A critical role for the adult edu-cator.* New York: Routledge.

Foucault, M. (1980). *Power/knowledge: Selected interviews and other writings, 1972–1977.* New York: Pantheon Books.

Freire, P. (1994). *Pedagogy of hope.* New York: Continuum.

Giroux, H. A. (1983). *Theory and resistance in education.* New York: Bergin & Garvey.

Giroux, H. A. (1988). *Teachers as intellectuals.* New York: Bergin & Garvey.

Gore, J. M. (1993). *The struggle for pedagogies: Critical and feminist discourses as regimes of truth.* New York: Routledge.

hooks, b. (1994). *Teaching to transgress: Education as the practice of freedom.* New York: Routledge.

Horton, M. (1990). *The long haul.* New York: Doubleday.

Lindeman, E.C.L. (1926). *The meaning of adult education.* New York: New Republic.

McLaren, P. (1994). *Life in schools.* White Plains, NY: Longman.

McLaren, P. (1995). *Critical pedagogy and predatory culture.* New York: Routledge.

Mezirow, J. (1991). *Transformative dimensions of adult learning.* San Francisco: Jossey-Bass.

Shor, I. (1996). *When students have power: Negotiating authority in critical pedagogy.* Chicago: University of Chicago Press.

Shor, I., & Freire, P. (1987). *A pedagogy for liberation.* New York: Bergin & Garvey.

Usher, R., & Edwards, R. (1994). *Postmodernism and education.* New York: Routledge.

Willis, P. (1977). *Learning to labor: How working class kids get working class jobs.* Westmead, United Kingdom: Gower.

Chapter Twelve

The Politics of Place

Producing Power and Identity in Continuing Education

Arthur L. Wilson

The site seemed perfect: set adjacent to a major urban center with its transportation conveniences and recreational amenities, but located on a college campus in a quaint historic riverside town. Graced with expansive grassy and treed courtyards, intersecting brick walkways, and stately facades of academic and administrative buildings, this small liberal arts college seemed an auspicious setting for inaugurating an emerging professional association's national certification and continuing education program for its members. This stereotypically picturesque college campus, whose faculty and administration had actively collaborated with the professional association to inaugurate and house one of the first master's degrees in the occupation the association represented, was a place that signaled academic respectability. Its environs clearly constituted a space signifying knowledge, legitimacy, and authority, and were consequently well suited to an occupation struggling to legitimate itself professionally. Relying on such cultural assumptions tied to place can be risky, however, as the unfolding of the events of the actual continuing education program will reveal.

On the morning of the first day of the program, it was raining hard as I stepped out of the van that had just brought me and a dozen others to the college campus from the hotel, a hotel whose wild African animal motif was emblazoned on the van in black and white stripes, along with the hotel's name, "Noah's Ark." I knew I would catch hell for this more than once today. One prominent member of the professional association for which I worked as director of education had already testily remarked that he certainly did not care to grab the proboscis of an elephant to open his hotel room. Besides, my gray suit was getting grayer from rain as I slogged through the grass and hurdled puddles on the way to the campus auditorium, which was accessible only by walking some distance. Tactile images of wet shoes and socks all day were rapidly becoming a reality for me as well as for the 125 participants in this continuing education program, as they bolted out of other zebra-striped vans to scurry across the sopping courtyard to assemble for registration and orientation in the campus auditorium.

The rain was only one aspect of what appeared to be a rapidly diminishing return on the organization's investment of attempting to associate the profession it represented with an academic context. Many other seemingly technical programmatic miscues plagued this program, threatening any potential benefit hoped for in choosing this site. In addition to our having selected this little-known college with no continuing education center or staff, the campus program liaison, a professor of academic philosophy with whom the association had contracted to write its primary textbook on the profession's "theory" (another story in itself), turned out to be a typical academic. The liaison's understanding of planning and implementing continuing professional education (CPE), indeed his understanding of education itself, was faulty at best and downright disruptive too much of the time. For example, because the program liaison had failed to "request" the classrooms on which we had originally agreed, the program ended up on the fourth floor of a building with no elevators. This would prove quite an obstacle to more than one participant whose sedentary professional life had led to decidedly unathletic mobility. Furthermore, numerous other disruptions (some my responsibility, others not)—late-arriving or incomplete instructional materials, unprepared or late-arriving instructional staff, metal folding chairs, bad lighting, too few tables, Styrofoamed coffee, college campus dining hall food—coupled with the rain and the hotel and too many presumptions about what this place could mean to this group, contributed to everyone beginning to wonder why we were here.

Although I could go on with the messy details of our trying to produce this continuing education for these professionals at this college, I want to get right to the central questions of this chapter: Why did the program have to be *located here*, in this particular *place*, defined physically, socially, and culturally as a *college campus?* Why was it so important to me as director of the association's CPE, to the professional association sponsoring the program, to the profession itself to be in this place? Why did it matter to the many involved that this CPE program be associated and identified with the college's academic identity? How was the identity—the program's and thus the profession's professional legitimization—defined by this campus location as compared with the much more typical business resort hotels, with their pools, bars, golf courses, and countless other amenities that constitute their location and thus the privilege and power of the program's and the profession's identity, which we had given up to be *here?* To put the question more technically, how did the socially constructed, materially defined *place* of the college campus contribute to shaping the professional identity and power of the participants, association, and profession itself?

My response, the subject of this chapter, is that "place" plays a significant role in shaping CPE. People invest in place to empower themselves (Harvey, 1993b). Whereas many educators likely see program location as a straightforward logistical planning task, in my view where we "locate" our CPE programs profoundly shapes not only their purposes and process but also the power relations that in turn shape the identities of the participating professionals, of the professions themselves, and the power that professionals and professions exercise in society. Thus the less than auspicious events recounted in the introductory anecdote are not mere technical planning glitches but significant programming dilemmas whose immediate effect was to undermine the supposed benefits of associating the program with a college. Important as well, their ultimate arbitration has important consequences for the identity of professionals and their ability to exercise power in society.

I take the rest of this chapter to address the role of place in shaping power and identity in CPE in three interrelated dimensions and then illustrate with further examples elaborating on the introductory anecdote. First, I look at the role of physical place in continuing education. How did the physical location of the college campus contribute to constructing the professional identity and power of the participating professionals? Second, I try to show how the place of the campus helped to construct social networks associated with the prestige of academia rather than with the privilege of a resort. Third, I discuss the creation of professional discourse shaped by its location in an academic place. I conclude with suggestions for how we might rethink our roles as continuing educators in shaping professionals' power relations in society. To begin, I introduce the role of place in shaping power relations by discussing the analytical tools I use in this chapter.

Place Matters: Shaping Power and Identity

I draw on a specific theoretical discussion to analyze the relationship between place and CPE. Until recently, most "modern" (the allusion is both particular and discursive in referring to the dominance of technical rational thinking in adult education) adult education theory has tended to be functionalist, that is, structuralist, ahistorical, and apolitical. In recent decades there has been a decided attempt to historicize U.S. adult education as well as engage in a more "critical" analysis of it in order to understand better our political and ethical responsibilities as adult educators. Such analysis is certainly important to understanding how we have come to be who we are as adult educators (Wilson & Melichar, 1995) and contributes significantly to heightening our awareness of the political conditions of planning practice (Sork, 2000). Such analyses, though quite important, are limited because understanding the role of power in adult education practice is more than a matter of revealing its historical antecedents or theorizing its presence in the here and now. Both frames of analysis struggle with their perceived lack of utility. People in the everyday often find it too easy to dismiss their insights because the practical relevance of those insights remains unapparent. In an attempt to address that legitimate concern, I draw on a frame of social analysis to help understand the political consequences of everyday adult education practice, particularly in terms of how our practice contributes to shaping relations of power in society.

Specifically I will draw on related literatures focused, on the one hand, on reasserting "space" into social analysis (Bird, Curtis,

Putnam, Robertson, & Tickner, 1993; Friedland & Boden, 1994; Lefebvre, 1974/1991; Soja, 1989) and, on the other hand, on "locating the politics of identity" (Keith & Pile, 1993). These intersecting conversations are fascinating and quite rich, but I can only assert a couple of starting points for this chapter. First, place is a key component of social analysis, and place is fundamental to understanding the formation of identity. For understanding the role of place in creating a social geography of human identity and interaction, there are a number of insightful analyses; see in particular the edited volumes by Friedland and Boden (1994) and Keith and Pile (1993) as well as the works on space and postmodernity of Harvey (1989), Jameson (1989), Lefebvre (1974/1991), and Soja (1989). Second, place thus has to be seen as a constituting and constituted dimension of human interaction as well as a significant factor in the politics of identity. Practically, this leads to the agenda of looking at how place shapes adult education practice in continuing education. More specifically in this chapter, I argue that the social construction of place is directly implicated in the production and reproduction of power differentials (Harvey, 1993b) in CPE. I parrot Harvey's question (1993b), By what social processes is place constructed? in order to ask how place shapes and produces power and identity in continuing education for the professions. Thus the key issue I take on is how to understand the relationships among place, power, and identity. The practical problem I examine here is the way in which place is implicated in shaping what many take to be the apolitical, routine technical work of planning, producing, and managing CPE.

A Geography of Power: Place, Community Identity, and Discourse

David Harvey, a noted theorist of the postmodern (1989), outlines the key questions that I introduced earlier about the relationships among place, power, and identity. While he lodges his comments in an analysis of historical materialism's critique of capitalism (a tack I don't pursue here but that is necessarily a corollary analysis of this argument), he captures one of the central insights of the reassertion of space into social analysis in claiming "that there are real geographies of social action, real as well as metaphorical territories and spaces of power" (1993b, p. 3). Harvey argues that "place in whatever guise is, like space and time . . . a social construct. The only interesting question that can be asked is: by what social process(es) is place constructed?" (p. 5). Beginning with this contention, Harvey then asks "why and by what means do social beings invest places (localities, regions, states, communities, or whatever) with social power; and how and for what purposes is that power then deployed and used across a highly differentiated system of interlinked places?" (p. 21).

With that observation, Harvey configures the relationships I examine in this chapter. Harvey, as well as several others, such as Soja (1989), draws heavily from the noted French geographer Lefebvre (1974/1991). Describing what he terms the Lefebvrian matrix, Harvey outlines the frames of spatial analysis that I use in this chapter to analyze CPE. He begins with a premise that is then articulated as analytical categories and thus warrants citing at some length here:

> The material practices and experiences entailed in the construction and experiential qualities of place must be dialectically interrelated with the way places are both represented and imagined. This leads me . . . to think through how places are constructed and experienced as *material artifacts;* how they are represented in *discourse;* and how they are used in turn as representations, as *"symbolic places,"* in contemporary culture. The dialectical interplay between experience, perception and imagination in place construction then becomes the focus of attention. But we also need to work simultaneously" across the relations between distanciation (presence/absence and spatial scale), appropriation, domination and production of places. This may all seem rather daunting, especially when coupled with the fact that the matrix provides a mere framework across which social relations of class, gender, community, ethnicity or race operate. But this seems to me the only way to attack the rich complexity of social processes of place construction in a coherent way. [Harvey, 1993b, p. 17, emphasis added]

Daunting indeed! Such a series of claims needs some unpacking. Harvey, among many others, is deeply concerned with what is often termed the crisis in representation resulting from the disintegration, deconstruction, reconstruction, evolution—pick a school, any school of thought—of modernity in the late twentieth century (Friedland & Boden, 1994). With all our ways of "knowing" largely destabilized by the cacophony of contesting voices vying for a front-line claim on just what *is* happening at the millennium, the range of possibility of understanding seems at times to expand almost exponentially. Like so many in this turbulent time, Harvey (1993a) is having to reposition his materialist and critical theorist concerns with social justice to take into account the fragility of ever knowing anything with any certainty. Thus, within this crisis he looks to new forms of analysis to further an agenda of social justice without that agenda itself becoming calcified as dead rhetoric.

So just what is he trying to say here, and how should we go about understanding the problem? A recurring problem in the crisis in representation is the significant poststructuralist question of subjectivity. Harvey goes right after this with his analysis of place (as do many in the politics of identity conversation; see Keith & Pile, 1993). Harvey argues that there are complex interrelationships among what people actually do ("material practices"), how they understand what they do ("represent and imagine"), and how their doing and understanding are embedded in the actual places in which they occur ("the construction and experiential qualities of space"). In the debate between a sanctified cogito and an inscribed subjectivity, Harvey weighs in by saying that in efforts to understand the complex dimensions of human interaction, we have to recognize a "locality" to them, a "placeness" that is both constituted as well as constituting, or as Giddens (1979) would say, both medium and outcome.

With representation thus located (though reliably variable), we then have to ask in what ways it is located. Harvey's response (1989) is to outline the Lefebvrian matrix as a way: place as physical place, as a community of social interactions, and as discourse about physical and imagined place. Whereas Harvey's theoretical and political agenda is for historical materialism to "take its geography seriously" (1993b, p. 3), I am more interested in pursuing his analytical agenda of mapping "real geographies of social action . . . and spaces of power" (p. 3). To do that I am going to analytically appropriate his categories to ask how place is implicated in producing power and professional identity in CPE. By way of appropriating those categories, I will alter them somewhat to talk first about how people associate with specific places in order to establish community. Next I analyze how participants use the established community as a place in which they construct a discourse that defines their professional identity associated with the specific place. I then argue that these located human practices produce both professional identity and the power that professionals exercise in society. To do that I return to recounting more events from the opening anecdote to illustrate these categories. As I do so, I will also use these analytical categories of place, community, and discourse to comment on what role place, community, and discourse play in producing and reproducing the identity this group of professionals was trying to construct for itself as well as the professional power they were hoping to achieve through this process of locating their professional identity.

Place and Power in Continuing Professional Education

This section shows how place, community, and discourse come together to construct the identity and power of the participants and the profession, and how identity and power are played out through and in place.

Place

The idea of place may be the most commonsensically obvious of this analysis. After all, most of us do have a sense of our physical whereabouts. Yet our assumptions about what place *means* are often taken for granted and left undisclosed. When pressed we can say that our home means *this* or that the place we grew up means *that*. It gets more difficult when we semiotically wonder about where we work or why we gather in some places to do certain things as opposed to other places. For most of us, geography is associated with the "physicalness" of our world: hills, valleys, mountains, crops, water, seasons, land forms, and where and how people live in the midst of the planet's physical contours. Geographers, as well as postmodernists and feminists, however, have significantly stepped to the forefront of much social analysis in the last thirty years to offer insightful interpretations for understanding the meaning of place

(Soja, 1989) by seeing place "as a fusion of space and experience and a context for action" (Friedland & Boden, 1994, p. 24). I have introduced some of this analysis already. More directly though, I argue that place does more than provide the "settings of interaction" (Giddens, 1984), because place "is produced and reproduced and thus represents the site and outcome of social, political, and economic struggle" (Keith & Pile, 1993, p. 24). My starting point is that place itself is a fundamental constituent of knowledge/power regimes (Gordon, 1980; Lefebvre, 1974/1991; Soja, 1989). This means that we have to come to understand how place is represented, how its meaning is produced, who gets to produce that meaning, and how the meaning is used. So what was the role of place in this CPE program?

Much of my response is suggested in the opening anecdote, but I'll spin out the meaning of place in a bit more detail now. As I indicated earlier, the specific site of the college campus was a very important place for me, the participants, and the profession itself. In terms of seeing this place as a site for constituting certain social practices, the college campus represented certain significant connotations and values. We collectively presumed (as Harvey would say, we imagined the symbolic meaning) that by meeting physically in this place we could then become deliberately associated with the putative authority and legitimacy of academic enterprises. Now I say "we" here somewhat grandly, for only some of us involved in the planning and production of the program actually were able to articulate this attempt to associate the profession and our organization with the college. For example, some members of the organization had already helped establish a concentrated cohort master's degree program at this college, one of the first intact graduate degree programs in the country. These leaders responsible for planning the association's education programs knew practically what the history of higher education has demonstrated dramatically: that for the past 150 years, any occupation that had successfully elevated itself in the public's eye to the status of "profession" had done so by locating itself specifically in universities that explicitly took on the role of producing (in other words, researching) the scientific knowledge needed to identify the expertise of the profession as well as the role of training the practitioners in the use of that expertise in the pursuit of the profession (Larson, 1979;

Schön, 1983). This formula of linking knowledge production with professional training is so well established that most of us take it for granted. However, a number of leaders in this organization did not. They explicitly worked to locate their programs on academic campuses because they believed it would be instrumental in professionalizing the occupation, and I was quite supportive of that strategy at the time. Indeed, I was often a spokesperson for and to the organization in presenting the case for why our programs *had* to be located across the country on college campuses whenever possible, rather than at the resort hotels that participants often listed on evaluations as their preferred location. In fact, this concept of linking the profession with academic research and training was typically a significant topic in my orientation talk at programs' plenary introductory sessions; my job was to convince participants of the significance of our decision to locate these programs in these places.

So the importance of locating, of placing the program physically, on a college campus had real as well as symbolic meaning. In deliberately associating the continuing education programs with the legitimacy bestowed by academic auspices, the association was signaling to its members and the public that practitioners who received their training from the association had acquired the requisite knowledge and skills, and therefore power, to do their work as professionals. Given that historically this occupation had not successfully managed this transition from trade to profession, the use of the "college" was quite significant in establishing its professional legitimacy, which depended, as Foucault would say, on establishing a productive relationship between knowledge and power. (And universities have—until recently—quite successfully cornered the market on such relationships.)

Community Identity

Community is of course a notoriously difficult notion to define. For much traditional sociology and anthropology, community has consisted of the place in which face-to-face social interaction happens on a recurring basis (Giddens, 1990). Although some might put forth the notion that such face-to-faceness has become both undermined and fragmented in our globalizing and telecommunicating world, for many humans the "compulsion of proximity"

(Boden & Molotch, 1994) still remains an essential dimension to constituting human community. Boden and Molotch argue that community depends on "the robust nature and enduring necessity of traditional [meaning face-to-face] human communication procedures" (1994, p. 258). They argue that for biographical and historical reasons, "copresence," although mediated in a modern-postmodern world of digitalism, remains "the fundamental mode of human intercourse and socialization. . . . When people can't actually secure a needed state of copresence, they ordinarily strive to approximate it as best they can: the phone, for example, is better than a memo, a swift e-mail exchange better than a letter. This preference for 'upgrade' toward more personal forms of communication has consequences for how individuals structure their daily calendar and how human activity is organized geographically" (p. 258). As E. P. Thompson's classic study (1963) of the rise of English working-class communities demonstrates historically, and despite claims to the contrary, such "proximity" remains central to human community. As Revill (1993) says, community "has been championed as a source of identity, of moral and social stability, of shared meaning and mutual co-operation" (p. 119) and does have an important "part to play in the way people think about themselves, in the construction of subjectivity" (p. 120). Revill further argues that the "social and physical boundaries and the rituals" that define communities "therefore become of paramount importance to the construction of community" because it is about "defining and ordering relationships between you and me, us and them" (p. 130). Revill suggests that communities shape the production of identity through informal social networks, the shared experience of people, and a sense of history. Let me illustrate in terms of this continuing education program.

The real physical location of the college campus was important for establishing the symbolic meaning of the program. The physical place was also important for creating space for copresence. Now, of course, that copresence would be possible at any site chosen for the program. But in this case, the need to legitimize the occupation as a profession by locating the program on a college campus was crucial to shaping the sense of community identity the participants were constructing. So it was important for that copresence to occur in a place that would define the meaning of the community in such a way that would promote a professional identity. Now it is fairly routine to hear professionals proclaim that although the organized events of any program or conference are important, the "real" reason they go is for the professional networking, the collegiality, the "informal" interacting with others so as to make or continue important professional contacts. Thus our strategy as programmers was to provide a place in which those significant interactions could occur but would have a specific meaning that would contribute to developing a sense of professional community identity. Although we were routinely challenged on this, a college was essential to us in establishing the legitimacy of the profession in a different way than a resort hotel, which would only speak to the privilege of established professions.

Such a strategy is so commonplace that its enactment is too simply seen as a technical, logistical planning task. Not so here, for we specifically created conditions on this campus that would favor, indeed perhaps accelerate, the construction of a professional community through face-to-face interaction. That meant concentrating the interaction in several ways. First, the program was an intensive "short" course, a common tactic in business and professional contexts. Classes ran for eight seat hours a day for four days. All breaks (scheduled to be thirty minutes but often running forty-five) and meals were communal. In this case, as already alluded to, there was only one site for accommodations. (Whenever possible, we tried to locate accommodations on the campuses themselves.) The point is that the program participants were spending approximately twelve to fourteen hours a day together for four days of intense face-to-face interaction in a highly charged professional and academic learning context. It is also important to know that even though the programs were presented regionally at multiple sites across the United States, program participants at any one program were likely to come from all over the country. That was the case for the program described here. Even though this program was located adjacent to a major midwestern city, among the 125 participants some thirty states were represented, and only about twenty-five participants came from the immediate urban area.

Another programmatic dimension also contributed to the professional community aspects we were trying to develop. Like most professions, the participants represented a number of subsets of professional practice. So we really were not producing a single course for a profession but a series of simultaneous courses for multiple subdisciplines. Creating a place of community development was thus particularly significant, because members of the various subsets had historically been given little opportunity for cross-discipline interaction or, for that matter, much allegiance to the umbrella occupation itself. In other words, participants tended to identify only with their market- or expertise-defined subdiscipline rather than with the occupation as a whole. It was therefore important for these programs to run simultaneously in the same site so as to create opportunities for interdiscipline as well as intra-discipline interactions.

So by using both the organization's and participants' professed interests in CPE, we devised specific conditions that would also enhance the development of professional community by using the specific meanings associated with the college campus site. Creating these conditions for copresence thus contributed directly to the development of a national community identity. These regional sites, with national participation, provided the opportunities on an accelerated basis for intense face-to-face community formation that was often easily sustained and furthered by the digital conveniences on which we have now come to routinely rely. But the meaning of the site itself was important too in forming this community. At a resort complex, CPE is typically considered "routine business" and viewed by many as a sign of privilege. On a college campus, however, the same types of activity are couched as "professional learning" and "professional development" that has a formal education imprimatur (that is, participation in the association's continuing education could be accrued for formal graduate credit). Thus the identity of the participants is shaped by the location of their programmatic participation.

Discourse

A central solidifier of place and community is discourse. The analysis of discourse, a multifaceted field of inquiry with seemingly endless contradictory intentions (Schiffrin, 1994), has nonetheless in certain guises led to significant insights into understanding how hegemonic social practices are played out (Luke, 1995). Harvey's notion of discourse is an implicit one that he uses to relate "how places are constructed and experienced" to how they are represented symbolically (1993b, p. 17). Places are "represented in discourse" by the "dialectical interplay between experience, perception, and imagination." But I want to push his notion more explicitly to say that discourse shapes "the logic of relations of contiguity in space and time and, in so doing, pattern[s] the organization and meaning of our lives" (Friedland & Boden, 1994, p. 24). So how does discourse pattern meaning and life, and in what ways is it associated with place? Foucault has perhaps been most prominent in "archaeologically" constructing "genealogies" of modern science discourses in terms of how those discourses underlie and produce knowledge/power regimes (1970, 1972, 1977; Gordon, 1980; Rabinow, 1984). Throughout his work, Foucault repeatedly returned to the theme that different historical periods define different modalities of "truth." Modernity's truth, as he would say, is disciplinary (1970). Disciplines are productive relations of discourses and power (the knowledge/power couplet, as it has become known): "the exercise of power perpetually creates knowledge and, conversely, knowledge constantly induces effects of power" (quoted in Gordon, 1980, p. 52).

Two points are relevant for the discussion here. First, "power and discourse are integral, not exterior, to one another" (Friedland & Boden, 1994, p. 24). In Foucault's analysis, modernity can best be characterized as the rise of disciplinary bodies of knowledge that are used to replace the more traditional forms of power in society. Disciplinary knowledge (such as psychoanalysis, medicine, architecture, military science, education, and law—the disciplines are the professions of the twentieth century) is created to organize power, to make it more productive. Disciplines do so by using knowledge to create hierarchies of power in which discipline experts ("practitioners") use discipline knowledge to say who is sick and who is not, who is criminal and how prisons operate, who is mad and who sane, and who builds buildings and how they function—in a word, to create "subjects" of humans through the exercise of disciplinary knowledge/power. Second, "the knowledge/power couplet has a distinctive spatiotemporal base" (Friedland & Boden, 1994, p. 25). Another essential Foucault insight is his historical observation that power's place, once a visible, visceral manifestation of the state (public punishment, armies, fortifications, thrones), is now by way of the disciplines diffused through less visible workings of bureaucracies and institutions (schools, prisons, hospitals). Thus the place of power has changed in modern times; the chief modality of power now is its exercise by professionals through observation—surveillance—rather than overt coercion (Foucault, 1970; Gordon, 1980). Professional discourse represents dominant understandings of how the world works and of people's relations to each other in the world. Power emanates from these structures of knowledge that allow practitioners of disciplines ("professionals") to define others as "objects" of professional knowledge and manipulation (Wilson, 1999). And for the last 150 years, the font of that disciplinary power has increasingly resided in academic places.

Using Foucault, I suggest that the construction of a specific occupational discourse focused on producing a body of knowledge was essential to creating the community identity of professionals and the knowledge/power they needed in order to identify themselves to themselves and to the public as professionals. The relationship between place and community becomes more significant when tied into the creation of a specific disciplinary discourse. As I have insinuated, the difficulty facing this occupation in establishing its identity and power had been its historical failure to develop a disciplinary body of knowledge. As is the case with most professions, producing disciplinary knowledge and training practitioners has to be located in an academic setting; otherwise the knowledge and training are not considered legitimate by the profession or the public. Thus the program was deliberately placed on an academic campus to frame its community in a discursive fashion.

Now back to the story. A key player also happened to be a nemesis in our attempts to build these relationships among place, power, and identity. I indicated earlier that the program liaison had other forms of involvement beyond programmatic responsibilities for this program; the nature of these other forms is significant for understanding the relationships, events, and intended outcomes. The program liaison was a professor of classical philosophy for this college. When the association leaders decided to depend on this professor for educational guidance, their cultural assumptions about place and power misfired. The educational leaders of the association contracted with this professor to produce a book of the disciplinary "theory," which they believed essential to establishing the occupation's credentials. (They did this after failing in an attempt to purchase the rights to an out-of-print text on their knowledge base.) Of course, the immediate problem was that the professor, because he had neither training nor field experience in the occupation, had little working knowledge of what constituted the discipline's base nor what Foucault would refer to as its "technologies," the professional mechanisms of practical knowledge use. So he proceeded in typical academic fashion to write a book based on his review of other people's work in this occupation. In my view this was a significant miscue but was beyond my influence, for the contractual agreements were in place before I became involved. The situation was further misfigured by having the professor—precisely because he represented the authority and legitimacy of academics—do introductory "theory" lectures to plenary sessions. The logic behind having him do this was reasonable with regard to the analysis I present here; it was the execution that disabled the production of these relations. The plenary lecture for this program, in its effort to infuse practitioners with a sense of community and discipline knowledge, actually produced the opposite. For this specific program, the professor insisted on forwarding incomplete drafts of isolated chapters from the disciplinary text, from which he then lectured rather inchoately in the plenary session. It was, of course, immediately obvious to seasoned practitioners that the professor's efforts were rather distanced from the actual knowledge needs of practitioners; more novice participants were simply befuddled. So instead of promoting the production of community through the dissemination of general professional knowledge, the session instead reinforced the subdisciplines' proclivities to think that their own market-defined focus was more important than the overall disciplinary knowledge being touted as necessary for community identity and professional power. As might be expected, the result in this instance was that the typical practitioner's suspicions of academic knowledge were confirmed, which meant that the attempt to fuse place, community, and discourse so as to build professional power and identity was not particularly successful. Indeed, in my tenure with this organization, this discursive strategy never really worked because it consistently tended to alienate practitioners. For both reasonable and unreasonable reasons, practitioners in this occupation tended to insist on their idiosyncratic contextual experience as more valuable knowledge.

The Role of Place in Shaping Professional Power and Identity

It is not my intent to critique this specific instance for good or bad continuing education planning practices. There are other examples of this organization's programming in which these relations worked more effectively (but never without considerable tension). Rather my interest is in using the events to understand the complex relations involved in creating identity tied to place to produce disciplinary power. How is place interwoven in the production and reproduction of power and identity? By way of introduction to the previous section, I indicated that I was using Harvey's analytical categories of place, community, and discourse in order to understand the relations among place, professional identity/power, and educational processes. The point of the anecdote is to show how the construction of power depends on creating discourse linked to locating communities in specific places. Put differently, locating a program is not simply a matter of logistical planning. It is clear to me that, although there were significant miscues in the planning, this production of this specific program was drawing both subliminally and overtly on significant cultural assumptions and practices central to establishing power and identity. At an analytical level, I think the discussion uses certain insights of the new geography and locational politics of identity to better understand the complex social processes by which we create power and identity. Much of the programmatic effort in this case was intentionally directed at producing and enhancing the discipline power of the occupation in order for the profession to be better able to exercise that power in its practices. Thus I would support the notion that there are significant spatial dimensions to human interaction and that the production of professional power is indeed embedded in the spatial definition of our professional communities.

These observations have distinct practical ramifications for planning CPE. To this day I remain quite ambivalent about my activities as an educator in this and similar programs. Consequently, a significant question for me has been the role of continuing educators in producing such programs, particularly in terms of how our programmatic actions are linked to shaping relations of power. I think it is apparent that we do have a role in producing and shaping these relations of power and identity whether we want to or not. In the human geography I have attempted to sketch here, as educators we are quite involved in producing and altering relations of power. In my view there is no way to escape such complicity. It appears quite clear in this anecdote that planning and production decisions (both deliberate and accidental) regarding what are too often considered technical programmatic issues had significant effects on how the place, community, and discourse dimensions shaped the power and identity of the participating professionals. These are not issues that can be safely subsumed under the guise of technical expertise, nor can they be ignored. The question is, what do we do about them?

Where Lies Responsibility?

Presumptions about how the world works and about adult education's contributions are built into much adult education practice, including CPE. As is more and more frequently pointed out, adult educators have attempted for too long to define themselves professionally as technicians of educational process. Building on previous work (Cervero & Wilson, 1994, 1996), I am using this chapter to argue for a specific politicalness to our practice—which leads to the necessity of naming and standing our ethical ground. If theory is to be plausible, strategic, and morally grounded (Cervero & Wilson, 1994; Forester, 1989), then we must work to make clear the politics and ethics that illuminate our technical expertise.

"Responsibility for the world we make" is a phrase Cervero and I coined a few years ago (1994) to highlight the political and ethical demands of adult education program planning, indeed our practical work as educators in general. In that formulation we argued for a "pragmatics with vision" that entails linking "how to" with "what for." Our point was that adult educators must recognize and take responsibility for the political ethical consequences of their educational actions. A formative principle for seeing and enacting that responsibility was our promotion of substantive democratic participation. Subsequently, we have begun working out such a pragmatics under the rubric of "working the planning table" (Cervero & Wilson, 1996, 1998). Recently I have argued that continuing professional educators, because of the increasing professional systemization and concomitant decrease of professional autonomy, must take on deliberate client advocacy roles (Wilson, 2000). Here I want to expand those obligations with a sense of place, power, and identity, to enlarge our sense of responsibility by becoming aware of the semiotic significance of what too many of us take to be routine technical dimensions to continuing education work. This is a daunting task from which many educators will clearly shy away, for it is difficult, first, to see these deeply embedded, often hegemonic cultural practices and, second, to have the political skill and ethical vision to challenge them. Yet if we are to become responsible educators, we must take up these challenges. For if we do not, we become unwitting accomplices in the differentiated production of power through our educational efforts, and all our philosophical and historical rhetoric about social change and democratic participation is for naught.

References

Bird, J., Curtis, B., Putnam, T., Robertson, G., & Tickner, L. (Eds.). (1993). *Mapping the futures: Local cultures, global change.* London: Routledge.

Boden, D., & Molotch, H. (1994). The compulsion of proximity. In R. Friedland & D. Boden (Eds.), *NowHere: Space, time and modernity* (pp. 257–286). Berkeley: University of California Press.

Cervero, R. M., & Wilson, A. L. (1994). *Planning responsibly for adult education: A guide to negotiating power and interests.* San Francisco: Jossey-Bass.

Cervero, R. M., & Wilson, A. L. (1996). *What really matters in adult education program planning: Lessons in negotiating power and interests.* New Directions for Adult and Continuing Education, no. 69. San Francisco: Jossey-Bass.

Cervero, R. M., & Wilson, A. L. (1998). Working the planning table: The political practice of adult education. *Studies in Continuing Education, 20*(1), 5–22.

Forester, J. (1989). *Planning in the face of power.* Berkeley: University of California.

Foucault, M. (1970). *The order of things.* New York: Random House.

Foucault, M. (1972). *The archaeology of knowledge and the discourse on language* (A. Sheridan, Trans.). New York: Pantheon Books.

Foucault, M. (1977). *Discipline and punish* (A. Sheridan, Trans.). New York: Vintage Books.

Friedland, R., & Boden, D. (Eds.). (1994). *NowHere: Space, time and modernity.* Berkeley: University of California Press.

Giddens, A. (1979). *Central problems in social theory.* Berkeley: University of California Press.

Giddens, A. (1984). *The constitution of society.* Berkeley: University of California Press.

Giddens, A. (1990). *The consequences of modernity.* Stanford, CA: Stanford University Press.

Gordon, C. (Ed.). (1980). *Power/knowledge: Selected interviews and other writings, 1972–1977.* New York: Pantheon Books.

Harvey, D. (1989). *The condition of postmodernity.* Cambridge, MA: Blackwell.

Harvey, D. (1993a). Class relations, social justice and the politics of difference. In M. Keith & S. Pile (Eds.), *Place and the politics of identity* (pp. 41–65). London: Routledge.

Harvey, D. (1993b). From space to place and back again: Reflections on the condition of postmodernity. In J. Bird (Ed.), *Mapping the futures: Local cultures, global change* (pp. 3–30). London: Routledge.

Jameson, F. (1989). *Postmodernism, or the cultural logic of late capitalism.* Durham, NC: Duke University Press.

Keith, M., & Pile, S. (Eds.). (1993). *Place and the politics of identity.* London: Routledge.

Larson, M. (1979). *The rise of professionalism.* Berkeley: University of California Press.

Lefebvre, H. (1991). *The production of space* (D. Nicholson-Smith, Trans.). Oxford, England: Blackwell. (Original work published 1974)

Luke, A. (1995). Text and discourse in education: An introduction to critical discourse analysis. In M. W. Apple (Ed.), *Review of research in education* (Vol. 21, pp. 3–48). Washington, DC: American Educational Research Association.

Rabinow, P. (Ed.). (1984). *The Foucault reader.* New York: Pantheon Books.

Revill, G. (1993). Reading Rosehill: Community, identity and inner-city Derby. In M. Keith & S. Pile (Eds.), *Place and the politics of identity* (pp. 117–140). London: Routledge.

Schiffrin, D. (1994). *Approaches to discourse.* Cambridge, MA: Blackwell.

Schön, D. (1983). *The reflective practitioner.* New York: Basic Books.

Soja, E. (1989). *Postmodern geographies: The reassertion of space in critical social theory.* London: Verso.

Sork, T. (2000). Planning educational programs. In A. L. Wilson & E. R. Hayes (Eds.), *Handbook of adult and continuing education: New edition* (pp. 171–190). San Francisco: Jossey-Bass.

Thompson, E. P. (1963). *The making of the English working class.* New York: Vintage Books.

Wilson, A. L. (1999). Creating identities of dependency: Adult education as a knowledge-power regime. *International Journal of Lifelong Education, 18*(2), 85–93.

Wilson, A. L. (2000). Professional practice in the modern world. In V. W. Mott & B. J. Daley (Eds.), *Charting a course for continuing professional education: Reframing professional practice* (pp. 71–79). New Directions for Adult and Continuing Education, no. 86. San Francisco: Jossey-Bass.

Wilson, A. L., & Melichar, K. (1995). A "rhetoric of disruption": Remembering the past by way of challenging our present educational practices. *International Journal of Lifelong Education, 14*(6), 422–433.

Chapter Thirteen

Solidarity and Power in Urban Gay Communities

Planning HIV Prevention Education

Kimberly B. Sessions, Ronald M. Cervero

One pleasant afternoon three years ago, Kimberly's friend Daniel was offered a job as an adult educator. Not a greatly unusual event perhaps, except that the offer came while he was standing in the lobby of a hotel in Washington, D.C. The timing of the offer couldn't have been better, though. Daniel was at the hotel attending a conference on HIV/AIDS education as one part of an effort to reengage in the world after the AIDS-related death of his life partner. The conference had proven to be unexpectedly exhilarating, and Daniel began to find himself intrigued by the possibility of reinstilling meaning in his own life by making a difference in the lives of other people. So when Greg, the education director of Helping Hearts, Inc., talked, Daniel listened. On the surface, the job Greg was offering sounded interesting: Helping Hearts is a major AIDS service organization in the Southeast, and they were looking for a director of gay outreach. If he took the job, Daniel would have wide latitude in devising and implementing HIV/AIDS prevention programs targeting urban gay men—an important component of the agency's larger mission to reduce the total number of new HIV infections occurring in the general population. It sounded, in short, like a dream opportunity. And because of that, Daniel was pulled up short by something Greg said almost in passing as the impromptu job interview was drawing to a close. "By the way, you're HIV-positive, aren't you?" Greg asked, more as a statement than a question.

"Uh, no," answered Daniel after a short hesitation. "Is that a problem?"

"No . . . of course not," Greg responded after a longer hesitation and a quick laugh. "It's just that all the rest of us at the upper management level *are*, and it would have been nice if you belonged to the club too."

The club. With just two words, that phrase—with all its connotations of exclusion, vested self-interest, and power—puts a label on one of the most closeted but powerful realities of HIV-prevention education for gay men in the United States: in large urban settings, HIV-positive gay men form a self-aware community of necessarily and rightfully protected individuals whose interests have come to define how HIV/AIDS is addressed among gay men. As "first among equals," HIV-positive men are the ones whose interests determine what is said and what is hidden from view, determine whose interests are primary and whose are subordinated when planning HIV prevention programs in the gay community.

As Daniel quickly discovered, this dynamic was particularly clear at Helping Hearts. When he arrived, the only organization in town dedicated to providing education to those most affected by the AIDS epidemic was not fielding a single prevention program targeting uninfected gay men. Not one. As Greg admitted to Kimberly at the time, "We have yet to do a program that is specifically for HIV-negative men. Specifically and uniquely." Remarkably, two years later, when Daniel left the organization in frustration over his inability to stem the rising tide of newly infected gay men, there were still no programs in place that "specifically and uniquely" targeted this high-risk group.

At first glance this phenomenon appears to make no sense at all. After all, who else would be the target of prevention education if not the uninfected? But as the discussion that follows makes clear, HIV prevention education in the gay community is fully subject to the larger political forces driving that community; it does not and cannot exist in a vacuum. And in the lived experience of the community in which Helping Hearts is located, the bulk of material, symbolic, and financial resources is reserved first and foremost for the needs of HIV-positive men. This is no secret to anyone. As the executive director of Helping Hearts—himself an HIV-infected gay man—said, "HIV-negative men don't fully fit in; they don't belong. The sense of community is built around the people who have HIV." Kyle, an HIV-negative participant in one of Helping Hearts' educational programs agreed: "I am sure it's like this golden door opening [when you become infected]. Maybe I am romanticizing it, but it seems totally wonderful: you enter this wonderful world of open arms and loving people when you become positive, but when you are negative there is nothing. There is no one; there is nothing out there."

Although it is the result of intentional actions, this jarring reality is by no means maliciously intended. HIV-positive men have a necessary and rightful place at the protected heart of gay community life. There is no dispute that discrimination against people with HIV is still a fact of life in the United States, and HIV-positive gay men have borne more than their share of the burden. Nevertheless, a fiercely enforced, if unintended, result of this necessary altruism is that in making sure that men with HIV are sheltered inside the circle of community support and attention, AIDS activists have all but closed that circle to others who are still struggling to remain uninfected. Culturally, symbolically, and materially, HIV-negative gay men have become the "Other." For this reason, gay men do not experience the results of prevention education as abstract events but as extensions of a culture in which HIV-negative gay men face a daily choice between remaining uninfected and finally fitting in. At Helping Hearts, as elsewhere in the gay community, if you want to take full advantage of the education, care, and compassion available to you, it's best to be infected.

Since its first documented appearance among gay men in the early 1980s, HIV in the United States has spread across all boundaries of race, gender, sexual orientation, ethnicity, and religion. In the year 2000 there is no longer any social group in the United States completely untouched by HIV/AIDS. This chapter is intended to discuss how one group—urban gay men—has incorporated one response to the epidemic—prevention education—into the politics of everyday life. Specifically, the purpose of this chapter is to explore the various compelling and legitimate pressures that have acted to shape a prevention curriculum that is designed, ironically enough, around the interests of men for whom the primary benefits of prevention are no longer relevant. This chapter will show how acting on the pragmatic need to protect men with HIV has unintentionally served to replace one disenfranchised group with another and created a situation in which education planners have little choice but to act against the interests of those persons who most stand to benefit from their education. Much of the material in the chapter is taken from a larger study of Helping Hearts' educational programming (Sessions, 1998; Sessions & Cervero, 1999). Although the names of the people and the agency have been changed, all of the descriptions of the agency and the quotes are real.

The Politics of Planning HIV Education in Urban Gay Communities

As we have asserted, it is vital that the gay community protect the interests of men with HIV, if for no other reason than that society at large has shown a reluctance to provide that protection itself. But formulating policy based on serving the interests of HIV-positive gay men above all else has created an unintended irony. By reinforcing the idea that HIV-negative men stand outside the circle of gay community support and attention, planners of prevention programs have successfully reproduced the dynamic that gay men generally face in relation to the larger heterosexual society. This can leave HIV-negative gay men feeling doubly excluded—an overwhelmingly hurtful experience for those who may have sought a sense of gay community in the first place precisely because they had spent a lifetime being the Other.

How did this come to be? How have Helping Hearts' program planners—compassionate and committed individuals with the best interests of their constituents at heart—find themselves responsible for creating the situation described here? We believe the answer lies in the politics that ground planning HIV prevention education in urban gay communities.

A Political Theory of Program Planning

Program planning for HIV prevention education, as in all other arenas of program planning practice (Cervero & Wilson, 1994, 1996,
1998), occurs in a turbulent world of multiple and conflicting pressures. Those pressures have been widely interpreted by prevention
educators at Helping Hearts as dictating that HIV-negative gay men
should not be singled out for special attention. This despite a ready
agreement that gay men are still at high risk for exposure to HIV
and that uninfected persons, if they are exposed to HIV, have
potentially more to lose than do already infected persons.

This seeming dichotomy—understanding versus action—
makes sense, however, if you realize that adult education is not
merely a process of meeting the needs of adult learners. Rather,
adult education is a struggle for and about the distribution of symbolic, cultural, and material resources. Envisioned in this way, the
production and implementation of adult education programs can
be seen as a fundamentally political process that occurs at the intersection of socially structured relations of power and people's
interests. Thus the political dynamics of Helping Hearts' social and
organizational context have as much, if not more, to do with creating the prevention education that exists today as do the ideals of
any individual program planner. The result of these dynamics at
Helping Hearts is a prevention philosophy that takes serostatus
into account only when the serostatus in question is HIV-positive.
There are programs at Helping Hearts that are specifically intended to help HIV-positive people cope with the reality of their
lives with HIV, but no programs that are specifically intended to
help HIV-negative men cope with the reality of theirs.

Drawing on theories of power in other areas of social life
(Forester, 1989; Giddens, 1979; Isaac, 1987), Cervero and Wilson
(1994, 1996, 1998) have theorized planning as a social activity
whereby people construct educational programs by negotiating personal, organizational, and social interests in contexts marked by
socially structured relations of power. A body of research (Archie-
Booker, Cervero, & Langone, 1999; Cervero & Wilson, 1996, 1998;
Mills, Cervero, Langone, & Wilson, 1995; Rees, Cervero, Moshi, &
Wilson, 1997; Sessions, 1998; Umble, 1998) has demonstrated that

adult educators consistently represent many interests in addition to those of the hypothetical "learner" in their planning and that these various interests inevitably form the basis of whatever programs are eventually produced. Furthermore, educators negotiate both *with* and *about* those various interests when planning programs. In short, negotiating interests constitutes the political process by which power is exercised in program planning. As a result, people's interests are causally related to all features—including the content and audience—of any adult education program.

Substantive Negotiations and Metanegotiations at Helping Hearts

Within this frame of reference, our explanation of planning at Helping Hearts focuses on the forms of negotiation that Elgstrom and Riis (1992) characterize as occurring at two levels: (1) *substantive negotiations* whereby people act *in* the web of power relations and interests to construct a program's purpose, content, and methods; and (2) *metanegotiations* whereby people act *on* the power relations and interests themselves, either maintaining or changing those macro-level boundaries. At Helping Hearts, the substantive negotiations produce the specific prevention education programs the agency sponsors, while leaving the power relations themselves untouched. These negotiations are influenced by three distinct sociocentric interests held by powerful stakeholders: first, that it is important to promote at least the outward appearance of gay community solidarity; second, that HIV-positive men should be protected from being disenfranchised by gay men themselves; and third, that the agency needs to have strong support within the communities that provide a significant proportion of its funding and volunteers.

At the level of substantive negotiations, these three interests have proven to be a stronger force in driving program design than any alternate interests have been. If this were not so, the program planners' oft-articulated interest in keeping HIV-negative gay men uninfected would certainly have resulted in programs specifically targeting those men. But there are no programs of this sort at Helping Hearts, nor are any planned. This fact alone—that programs targeting the most logical beneficiaries of primary prevention *still* do not exist seventeen years after the agency opened—reveals with startling clarity just how strong the need is to subordinate the unique interests of HIV-negative gay men to other, more pressing interests.

These essential political dynamics are complemented by negotiation at a more fundamental level: educators also negotiate *about* the interests and power relationships of the multiple stakeholders at the planning table. Thus the actions of planners at Helping Hearts, while directed toward constructing programs, are also directed toward reconstructing or maintaining the power relationships and interests themselves. Put another way, people's interests and power relations are not static but are continually affected by the very act of negotiation. As Forester (1989, p. 71) says, "Every organizational interaction or practical communication (including the nonverbal) not only produces a result, it reproduces, strengthening or weakening, the specific social working relations of those who interact." Thus the negotiations that people undertake to construct an adult education program always have two outcomes: the educational program itself (the negotiated intersection of personal and organizational interests) and the maintenance or transformation of the power relations and interests that drive the program. At Helping Hearts, not only do the three interests described earlier contribute to determining prevention program design; the resulting prevention program design also contributes to maintaining the strength of these three interests in the gay community.

The Politics of Planning Prevention Education at Helping Hearts

This section provides a social and historical background of the three sociocentric interests driving the planning of prevention education at Helping Hearts. It further shows how those interests are central to the process of constructing prevention education that inadvertently serves to disadvantage HIV-negative gay men.

Prevention Education and the Need for Community Solidarity

For all gay men, the challenges of living in the midst of the AIDS epidemic are highly personal. Coming from small towns or big cities across the country, many gay men still bear the scars of growing up outside the inner circle of community life, feeling isolated by an invisible but heavily stigmatized difference from "normal" (that is, heterosexual) people (Ball, 1996). In the late 1970s and early 1980s, San Francisco, New York, and other cities with large gay populations offered a place where gay men and women could find the acceptance they sought, a society where they could step inside the circle of community life and truly belong.

HIV threatened the solidarity of that community to the core. Not only did it reveal how fragile recently won civil liberties for gay men and women were (Rotello, 1997), but the earliest reports publicizing the emerging syndrome (for example, "Kaposi's Sarcoma and *Pneumocystis* Pneumonia Among Homosexual Men—New York City and California" [Centers for Disease Control and Prevention, 1981]) and the first terms used to describe the illness, *gay cancer* and GRID (Gay Related Immune Dysfunction), essentially welded the disease to gay identity both in the minds of the general public and in the minds of gay men themselves (Johnston, 1995; Rofes, 1996; Shilts, 1988). As a result, anything related to GRID—later known as AIDS—that threatened one member of the gay community was perceived as threatening the community as a whole. Where that threat originated from was irrelevant. As a result, disenfranchising gay men with AIDS—excluding them from the inner circle of community life—was perceived by the leadership of the gay community as being equally wrong whether it was the act of Senator Jesse Helms or of frightened gay men themselves.

Eighteen years later, many of the gay men planning education programs can barely remember a time before AIDS, but the psychic scarring continues. Educational programs result from the work of individuals who are doing the best job they can in the face of a very personal threat. The responses to these perceived threats—circle the wagons, protect the infected, and present at least the appearance of a unified front to the outside world (Patton, 1990; Rofes, 1996; Rotello, 1997)—have had tremendous implications for the way prevention education programs have been conceptualized and presented. These responses have, for one, required prevention education campaigns to insist that gay men treat each other equally— as equally dangerous, that is. For the entire history of the epidemic, gay men have been told that their best chance of preventing infection is to be "100 percent safe, 100 percent of the time." Unfortunately, there is a flaw in the assumption that undergirds this mantra. The advice to be 100 percent safe, 100 percent of the time is grounded on the simplistic premise that one is in danger from, or poses a danger to, every potential sexual partner encountered. Hence, if you are to remain protected from them (or they from you), it is absolutely essential to practice ceaseless vigilance, with no exceptions. In reality, not all gay men *are* at risk from (or pose a risk to) others, and institutionally ignoring this fact for the purposes of community solidarity dangerously disadvantages HIV-negative men. Why? Because ceaseless vigilance is impossible to maintain, because condoms are no less problematic for gay men than they are for men as a group (Odets, 1994; 1995), and because sharing responsibility equally sometimes means that no one actually accepts ownership of that responsibility. What the "100 percent safe, 100 percent of the time" educational mantra *does* do is discourage the public or private negotiation of sexual expression. In short, it preserves the illusion of community solidarity through the institutionalization of individual silence. And because HIV-negative men have potentially more to lose from unprotected exposure to HIV than do HIV-positive men, silence disproportionately oppresses the uninfected.

Program planners at Helping Hearts have mixed emotions about the ultimate utility of pushing the "100 percent safe, 100 percent of the time" mantra. Although they feel an obligation to support it professionally, they also acknowledge a personal inability to live consistently by its stringent dictates. For some individuals, this cognitive dissonance occasionally reveals itself as wildly inconsistent messages given during educational programs. For instance, after giving a standard lecture on the need for being 100 percent safe, 100 percent of the time, one HIV educator found himself advocating for gay men to negotiate trust as well as safety, because "HIV shouldn't be allowed to define our lives." As a way of emphasizing this, he then posed a question to the group about whether a hypothetical uninfected couple should engage in safer sex. And when one participant said—insisted—that they *should* engage in safer sex, regardless of their serostatus, the facilitator became angry and accused the participant of not valuing gay male relationships. The exchange left the (HIV-negative) program participant feeling hurt and confused. He had the strong impression, he said, that as far as safe sex was concerned the lesson was, "Let's not, and say we did." It is reasonable to suppose, however, that this was not the lesson the facilitator intended to give. Unfortunately the agency's institutionalized interest in promoting an appearance of solidarity about how gay men respond to the threat of HIV created an opportunity for intellectual and educational chaos when that interest collided with the realities of practice. Discussion was stifled in the name of quelling dissension, and at least one HIV-negative man was left feeling that he had received absolutely no support for practicing what was preached—that is, to consistently practice safer sex, regardless of the circumstances.

The need to promote at least the illusion of community solidarity also leaves institutional leaders feeling uncomfortable about being seen diverting resources to HIV-negative gay men from HIV-positive men or from programs targeting generic men, that is, men undifferentiated by serostatus. Doing so would be a betrayal of the "all for one and one for all" spirit of community solidarity. Historically, this discomfort has valid roots. When other agencies tried to single out HIV-negative people for support and attention, they were roundly criticized for it. For example, an article in the *St. Louis News-Telegraph* (Barnet, 1994) discusses an ACT UP/Kansas City advertisement in a local gay publication that "depicts money being flushed down a toilet" and has text that reads, "If you are spending one dime to support this HIV-negative group, this is one dime you are taking away from an HIV-positive person in need" (p. 2). Leaflets signed only "an HIV victim" that expressed similar views were distributed in Boston after the Boston AIDS Action Committee and Fenway Community Health Center publicized their sponsorship of an HIV-negative support and discussion group in December 1994 (Rofes, 1996).

Prevention Education and the Politics of Serostatus

Beyond the need for community solidarity is the even deeper need to protect the infected from being disenfranchised by gay men themselves. At the beginning of the epidemic this was difficult. Knowledge was scarce, and gay men were just as prone as anyone to fear and distrust people with AIDS. But that fear began to give way as members of the gay community's elite social and political leadership became known to be infected (Rofes, 1996). Because of their high profile, these men lent an air of heroic tragedy to the disease that went a long way toward turning people with HIV from objects of fear into human beings deserving of compassionate concern. Later, as more and more gay men went public with their HIV infection, and as advances in medical science were able to transmute the mantle of heroic suffering into one of heroic survival, the public identity boundaries between demigod and disease began to blur. Where once a person might have been influential despite having HIV, now he might be influential *because* he had HIV. For example, Odets (1995, p. 12) quotes one of his therapy patients as saying, "Matt and I were sitting around reading the [*POZ* magazine] interview [about the official spokesman of a San Francisco AIDS prevention campaign], and talking about how hot he is. And Matt said to me 'I'd like to be exactly like him—he's got everything a queer queen could want. He's got it made.' And I said 'Yeah, but he's got AIDS too.' And Matt said, 'So what? A lot of guys have AIDS. I mean, he wouldn't be where he is if he didn't have AIDS. He'd be hot, but that's a dime a dozen. Guys who have AIDS get a lot more attention.'"

The social and epidemiological implications of this perspective are far reaching. After all, when even the official spokesman for a campaign targeting HIV-negative men is not himself uninfected, it is a clear indication of the social status that HIV-infected men hold in the gay community. Furthermore, it goes a long way toward explaining why some men report that they have intentionally tried to become infected (Scarce, 1999; Schacker, Collier, Hughes, Shea, & Corey, 1996). "[This] is worrying," Daniel pointed out, "because it seems like the only way [for HIV-negative gay men] to become visible is to become infected. And they want to be visible."

He should know. When the story of Daniel's hotel lobby job interview got back to Richard, another HIV-negative division director at Helping Hearts, the "serostatist" perspective that Greg had displayed regarding Daniel's not being in the "club" dismayed but didn't particularly surprise him. As Richard reported later: "Well, the whole thing was presented as a disappointment that [Daniel] wouldn't be part of the head management club. And that hurt, because it really implied that *I* wasn't part of the club, and I had already been [at Helping Hearts] a while. But we brought some of this on ourselves; it is just a manifestation of the mind-set that we created by protecting HIV politically—people with HIV—so much that people with HIV gained the power to define who was and wasn't in the club by serostatus, not by something else." In short, AIDS educators have succeeded beyond their wildest dreams in protecting the infected from disenfranchisement by gay men. But in the calculus of community influence, lessening the disenfranchisement of HIV-positive men may have served only to increase the disenfranchisement of those who are HIV-negative.

Prevention Education and the Politics of Urban Gay Communities

The drive for at least the appearance of community solidarity and the related need to protect infected men from disenfranchisement are only two of the interests that have created a prevention agenda that disadvantages HIV-negative gay men. The power that local communities can wield over community-based AIDS service organizations (ASOs) has also played a role. From the beginning of the epidemic, there has been very little public funding for HIV/AIDS education targeting the gay community. Beginning in 1987 with the passing of the Helms amendment denying funding to any activities that "promote" homosexuality and promiscuity, the little education that has been developed by public health officials has been subject to severe restrictions and the continuing threat of censorship by local community standards boards (Patton, 1996).

Helping Hearts is familiar with the tension. In fact, the agency's executive director sees a major part of his job as serving as a buffer between the desires of the Helping Hearts education department and the sensibilities of funders from outside the gay community. As he notes, a sexually explicit ad campaign that educators might take for granted could absolutely appall a donor who never sees the campaign except when he or she comes to a board meeting. And an appalled donor is a reluctant one. "So as much as I'd like to say, 'That's life! That's the message we are trying to get across!'" says the director, "the truth is that without funding, *no* messages get out. So there needs to be a balance, and it is my job to provide that balance."

In real terms this has meant that Helping Hearts has handled the challenge of funding gay-targeted prevention programming just as many other large ASOs have (Rofes, 1996): with money donated by local gay men and organizations. This approach has both positive and negative ramifications, though. On the one hand, locally produced programs are likely to more accurately reflect the needs and realities of Helping Hearts' constituents than a canned national program would. This is the positive side of community-based programming, and it has a long history of success in adult education (Bell, Gaventa, & Peters, 1990). On the other hand, this process also places a great deal of power for defining an ASO's educational response to the AIDS epidemic in the hands of a small number of influential stakeholders. Put another way, because Helping Hearts' power in the gay community derives from the community itself, the agency's prevention planners cannot afford to alienate the individuals who grant them authority. As one education planner at Helping Hearts said, "We would love to be a little bit stronger, but all of us are afraid of maybe turning people off to the message or sounding as if we don't want people to have a good time. We'd never see them or their dollars again."

As a result, the educational and institutional leaders at Helping Hearts are extremely sensitive about the need to avoid giving offense to gay men, specifically to HIV-positive gay men. This is true because the interests of those who are infected are widely, if silently, acknowledged to have greater weight than even the concrete prevention needs of men who are uninfected. How else to explain why, during his tenure as director of gay outreach, Daniel would assert, "I have a problem with us saying, 'You are a bad person if you have unprotected anal intercourse knowing you have HIV.' Because I think that if we call people bad, or even imply that they are not living up to our standards, then they reject us and our standards. And that gives them even more free rein to behave in what we consider to be an unethical way! So I think that we need to be very careful of our language and—as much as I hate it—pander to gay political correctness." In this case, gay political correctness means that one must treat sexual behaviors as if they have no bearing on the transmission of sexually transmitted diseases and are, therefore, unfit topics for conversation, even by AIDS educators.

What does this say about the power of vested interests in adult education program planning? Simply that when even a passionately committed prevention leader such as Daniel does not feel comfortable telling HIV-positive gay men that they should get serious about protecting their sexual partners, it is clear that community solidarity ("all for one and one for all") and community influence ("as long as the 'one' is HIV-positive") are more compelling interests in determining program design than any hypothetical need to keep HIV-negative gay men uninfected.

Prevention Education, Power, and Planning

As we have illustrated through the example of one HIV/AIDS education and service agency, ignoring the specific prevention education needs of a group of people who could benefit deeply from targeted prevention education does not just happen; it is deliberately planned to happen. Real people, trying to put together a coherent, effective, and rational response to the epidemic, plan programs in complex social and organizational environments whose power relations, traditions, and interests profoundly influence that response.

We have shown that three specific interests—that the appearance of gay community solidarity must be maintained, that HIV-positive men should not be disenfranchised, and that the agency needs to maintain its funding support within the community—are not just abstract considerations to program planners. These interests are at the core of a political process that refuses to single out HIV-negative gay men for special support and attention. They are also perceived realities that form the basis for personal and professional self-evaluation. For example, Daniel resigned after two years at Helping Hearts because he was no longer able to bear his personal sense of failure in the face of a rising tide of newly infected gay men. Gay men, he concluded, felt they had little to gain by remaining uninfected, and nothing he had done had affected that. Of course he would be the first to agree that various personal and institutional agendas had consistently hobbled his efforts to effect change in the community. As we have described, despite his personal commitment to helping prevent new infections, even he felt that it went too far against agency culture to tell HIV-positive men that protecting their sex partners was the right and necessary thing to do.

In forcing dilemmas like these on the Helping Hearts staff, the political dynamics of this organization expose a fundamental conflict between individual and collective interests that lurks beneath almost all HIV prevention planning negotiations. Silin (1987, p. 36) does an excellent job of summing up the tension faced by prevention planners: "How is it possible for safer sex programs, so often planned and implemented by gay professionals, to foster desires and behaviors in us that reinforce rather than challenge a sociopolitical system that is so obviously oppressive to us? Can those who are instructing us in survival techniques be allowing their professional commitments to take precedence over their own best political interests? What are the alternative strategies that would not only teach individuals how to protect themselves but also how to strengthen the entire community in the future?"

Helping Hearts has not yet resolved this tension. Instead, it behaves schizophrenically, consistently promoting educational approaches that downplay serostatus differences among gay men while simultaneously awarding HIV-infected men a higher status than their uninfected counterparts. But by focusing on interests only when those interests serve someone with HIV, program planners working within the political culture of Helping Hearts find themselves continuing to reproduce, rather than challenge, the community's existing power relations and interests. These power relations and interests offer special reverence for the sensibilities and concerns of HIV-positive individuals at the expense of individuals without HIV. As Kyle summed up in his plaintive musings on how wonderful it must be to have HIV, this special reverence for the needs of people with HIV can come at a price. And that price is most often borne by those who have an equally legitimate claim on our educational attention: men who face a daily decision about remaining uninfected and a daily struggle to remember why they should bother doing so.

Addressing the Dilemmas of Practice

Is it possible for educators at Helping Hearts to serve the interests of community solidarity and institutional culture, *as well as* the interests of HIV-negative men? We would like to think so, although we fully acknowledge how complicated the issue is. In some ways, HIV-negative gay men are where gay men in general were two decades ago, closeted participants in a community that refuses to acknowledge the legitimacy of their presence. Unlike gay men of two decades ago, however, no one seems willing to "out" the HIV-negative. But if HIV-negative gay men as individuals and gay society as a whole are to survive and thrive in the coming years, institutional and community leaders will need to negotiate now for education that supports the value of being uninfected as well as the value of *people* who are uninfected.

This is a community issue, not just an individual one, and educators should treat it that way. Without a concept of the value of being gay that is developed *in*, not apart from, the context of all the different communities with which gay men identify, the tragedy of HIV will never be dealt with effectively. It is not enough to show men why they should not get infected; it is also necessary to help them want to stay uninfected. Doing this requires providing societal cachet for the effort that staying uninfected takes.

It is unlikely that such a shift in educational priorities will happen until educators themselves acknowledge the primacy of that interest. And given how severe the repercussions of ignoring it are, it *is* a valid interest for us as a society. For example, of the almost 360,000 cases of AIDS reported through June 1998 among men having sex with men (Centers for Disease Control and Prevention, 1998), all but about 6,000 were reported during or after January 1989. Given the normal length of delay between infection with HIV and an AIDS diagnosis, it can be inferred that most gay men with AIDS were probably infected after 1985, the first year that antibody testing made it possible to determine if a healthy-looking person was or was not infected with HIV. Under best-case conditions then, if antibody testing had been encouraged from the time it first became available, and if this testing had been functionally linked to a 100 percent effective program of prevention education specifically targeting uninfected gay men, it is possible that up to 354,000 cases of AIDS could have been prevented.

This scenario is naively simplistic of course. For one thing, there is no such thing as a 100 percent effective prevention program. But the point is still valid. We have been squandering an opportunity to save hundreds of thousands of lives. If prevention educators operated in a political vacuum, the greatest collective benefit would come from focusing their efforts exclusively on HIV-negative men. Because if it is true that the uninfected have more to lose from exposure to HIV, they also have more to gain from education efforts aimed at interrupting that exposure. Or to put it more baldly, if you had to prioritize between preventing new infections and preventing reinfections, more lives would be saved in the long run by preventing new infections.

As we have made clear, program planners do *not* operate in a political vacuum. Their decision making occurs in a larger context that holds much more than the interests of HIV-negative gay men as central to agency action. For reasons that we have explained in this chapter, this situation is understandable and, to some extent, unavoidable. But it doesn't have to be *completely* unavoidable. There is, we believe, still room for some change. For example, the Helping Hearts outpatient clinic offers HIV testing. As a matter of course, individuals whose test results come back HIV-positive meet immediately with counselors and peer educators to assess their immediate and long-term emotional, educational, and physical needs. We believe that HIV-negative clients would profit from access to a similar support system. We also believe that providing such a system would complement, not threaten, services provided to HIV-positive clients.

We suggest that like their HIV-positive friends, gay men who test negative at an ASO test site could also immediately meet with a counselor for assessment and referrals to appropriate prevention education and support services. They could also meet with an HIV-negative peer educator for congratulations and encouragement as well as to receive a small token marking the occasion of their enrollment or continued inclusion in a support group that might be called "The IN [I'm Negative] Crowd." Programs available through what might be termed the Life Preserver initiative (an arm of gay outreach intended to target HIV-negative men) would include behavior modification classes designed around the unique needs and perspectives of uninfected men. Every third meeting, these classes would join with an analogous class targeting the prevention needs of HIV-positive men to discuss common interests and concerns as well as to promote communication and help heal the rift between gay men of differing serostatus. Other available programs through Life Preserver could include the following:

- Discussion groups for serodiscordant couples to deal with practical and emotional issues unique to that group
- Discussion groups to help HIV-negative couples deal with issues of negotiated trust
- Reality-check education that would include opportunities to talk to HIV-positive people who are taking the new "miracle" drug regimen and having physical, emotional, or financial problems with it, or with infected gay men who are willing to talk about what they would do differently if given the chance to go back in time and be uninfected
- Positive reinforcement education that would include the establishment and maintenance of a peer educator and support network as well as rituals of celebration for remaining HIV-negative
- A discussion group to brainstorm ways in which the agency and the local gay community might be encouraged to become more supportive of HIV-negative men's efforts to remain uninfected and provide value for *being* uninfected

The whole point is to create both the perception and the reality of a vibrant and inclusionary role for HIV-negative gay men who are coping with their participation in the epidemic from inside, not outside, the gay community.

HIV educators can play a fundamental role in bringing this situation about. Alternatively, they can continue to play a fundamental role in reinforcing existing mores that close HIV-negative men out of the circle of gay community services, support, and attention. Although the choice is theirs, we acknowledge that HIV educators who *would* choose to alter the system will have to face considerable personal, professional, and societal obstacles to do so. Nevertheless, the ultimate benefit of taking that risk is compelling when weighed against almost any measure of the threat that HIV/AIDS poses in gay society today.

References

Archie-Booker, E., Cervero, R. M., & Langone, C. (1999). The politics of planning culturally-relevant AIDS prevention education for African-American women. *Adult Education Quarterly, 49,* 163–175.

Ball, S. (1996). Serostatus and counseling. FOCUS: *A Guide to AIDS Research and Counseling, 11*(8), 1–4.

Barnet, J. B. (1994, February 11). HIV-negative support group formed. *St. Louis News-Telegraph,* pp. 2–4.

Bell, B., Gaventa, J., & Peters, J. (Eds.). (1990). *We make the road by walking: Conversations on educational and social change with Myles Horton and Paulo Freire.* Philadelphia: Temple University Press.

Centers for Disease Control and Prevention. (1981). Kaposi's sarcoma and *Pneumocystis* pneumonia among homosexual men—New York City and California. *Morbidity & Mortality Weekly Report, 30*(25), 305–308.

Centers for Disease Control and Prevention. (1998). *HIV/AIDS Surveillance Report, 10*(1).

Cervero, R. M., & Wilson, A. L. (1994). *Planning responsibly for adult education: A guide to negotiating power and interests.* San Francisco: Jossey-Bass.

Cervero, R. M., & Wilson, A. L. (Eds.). (1996). *What really matters in adult education program planning: Lessons in negotiating power and interests.* New Directions for Adult and Continuing Education, no. 69. San Francisco: Jossey-Bass.

Cervero, R. M., & Wilson, A. L. (1998). Working the planning table: The political practice of adult education. *Studies in Continuing Education, 20*(1), 5–21.

Elgstrom, O., & Riis, U. (1992). Framed negotiations and negotiated frames. *Scandinavian Journal of Education Research, 36*(2), 99–120.

Forester, J. (1989). *Planning in the face of power.* Berkeley: University of California Press.

Giddens, A. (1979). *Central problems in social theory: Action, structure, and contradiction in social analysis.* Berkeley: University of California Press.

Isaac, J. (1987). *Power and Marxist theory: A realist view.* Ithaca, NY: Cornell University Press.

Johnston, W. I. (1995). *HIV-negative: How the uninfected are affected by AIDS.* New York: Insight Books.

Mills, D. P., Cervero, R. M., Langone, C. A., & Wilson, A. L. (1995). The impact of interests, power relationships, and organizational structure on program planning practice. *Adult Education Quarterly, 46,* 1–16.

Odets, W. (1994). AIDS education and harm reduction for gay men: Psychological approaches for the twenty-first century. *AIDS and Public Policy Journal, 9*(1), 3–15.

Odets, W. (1995). Why we stopped doing primary prevention for gay men in 1985. *AIDS and Public Policy Journal, 10*(1), 3–21.

Patton, C. (1990). *Inventing AIDS.* New York: Routledge.

Patton, C. (1996). *Fatal advice: How safe sex education went wrong.* Durham, NC: Duke University Press.

Rees, E. F., Cervero, R. M., Moshi, L., & Wilson, A. L. (1997). Language, power, and the construction of adult education programs. *Adult Education Quarterly, 47,* 63–77.

Rofes, E. (1996). *Reviving the tribe: Regenerating gay men's sexuality and culture in the ongoing epidemic.* New York: Haworth Press.

Rotello, G. (1997). *Sexual ecology: AIDS and the destiny of gay men.* New York: Penguin Books.

Scarce, M. (1999, February). A ride on the wild side. *POZ,* pp. 52–55, 70–71.

Schacker, T., Collier, A. C., Hughes, J., Shea, T., & Corey, L. (1996). Clinical and epidemiologic features of primary HIV infection. *Annals of Internal Medicine, 125*(4), 257–264.

Sessions, K. B. (1998). *Living outside the circle: The politics of HIV/AIDS education and the disenfranchisement of HIV-negative gay men.* Unpublished doctoral dissertation, University of Georgia, Athens.

Sessions, K. B., & Cervero, R. M. (1999). The politics of planning HIV/AIDS education and the disenfranchisement of HIV negative men. *Studies in Continuing Education, 21*(1), 3–19.

Shilts, R. (1988). *And the band played on: Politics, people and the AIDS epidemic.* New York: Penguin Books.

Silin, J. G. (1987). Dangerous knowledge. *Christopher Street, 10*(5), 36.

Umble, K. E. (1998). *Negotiation of power and interests in continuing education program planning: A case from public health.* Unpublished doctoral dissertation, University of Georgia, Athens.

Chapter Fourteen

Power in Practice
A New Foundation for Adult Education
Arthur L. Wilson, Ronald M. Cervero

In the opening lines of Chapter One, we sketched a view of adult education as deeply embedded in the production and distribution of knowledge and power: businesses spending billions on training, campesinos educating themselves for political and social transformation, politicians rewriting welfare-to-work programs, post-apartheid unions using education to reshape political alliances, race relations groups using adult education to address prejudice and privilege. For those who might share our point of view, we have been making superfluous claims about adult education as a significant site of struggle for knowledge and power; it is obvious, they would say. Without day-to-day, on-the-ground engagement with such sites, however, such examples may seem distant, even otherworldly when compared to what we believe we do as adult educators. Yes, we say, these are probably very important issues, and, yes, maybe even adult educators are involved. But in our work, we say, we are just trying to keep our company competitive, help someone get or keep a job, teach somebody what they need to pass a test, encourage self-development, teach courses in graduate adult education, help someone learn English or become a citizen. So for many adult educators, even those of us who might be sympathetic to the broad social realities sketched in this volume, it is often difficult to see how the struggles for knowledge and power play out in practice. We think the chapters in this book change that situation. Just as each chapter has as its starting place very real adult education programs, practices, or policies, each also has at its heart the struggle for knowledge and power.

In these very real places, the questions Who benefits? and Who should benefit? embody much of what is at stake in adult education. Although there never have been simple answers to these questions, too many adult educators continue to indulge in the luxury of believing that there are. At stake for us in producing this volume is to take heed on these questions of politics and ethics in adult education. We believe it quite important that as adult educators we recognize the significance of these questions and take responsibility for them in our practice. Doing so means we have to escape the timeworn traps of professional adult education caught between a naïve disavowal of ideology and an uncritical overvaluation of "what works" for whomever tells us to do it. To do that, we have set about engaging "the polymorphous unruliness of our world to gain a greater understanding of its shifting tectonics of power and the fault lines they generate" (Ó Tuathail, Herod, & Roberts, 1998, p. 2). If we adult educators are ever to dismantle our self-enshrouded innocence, to question our long-touted preference for process over consequence, to challenge our unwillingness to engage forthrightly in struggles for knowledge and power, then we have to begin to substantively change the way we see our world and how we act in it.

We began this book with our critique of the dominant notion of the generic, disembodied adult learner as the foundation of adult education practice. The field is not there anymore. The subsequent chapters clearly showed that the adult learners we work with have to be understood relationally within the particular material, social, and political locations of their participation, not as some generic precipitate of research or imagined embodiment of ideological wishful thinking. Along these lines, the field has witnessed the emergence of a continuing stream of ideological critique over the past two decades. The thrust of that work has been to show that adult education is indeed a critical site for the struggle of knowledge and power, and our purpose in this book was to collect a number of these analyses in one place. We share, however, a continuing concern (Apple, 1988; Newman, 1999; Walters, 1996) that our actual practices in distributing knowledge, reshaping power structures, and changing who benefits remain idiosyncratic and undeveloped.

At the end of such an effort we ask, What now? What is now possible if we choose to see adult education as a political struggle for knowledge and power? Our core response is this: because the struggle for knowledge and power is foundational to practice, we have to see our practice as political and therefore strategic, not simply technical or facilitative, in terms of shaping who should benefit. And once we see such a foundational struggle defining the terrain of practice, we have to see the brokering of knowledge and power as our central role in such a practice. Under these conditions, we finally must ask, To whom and for what are we responsible?

First, to develop this argument, we use the questions Who benefits? and Who should benefit? to shift the notion of foundations from its technical origin in "knowledge applied to professional practice" to an analysis of our work as social change actors in the structural conditions that ground the material and ideological practice of adult education. Second, we pursue the argument in order to replace the classic image of the adult educator as innocent facilitator with the notion of adult educators as knowledge and power brokers. We conclude with a view toward a "politics of possibility" (Harvey, 1996). If we are to change the way we act, we must change the way we see our world and the way we see ourselves in it.

A note of caution about what this chapter is not: expect neither a succinct synopsis nor a grand synthesis of the various viewpoints about power discussed in these chapters. Such a move seems unwarranted to us. It seems too early in the conversation for such attempts, because these investigations, in adult education at least, are still quite formative. Further, the very array of viewpoints expressed here belies any simple taxonomy or concatenation of ideas about power and practice, even if we were inclined to search out grand unifying notions of how power works (which we are not). Although we do draw on the preceding chapters to briefly illustrate our argument, our move here is not to present panaceas but to begin reframing what and how we see our work as adult educators, so as to begin imagining new possibilities for action.

Toward a New Foundation of Practice: The Struggle for Knowledge and Power

Since the origins of formal adult education work in the 1920s, a single view of understanding adult education as a scientifically validated technical profession has dominated the mainstream, self-identified manifestations of the field in the United States (Wilson, 1993; Wilson & Cervero, 1997). That orientation lies behind much of what we critiqued earlier as the romancing-the-adult-learner tradition. In Chapter One we used the metaphor "at the heart of practice" to signal what we considered to be the core involvement of adult education in struggles for knowledge and power. That metaphor is a reference to our continuing concern for "what really matters" (Cervero & Wilson, 1994a, 1996, 1998). So as a starting point, we propose that the traditional foundations of practice based on constructing a body of scientific knowledge that romanticized the adult learner and sought neutral-seeming facilitation techniques are inadequate for understanding the high stakes of adult education. It is not so much that we eschew technical rationalist understandings of practice, for we have routinely maintained (1994a, 1996) that technical expertise plays a significant role in the power-enshrouded and ethically charged practice of adult education. But as we introduced in Chapter One and as is abundantly evident throughout the book, we propose instead three starting points as foundational for understanding the shifting terrain of work and for mapping our actions in adult education: (1) adult education is a significant site in the struggle for knowledge and power, (2) there is a reciprocal relationship between adult education and power, and (3) adult educators are social activists. Thus adult education practice is not simply technical but is better characterized as a social practice (Cervero & Wilson, 1994a, 1994b) whose political and ethical dilemmas define its heart and soul. Thus what is foundational to good practice is not simply technical expertise but the capacity for wise and prudent action (Cervero, 1992; Wilson & Hayes, 2000).

We use this section to extend and explain our core argument. First, we amplify our claim that the struggle for knowledge and power is fundamental to adult education practice. Second, we investigate the question of what it means to act once we choose to see the political reality of adult education practice in terms of managing, confronting, and transforming relations of knowledge and power. Third, we seek to replace the innocent images of adult educators as facilitators, process experts, mentors, andragogues, and individual empowerers with the politically astute and ethically charged image of adult educators as knowledge and power brokers. We believe that developing such an image is central to developing practical strategies that make sense in negotiating power relations (Cervero & Wilson, 1994a) and for affixing responsibility (Forester, 1989; Isaac, 1987; Luke, 1996; Winter, 1996) for who should benefit from the practice of adult education.

The Politics of Practice

At stake in the political practice of adult education is the central place adult education has in struggles for knowledge and power. To grasp the importance of our role in these struggles, we must first see what the struggles are about. In many of the discussions in this book about programs, policies, and practices—whether they describe the consequences of using adult education's traditional technologies (Part Three), the role of higher education in maintaining and challenging privilege (Part Two), or the crucial place of adult education in shaping the workplace (Part One)—the struggle for knowledge and power is always at issue. Adult education always benefits some groups more than others, and in structural terms it typically reinforces the way things are (Rubenson, 1989). Every chapter, even those that address seemingly esoteric topics such as policy and discourse, presents situations in which people with specific interests actively use adult education to maintain or transform relations of knowledge and power. If there is any doubt, consider how each chapter addresses the question of benefits. If not for the specific contesting actions prescribed or suggested by chapter authors, what normally and routinely happens through adult education practice? Corporations, under the guise of "anything for the bottom line" and often in clear collusion with the state, increase their power in the workplace to say who should receive education and for what purpose; colleges and universities hegemonically reproduce systems of access and privilege; and perhaps most insidiously, classic adult education practices, those through which we most often proclaim our innocence, become vehicles for maintaining the power and privilege of those with structural access and cultural capital. To put it another way, take away the analysis of power embedded in each chapter, and what we would have left is that which is often described as "good" adult education practice: serving the organization, maintaining and improving society, facilitating individual growth and development, or employing adult education principles of expertise (Beder, 1989; Courtney, 1989; Darkenwald & Merriam, 1982; Merriam & Brockett, 1997). Such classically defined good adult education can be understood, through the relational analyses presented throughout the book, as collusive with and reproductive of dominant knowledge and power structures. We can see that when an analysis of power is brought into play, the answers to the benefits question change significantly from our traditional presumptions.

In order to see the fundamental politics of adult education practice, we have to see the struggle for knowledge and power as a foundational constituent of that practice, which consists of structuring and (re)structurable conditions that shape our work. Foundational does not mean essentialist (in the manner reminiscent of the generic adult learner) but conditional; that is, struggle structures, and is structured by, practice. With that premise in place, we want to make two points. First, in examining the question of who benefits from adult education, these everyday experiences of the workplace, higher education, and using adult education technologies (as well as numerous other examples of adult education not addressed here) revealingly illustrate the high-stakes position adult education plays in the distribution of knowledge, power, resources, and opportunities. Central to understanding these high stakes are pervasive questions that tend to underlie nearly every situation described in this book: Who gets to learn what, and who gets to decide who learns what? Second, when adult education is viewed relationally, that is, when it is seen as deeply embedded in, not separated or marginalized from, the distribution of knowledge and power through the structural arrangements of society and its institutions, it becomes quite evident which high stakes are negotiated through and in the practice of adult education. Without confrontation, privileged access is reproduced in higher education (Johnson-Bailey, Chapter Seven; Hart, Chapter Nine); corporations and the state continue to control the learning agendas of adults to fit their own economic and political interests (Butler, Chapter Four; Rubenson, Chapter Five; Schied, Carter, and Howell, Chapter Three); even innocuous-sounding decisions—for example, choosing to use group learning processes or selecting program sites—lead to reproducing social capital and professional power (Brookfield, Chapter Eleven; Wilson, Chapter Twelve). In our view, a relational analysis enables us to see the reciprocal role adult education plays in the distribution of power and knowledge. Not only does adult education benefit some while denying opportunity to others, it also reproduces the conditions and circumstances that support that inequitable distribution, as many chapter authors point out. Thus a relational analysis enables us to see these productive and reproductive relations of power as foundational to and in adult education practice.

Understanding who benefits depends on how we understand social reality and how we understand the workings of power (Youngman, 1996). The chapters offer a rich array of such understandings. But even though there are many ways to see these relations, one thing remains clear: in each case there are those who gain from the use of adult education and those who do not. This can no longer be denied. We can no longer maintain our neutrality, our innocence, our supposition that we have no stake in any of these struggles except to facilitate adults' learning in whatever guise they choose. We cannot get any more direct than this: not only is adult education a significant distributor of knowledge and power, it also plays a central role in maintaining the relations of knowledge and power that structure access and benefits. Adult education does matter in terms of who gets what and who does not. So our first move is to describe the politics of practice by seeing practice as the struggle for knowledge and power. Given a practice that is embedded and embodied in such struggles, what do we do now?

The Practice of Politics

Given the multiple views of the politics of practice in the previous chapters, what then does the practice of politics look like? Youngman (1996) has argued that social action requires theories of social transformation. For us to raise questions about how adult education either supports or undermines dominant relations of power means we have to develop understandings of those relations in order to act meaningfully in changing them. If we understand the foundations of adult education practice as the struggle for knowledge and power (not as "applied procedural expertise"), then strategic educational practice means political action that forthrightly attempts to alter who benefits in such struggles by seeking to redistribute benefits to those who should. As in any high-stakes endeavor, strategy requires an ability to see and a willingness to commit to an end worth struggling for as well as specific practices for achieving that end. It is difficult to envision adult education in any lesser sense, as the chapters here amply warrant. In this section, we take on two aspects of strategic action in adult education. First, we return to the question of benefits to show that our action as adult educators is indeed strategic because our work always shapes who benefits. Second, by looking at how the authors envision who should benefit from adult education and how our practice is to be shaped to enact those visions, we argue that adult educators must act strategically. Understanding the political necessity for strategic action is necessary in order to dismantle the classic image of the innocent adult educator.

Despite the array of analyses of how power works, each chapter fundamentally illustrates the strategic role of adult educators in how their specific practices shape who benefits from adult education. When adult educators' analyses are strategic, as opposed to instrumental, the educators actively name and respond to the struggles for knowledge and power as they see them, and they deliberately try to alter who benefits. Thus each author also has implicitly or explicitly proposed strategic action for addressing the distribution of knowledge and power, which Walters (1996) and others (Apple, 1996) term *micropractices*. As with the understandings of power, the array of strategic actions is also varied, ranging from specific classroom practices that name in order to change relations of identity structured by social markers (Hart, Chapter Nine; Tisdell, Chapter Eight) to programmatic practices that attempt to restructure program outcomes (Miller, Chapter Ten; Sessions and Cervero, Chapter Thirteen) to policy and discourse analyses that reframe program purposes (Butler, Chapter Four; Rubenson, Chapter Five). The point is that the grounded, specific actions implied or prescribed in these examples (as well as in other chapters) directly respond to the specific power-structured conditions that the educators act in and seek to change. As we pointed out earlier, once we begin to see how adult education is central to distributing knowledge and power, it becomes clearer who tends to benefit as well as who should be benefiting. But just as there is no universal adult learner, we argue here that the broad conditions of struggle are acted out differentially in every case we face. There is a rich array of confrontational tactics to draw on in the face of power (Forester, 1989). Our strategic response lies in the specific analysis of the situation before us and how we choose to act to change who benefits in that situation. Within the broader foundational context of knowledge and power struggles, our visions of who should benefit and our efforts to alter who does benefit necessarily make our intentions and actions strategic, not simply procedural. Our politics are always embedded in our practice.

So too then is the question of micropractices deeply embedded in the question of who should benefit from adult education. This is no less a strategic question in the practice of politics. For without a notion of "what for" there are no reasonable grounds for saying "how to" (Forester, 1989). In every chapter in this book, the contributors, in naming who typically does benefit in a given situation, either implicitly or explicitly state who should benefit. Such struggles of power and justice are not reserved for "radical" forms of adult education, as many of us who practice in the conventional arenas depicted in this book are wont to believe. As we have noted, the range of specific struggles is quite varied (from immigrant working women to HIV-negative men, from those lacking social capital to those lacking technological access), but with few exceptions a recurring theme is social enfranchisement: those who should benefit are routinely the very ones who most often do not have access, privilege, and power in the struggles for the distribution of knowledge. Thus the social vision that informs the "what for" is one that can be subsumed under the umbrella of social justice that characterized almost all critical thinking and practice in the latter part of the twentieth century. Whether it is providing opportunities for voice, creating space for involvement, altering who gets to the table, crossing borders and boundaries, challenging practices—whatever works—all refer to strategic practices of recognizing the uneven distribution of power and knowledge and seeking practically and politically to alter that distribution in ways to change who typically benefits. What makes this position strategic is that the various strategies for increasing social enfranchisement do not make any sense without knowing to what end they are directed. Thus it makes little sense to enfranchise HIV-negative men or to create technological access for working-class women or to deconstruct work-related learning policy if the redistribution of power were not the agenda or if the practice of justice were not of central concern. And it is because these goals of social enfranchisement and redistribution of power are such important stakes that adult educators' action must be strategic.

The End of Innocence: Adult Educators as Knowledge-Power Brokers

These chapters show what is at stake in adult education. We no longer are free to say, "How can I help you?" without our own answers to the benefits questions shaping dramatically how we respond. Indeed, in the high-stakes contest of who does and who should benefit from adult education, it is our responsibility to take a stand on these questions. We can no longer see ourselves as innocently, patiently, and professionally waiting to offer our services to facilitate this or organize that (Cervero & Wilson, 1999). This is no secret, of course, for practitioners and theorists alike have known for decades (Brookfield, 1986; Clark, 1958; Griffith, 1976; Newman, 1994) that adult education matters, and they have been willing to organize, teach, or plan to shape the world the way they think it should be. So we cannot pretend that scientifically validated technical expertise defines practice or that we are neutral, innocent purveyors of such expertise (Cunningham, 1989). In our view, we must recast that foundational image into one of adult educators as knowledge-power brokers. What does that mean?

As a knowledge-power broker, the adult educator sees what is at stake and is willing to act to change who benefits and who should benefit from adult education. What is clear from both the grounded stories and the more abstract accounts in the chapters is that these authors understand how crucial their role is in brokering the distribution of knowledge and power. In their analysis of how power works and who benefits, the authors tell us how they understand the distribution of knowledge and power and how they respond to such distributions. Their actions are predicated on their analysis and on what explicit changes they seek. Whether it is developing political alliances with learners (Hart, Chapter Nine), seeking to enfranchise excluded members of communities (Sessions and Cervero, Chapter Thirteen), confronting the production of identity in the classroom (Tisdell, Chapter Eight; Johnson-Bailey, Chapter Seven), or calling into question the role of adult education in worker exploitation (Butler, Chapter Four; Hall, Chapter Six; Rubenson, Chapter Five), each author knowingly addresses who is benefiting from adult education's role in distributing knowledge and power and how they would seek to change that distribution. Although the discussion of micropractices—how they actually work to alter such distribution—is still embryonic as well as idiosyncratic and quite situational, these micropractices do illustrate directly the practice of politics in adult education: an understanding of what counts and a willingness to struggle in changing who benefits.

Being politically savvy is only part of the knowledge-power broker image. It is not enough to just be willing to strategically struggle to shape who benefits. We already know there is a strong "practical" tradition in adult education that values what works at any cost and too often chooses to ignore the consequences of who benefits from that practicality. So what also matters is the question of who should benefit. As we have already indicated, many authors depend on notions of social justice for defining who should benefit. From reading these accounts, we know who should benefit: immigrant women in jobless economies, HIV-negative men educationally disenfranchised in their communities, workers used as capital for the new global economy, black women fighting for visibility in higher education, working-class women without access to technology, learners unable to participate because of the power-reproducing practices of adult education discussion methods. Although there are some serious questions that might be raised around the often uncritical espousal of social justice, we nonetheless share the deep conviction that this is what adult education can and should be about. A significant aspect of this knowledge-power brokering image is the willingness to name who should benefit and to take responsible action that directs the distribution of knowledge and power that way.

But why the term *brokering?* Brokering has an usurious meaning in contemporary culture, one in which pecuniary interests prevail. The important point is that a broker is someone who does have specific interests and is willing to manage transactions defined by both self-interests and other interests. We think the suffixes *knowledge* and *power* build the political connotations of that image. In earlier work we had used the term *negotiating interests* (Cervero & Wilson, 1994a, 1994b) to highlight what is at stake in adult education, to begin redefining how we understand the characteristic activity of our work by way of confronting the classic innocent image of adult educators as neutral facilitators. Brokering knowledge and power adds to the politicalness of that negotiating image, for it invokes the high level of stakes involved and says more specifically what the practice of negotiating is all about. Not only does the broker image characterize a major contributor to such negotiations, it also names the stakes and interests the broker brings to the negotiated transactions: adult educators and adult education are fundamentally about brokering the distribution of knowledge and power. Again, all the chapter authors, through their anecdotal analysis, portray themselves or other adult educators as willingly engaged in managing knowledge and power transactions designed to limit who does benefit or increase the opportunities of who should benefit. Many of these micropractices need to be worked out, but what remains common to all of the chapters is the educator as someone brokering specific relations of power, thus redistributing opportunities, resources, and knowledge to change who typically has benefited. So for us the notion of brokering incorporates adult educators as social change activists who are able to see what is at stake, willing to act to change who benefits, and managing the negotiations of that redistribution of knowledge and power.

Adult Education as the Practice of Possibility

In our struggles for knowledge and power, our work in adult education is about trying to change the world, at least some part of it that we care about—otherwise, why do it (Cervero & Wilson, 1994a)? We have described the world we hope to change as one dominated by the struggle for knowledge and power. To confront and change this world of inequity, we need to understand the way it is, have a vision for what it should be, and have strategies for achieving our vision of what society should be (Livingstone, 1983). Further, we believe that "spaces can be found in all situations if adult educators are clear about their social goals and how these can be embodied in their day-to-day activities" (Youngman, 1996, p. 4). In responding to such challenges, we have argued that we must understand the politics of practice as founded on the struggle for knowledge and power, that the practice of politics is concerned with what we actually do to shape that distribution of knowledge and power, and that this "refounding" of adult education re-images the adult educator as a broker of knowledge-power negotiations. In our attempt to refigure the foundations of adult education practice, we have one more dimension to address: adult education as the practice of possibility. In this final discussion, we take on the question of the politics of power and responsibility to argue that because the construction and distribution of knowledge and power are social processes (that is, not unchangeable "forces of human nature"), they therefore can be disrupted, altered, refigured. We can change who benefits from adult education, and furthermore we have a responsibility to do so.

The Politics of Power and Responsibility

In this chapter, we have attempted to define a workable set of foundational concepts for adult education in the spirit of Harvey (1996, p. 2): "The task of critical analysis is not, surely, to prove the impossibility of foundational beliefs (or truths), but to find a more plausible and adequate basis for the foundational beliefs that make interpretation and political action meaningful, creative, and possible." The value of Harvey's insight is to warn directly of the dangers of oversimplifying the always evident complexity of human interaction. Although it is reasonable to long for certainty—indeed, this book is about promoting our own aspirations in this regard— we must not fall victim to the lure of easy solutions to the difficult choices and tasks that face us as we broker the distribution of knowledge and power in our adult education work. Thus, in a politics of power we must see what matters: that the struggle for knowledge and power is about the constitution of individual lives and the society we create.

In the struggle for constituting social life, we must create opportunities for taking control of and changing our lives and the conditions in which we live. So to a politics of power we must add a politics of responsibility. To pursue the political commitment for change advocated by many in this volume, we must also have a clear sense of what that vision is: "political movement has to make its choice and not reserve its judgment" (Harvey, 1996, pp. 11–12). The ideological debate in adult education regarding to what use it should be put is so long standing now as to be beyond the patience of too many adult educators. It should not be. To those who extol a selective past of adult education to promote a social practice of emancipation and to those who extol a selective present of adult education to promote technical and managerial competence, look at what adult educators say and do in this book. The questions of practices and purposes in adult education will not and cannot go away. Look to the anecdotes and analyses in this book to see how troubling our actual work is in these everyday sites of practice. As we noted earlier, adult educators knowingly or unknowingly take stands every day on what matters in their practice; they are always making "bets" on how the world works and what effect their actions will have. What distinguishes the commentators in this volume from the more dominant technical vision is the often explicit, although we would add contestable, evocation of social justice as the end toward which we should work. Thus we believe that this volume extends an emerging conversation in adult education that takes seriously the political and ethical demands of our work (Collins, 1991; Cunningham, 1989, 2000; Hart, 1991; Heaney, 1996, 2000; Newman, 1994, 1999; Wangoola & Youngman, 1996; Welton, 1995). The contributors to this volume clearly take stands on what our responsibility is, and the question of micropractices has everything to do with what that work looks like in their everyday practice. If we see adult educators as brokering the distribution of knowledge and power, then we must take responsibility for our actions in shaping how people take control of and change their lives.

Knowing what matters and why it matters means we also have to face the question of what to do. In Chapter One we sought to ground practice in a view that avoided overly deterministic or unfettered understandings of human interaction (Giddens, 1979).

All too often, our theoretical attempts to explain adult education and our technical efforts at doing adult education tend to fall prey to one extreme or another. That is, adult education, like many other practices engaged in by human beings, is remarkably under-theorized in terms of understanding human action. Drawing on Giddens, we have promoted an understanding of adult education as a social practice in which we simultaneously act and act on (Cervero & Wilson, 1994a, 1994b, 1998). We have worked to show that just as our practices produce substantive accomplishments (programs, policies, technologies), we simultaneously reproduce or alter the power relations in which we work. Thus the underlying problem of this volume is the question of how we produce and reproduce different social practices and who benefits from that uneven production. We think many of the chapters, through their explicit analyses of power and micropractices, provide a rich array of insights for thinking critically "about how differences in ecological, economic, political, and social conditions get produced (particularly through those human activities that we are in a position in principle to modify or control)" (Harvey, 1996, p. 5). Seeing adult education as both constituted by and constitutive of the differences produced by struggling for knowledge and power means that we face two questions in practice: What is the justness of these distributions, and what can we do about them? We believe the contributors to this volume make significant movement toward addressing such foundational issues with their responses to the benefits and micropractices questions.

Understanding human interactions as both the medium and outcome of social practices (Giddens, 1979, 1984) means also that because human interactions are socially constructed, they are disruptable and changeable. We can change who benefits. Further, we have a responsibility to change our practices to fit our views of justness. No longer can we presume that social conditions and our social practices are idiosyncratic or structural constraints to be deplored or ignored. Because the stakes are so high in the political practice of adult education, we have to make bets on how such differential struggles for power and knowledge affect access and benefits, how our practical action confronts such distributions, and who should benefit in making our political action meaningful. If we are to take seriously our role in such struggles and if we are to have a chance at changing such distributions, then we must take seriously our politics of power and responsibility.

The Practice of Possibility

Our goal has been to reframe the foundations of adult education in order to broaden our vision of what is possible. In identifying sites and technologies of struggle, presenting multiple ways of understanding power, and envisioning practical responses, what point have we come to? Rather than simply seeing adult education in practice in technical terms of serving adult learners, we have directed attention to what many already know: adult education is a high-stakes arena in which many actors use its seemingly innocent practices to structure opportunity and benefits. With the struggle for knowledge and power as a foundation of adult education practice, we know that multiple interests are always at stake; many interests crowd the table, but only a few voices command attention and action. The questions of benefits—"who does" and "who should"— are always answered in practice. Thus there is no innocent place from which adult educators can act, nor can we pretend that there is (Cervero & Wilson, 1999). As adult educators, we routinely broker access and benefits. If we did not, why would anyone care about adult education? What remains clear, however, is that many do care and are willing to struggle for selectively distributing access to and benefits of adult education. The contributors to this volume certainly understand this and routinely work to shape how these high stakes play out in their work. We have come some way in understanding how power works, and we have new insights into how to respond strategically to inequitable distributions, although micropractices clearly need further attention. We are also clearer on an increasingly well established, but difficult to enact, sense of responsibility.

It is self-evident that we cannot change what we do not see. This book is about changing what we can see, and we are only beginning to talk about doing. We have ended the book with a tentative response to the "doing" question: brokering knowledge and power. As Apple (1988), Walters (1996), and others have noted, there is vastly more abstract analysis of power and privilege than there is practical strategy on what to do about them. Harvey (1996) has reflected on the politics of possibility as a way to envision practice. In an intriguing spin on Marx's adage that humans make themselves but not under conditions of their own choosing, Harvey describes Marx's notion of revolutionary imagination as a way of creating responses to the question of what world we wish to create for ourselves. In trying to create new worlds, Harvey (1996, p. 14) says that he has struggled "to find foundational concepts for the human imaginary to contemplate our embeddedness" in what we have termed struggles for knowledge and power. In a related context, Hooper (1992) has described such a revolutionary imagination "as desire, imagined and worked out in sociospatial context" in which "the imaginative possibilities of what is not yet" are brought into "the concrete realm of what could be" (p. 53). The environmental slogan "Think globally, act locally" serves as a segue from Harvey's and Hooper's reflections on humans as actively creative agents in imagining their own futures to Gore's notion (1993) of how that imagining might work. Gore captures best the notion of a practice of possibility: "I argue that visions of different classrooms and different societies need not be rejected, just worked out locally" (p. xvi). As both Gore and Harvey suggest, the question is, How do we use foundational concepts directly in our education action? The answer is that we must seek a practice of possibility by engaging in specific practices, projects, and imaginings that embody our visions of who should benefit from adult education. To paraphrase Gore, local possibilities are places and opportunities where practitioners with specific social analyses engage in specific struggles to work out visions of how society might be. As we argued in Chapter One, the struggles for knowledge and power in society do not stop at the door of the adult education classroom. Thus it is through our engagement with specific imaginings and actions—ranging from reorganizing circles of learners, to challenging the social assumptions of our cultural positions, to confronting the commodification of lifelong learning by corporations and governments—that we must seek to engage the political practice of our responsibilities. The chapters thoroughly capture the possibility of such struggles of engagement in which we adult educators enact our own interpretations of the politics of practice and the practice of politics.

To practice the possible, we must first see what *is,* in order to imagine what we can do. Using the image of the adult educator as knowledge and power broker, we take seriously the political and ethical consequences of adult education. To practice the possible, though, may require an undoing of what seems imaginable and what seems reasonable and to do what may well be dangerous. This revolutionary imagination is possible because so much of what we describe as the foundations of adult education—the struggle for knowledge and power, the reciprocal relations between adult education and power, and our activist roles as brokering access and benefits—are socially constructed and therefore subject to disruption, altering, and refiguring. Furthermore, we believe it is our responsibility as adult educators to take sides in such struggles by working actively to redistribute access to and benefits from knowledge and power. We must take responsibility for the world we make, and we must choose deliberately what that world looks like.

We are under little illusion, though, that this book will in any great way lessen the continuing protestations of innocence that dominate much theoretical and practical discourse in adult education. We do hope, however, to have added meaningfully to the conversation through which we are valiantly trying to reshape how we see ourselves as adult educators so that we might reshape what we do and for whom we do it. As Youngman (1996) suggests, we can find space to act out our social vision of what matters in the work of adult education. Further, we have to take responsibility for the consequences of acting out a vision of redistribution and restructuring, for if we do not, we know who will: those who have learned so well what adult education can do for them. Because of what is at stake, we can no longer pretend innocence by reserving our judgment or suspending our action.

References

Apple, M. (1988). *Teachers and texts: A political economy of class and gender relations in education.* New York: Routledge.

Apple, M. (1996). Power, meaning, and identity: Critical sociology of education in the United States. *British Journal of Sociology of Education, 17*(2), 125–144.

Beder, H. (1989). Purposes and philosophies of adult education. In S. B. Merriam & P. M. Cunningham (Eds.), *Handbook of adult and continuing education* (pp. 37–50). San Francisco: Jossey-Bass.

Brookfield, S. D. (1986). *Understanding and facilitating adult learning: A comprehensive analysis of principles and effective practices.* San Francisco: Jossey-Bass.

Cervero, R. M. (1992). Professional practice, learning, and continuing education: An integrated perspective. *International Journal of Lifelong Education, 11,* 91–102.

Cervero, R. M., & Wilson, A. L. (1994a). *Planning responsibly for adult education: A guide to negotiating power and interests.* San Francisco: Jossey-Bass.

Cervero, R. M., & Wilson, A. L. (1994b). The politics of responsibility: A theory of program planning practice for adult education. *Adult Education Quarterly, 45,* 249–268.

Cervero, R. M., & Wilson, A. L. (Eds.). (1996). *What really matters in adult education program planning: Lessons in negotiating power and interests.* New Directions for Adult and Continuing Education, no. 69. San Francisco: Jossey-Bass.

Cervero, R. M., & Wilson, A. L. (1998). Working the planning table: The political practice of adult education. *Studies in Continuing Education, 20*(1), 5–21.

Cervero, R. M., & Wilson, A. L. (1999). Beyond learner-centered practice: Adult education, power, and society. *Canadian Journal for the Study of Adult Education, 13*(2), 27–38.

Clark, B. (1958). *The marginality of adult education.* Chicago: Center for the Study of Liberal Education for Adults.

Collins, M. (1991). *Adult education as vocation: A critical role for the adult educator.* London: Routledge.

Courtney, S. (1989). Defining adult and continuing education. In S. B. Merriam & P. M. Cunningham (Eds.), *Handbook of adult and continuing education* (pp. 15–25). San Francisco: Jossey-Bass.

Cunningham, P. M. (1989). Making a more significant impact on society. In B. A. Quigley (Ed.), *Fulfilling the promise of adult and continuing education* (pp. 33–46). New Directions for Continuing Education, no. 44. San Francisco: Jossey-Bass.

Cunningham, P. M. (2000). A sociology of adult education. In A. L. Wilson & E. R. Hayes (Eds.), *Handbook of adult and continuing education: New edition* (pp. 573–591). San Francisco: Jossey-Bass.

Darkenwald, G., & Merriam, S. B. (1982). *Adult education: Foundations of practice.* New York: HarperCollins.

Forester, J. (1989). *Planning in the face of power.* Berkeley: University of California Press.

Giddens, A. (1979). *Central problems in social theory: Action, structure, and contradiction in social analysis.* Berkeley: University of California Press.

Giddens, A. (1984). *The constitution of society*. Berkeley: University of California Press.

Gore, J. (1993). *The struggle for pedagogies: Critical and feminist discourses as regimes of truth*. London: Routledge.

Griffith, W. (1976). Adult educators and politics. *Adult Education, 26*(4), 270–297.

Hart, M. (1991). *Working and educating for life: Feminist and international perspectives on adult education*. London: Routledge.

Harvey, D. (1996). *Justice, nature, and the geography of difference*. Oxford, England: Blackwell.

Heaney, T. (1996). *Adult education for social change: From center stage to the wings and back again*. Columbus, OH: ERIC Clearinghouse on Adult, Career, and Vocational Education.

Heaney, T. (2000). The relationship between adult education and society. In A. L. Wilson & E. R. Hayes (Eds.), *Handbook of adult and continuing education: New edition* (pp. 559–572). San Francisco: Jossey-Bass.

Hooper, B. (1992). "Split at the roots": A critique of the philosophical and political sources of modern planning doctrine. *Frontiers, 13*(1), 45–80.

Isaac, J. (1987). *Power and Marxist theory: A realist view*. Ithaca, NY: Cornell University Press.

Livingstone, D. (1983). *Class ideologies and educational futures*. London: Falmer.

Luke, A. (1996). Text and discourse in education: An introduction to critical discourse analysis. In M. Apple (Ed.), *Review of Research in Education* (Vol. 21, pp. 3–48). Washington, DC: American Educational Research Association.

Merriam, S. B., & Brockett, R. G. (1997). *The profession and practice of adult education: An introduction*. San Francisco: Jossey-Bass.

Newman, M. (1994). *Defining the enemy: Adult education in social action*. Sydney: Stewart Victor.

Newman, M. (1999). *Maeler's regard: Images of adult learning*. Sydney: Steward Victor.

Ó Tuathail, G., Herod, A., & Roberts, S. M. (1998). Negotiating unruly problematics. In A. Herod, G. Ó Tuathail, & S. M. Roberts (Eds.), *An unruly world: Globalization, governance, and geography* (pp. 1–24). London: Routledge.

Rubenson, K. (1989). The sociology of adult education. In S. B. Merriam & P. M. Cunningham (Eds.), *Handbook of adult and continuing education* (pp. 51–69). San Francisco: Jossey-Bass.

Walters, S. (1996). Gender and adult education: Training gender-sensitive and feminist adult educators in South Africa—an emerging curriculum. In P. Wangoola & F. Youngman (Eds.), *Towards a transformative political economy of adult education: Theoretical and practical challenges* (pp. 293–319). De Kalb: LEPS Press, Northern Illinois University.

Wangoola, P., & Youngman, F. (Eds.). (1996). *Towards a transformative political economy of adult education: Theoretical and practical challenges.* De Kalb: LEPS Press, Northern Illinois University.

Welton, M. (Ed.). (1995). *In defense of the lifeworld: Critical perspectives on adult learning.* Albany: State University of New York Press.

Wilson, A. L. (1993). The common concern: Controlling the professionalization of adult education. *Adult Education Quarterly, 44,* 1–16.

Wilson, A. L., & Cervero, R. M. (1997). The song remains the same: The selective tradition of technical rationality in adult education program planning theory. *International Journal of Lifelong Education, 16*(2), 84–108.

Wilson, A. L., & Hayes, E. R. (2000). On thought and action in adult education. In A. L. Wilson & E. R. Hayes (Eds.), *Handbook of adult and continuing education: New edition.* San Francisco: Jossey-Bass.

Winter, S. (1996). The "power" thing. *Virginia Law Review, 82*(5), 721–835.

Youngman, F. (1996). A transformative political economy of adult education: An introduction. In P. Wangoola & F. Youngman (Eds.), *Towards a transformative political economy of adult education: Theoretical and practical challenges* (pp. 3–32). De Kalb: LEPS Press, Northern Illinois University.

Name Index

Subject Index

Printed in the United States
77168LV00002B/263

9 780787 947293